The Atlantic Slave Trade from West Central Africa, 1780–1867

The Atlantic Slave Trade from West Central Africa, 1780–1867 traces the inland origins of slaves leaving West Central Africa at the peak period of the transatlantic slave trade. Drawing on archival sources from Angola, Brazil, England, and Portugal, Daniel B. Domingues da Silva explores not only the origins of the slaves forced into the trade, but also the commodities for which they were exchanged and their methods of enslavement. Further, the book examines the evolution of the trade over time, its organization, the demographic profile of the population transported, the enslavers' motivations to participate in this activity, and the Africans' experience of enslavement and transportation across the Atlantic. Domingues da Silva also offers a detailed "geography of enslavement," including information on the homelands of the enslaved Africans and their destination in the Americas.

Daniel B. Domingues da Silva is Assistant Professor of African history at Rice University.

Cambridge Studies on the African Diaspora

General Editor

Michael A. Gomez,
New York University

Using the African Diaspora as its core defining and launching point for examining the historians and experiences of African-descended communities around the globe, this series unites books around the concept of migration of peoples and their cultures, politics, ideas, and other systems from or within Africa to other nations or regions, focusing particularly on transnational, transregional, and transcultural exchanges.

Titles in the Series

The Atlantic Slave Trade from West Central Africa, 1780–1867

DANIEL B. DOMINGUES DA SILVA

Rice University

To Dr. Karasch,

With respect and admiration;
a token of my work.
From a distant pupil.

Daniel

Houston, 19- Mar- 2018.

CAMBRIDGE
UNIVERSITY PRESS

CAMBRIDGE
UNIVERSITY PRESS

University Printing House, Cambridge CB2 8BS, United Kingdom

One Liberty Plaza, 20th Floor, New York, NY 10006, USA

477 Williamstown Road, Port Melbourne, VIC 3207, Australia

4843/24, 2nd Floor, Ansari Road, Daryaganj, Delhi – 110002, India

79 Anson Road, #06–04/06, Singapore 079906

Cambridge University Press is part of the University of Cambridge.

It furthers the University's mission by disseminating knowledge in the pursuit of education, learning, and research at the highest international levels of excellence.

www.cambridge.org
Information on this title: www.cambridge.org/9781107176263
DOI: 10.1017/9781316771501

First published 2017

Printed in the United States of America by Sheridan Books, Inc.

A catalogue record for this publication is available from the British Library.

Library of Congress Cataloging-in-Publication Data
NAMES: Domingues da Silva, Daniel B., author.
TITLE: The Atlantic slave trade from West Central Africa, 1780–1867 /
Daniel B. Domingues da Silva.
OTHER TITLES: Cambridge studies on the African diaspora.
DESCRIPTION: New York, NY : Cambridge University Press, 2017. | Series: Cambridge studies on the African diaspora | Based on the author's thesis (doctoral) – Emory University, Atlanta, 2011, titled: Crossroads : slave frontiers of Angola, c.1780–1867. | Includes bibliographical references and index.
IDENTIFIERS: LCCN 2017019026| ISBN 9781107176263 (alk. paper) | ISBN 1107176263 (alk. paper)
SUBJECTS: LCSH: Slave trade – Atlantic Coast (Africa, Central) – History. | Slave trade – Angola – History. | Slave trade – Africa, Central – History. | Slavery – Africa, Central – History. | Slavery – Angola – History.
Classification: LCC HT1427.A85 D66 2017 | DDC 306.3/6209673–dc23
LC record available at https://lccn.loc.gov/2017019026

ISBN 978-1-107-17626-3 Hardback

To Livia

Contents

Figures

Tables

Preface

The Atlantic Slave Trade from West Central Africa, 1780–1867 traces for
the first time the origins of slaves leaving West Central Africa at the peak
period of the transatlantic slave trade. West Central Africa was one of the
principal sources of slaves for the Americas. During the nineteenth century, the importance of the region as a supplier of slaves increased as
a result of the suppression of the trade north of the Equator. Although
some nations retreated from the business early in that century, others
remained active, expanding their activities along the coast of West
Central Africa. Some scholars of the slave trade claim that a quest for
political power motivated Africans to sell one another into the transatlantic commerce as prisoners of war. They argue that the expansion of the
slave trade from West Central Africa in the nineteenth century increased
the incidence of warfare in the region, which in turn spread the enslaving
frontiers further into the region's interior. However, as this book demonstrates, the rate of slaves leaving from West Central Africa remained
relatively constant from the late eighteenth until the mid-nineteenth century, with slaves originating from places much closer to the coast than
previously thought. Moreover, the book shows that cultural and economic motivations were also important factors shaping the participation
of Africans in the slave trade. More Africans engaged in this activity than
a handful of rulers and warlords, but their participation depended significantly on the ability of merchants in Europe and the Americas to
deliver the goods required for exchanging for slaves.

Daniel B. Domingues da Silva is Assistant Professor of African history
at Rice University. He received his Ph. D. in history in 2011 from Emory
University, Atlanta, and previously taught at the University of Missouri,

Columbia. His research focuses on the slave trade between West Central Africa and the Americas, especially Brazil and Cuba. It received funding from several institutions, including the National Endowment for the Humanities, the Andrew W. Mellon Foundation, the Calouste Gulbenkian Foundation, and the Luso-American Foundation for the Development of Portugal. Domingues is co-manager of "Voyages: The Trans-Atlantic Slave Trade Database" and his research is available to the public in peer-reviewed journals in English and Portuguese, such as *Journal of African History*, *Slavery and Abolition*, and *Revista Afro-Ásia*.

Acknowledgments

This book grew out of my Ph. D. dissertation, "Crossroads: Slave Frontiers of Angola, c.1780–1867," developed with support from the Andrew W. Mellon, the Calouste Gulbenkian, and the Luso-American foundations, and presented at Emory University, Atlanta, in 2011. The book could not have been possible without the generous support from the National Endowment for the Humanities and the Research Council of the University of Missouri, where I held an appointment as assistant professor of African history until recently. I am also in debt to several colleagues, friends, and family members. I wish to thank first my mentors, David Eltis, Kristin Mann, and Clifton Crais, and my colleagues from the University of Missouri History Department, specially Mark Smith and Robert Smale, who read the manuscript, offered suggestions for improvement, and released me from part of my teaching obligations to revise the manuscript in 2015. My colleagues from the Black Studies Department, Afro-Romance Institute, and the newly established African Interdisciplinary Studies Hub, all at the University of Missouri, created an engaging environment for intellectual exchange.

The work of historians is often a lonely enterprise, but I am fortunate to have counted on the support and encouragement of many friends and colleagues. John Thornton, Walter Hawthorne, and Douglas Chambers read earlier drafts of the manuscript and offered important criticisms. Joseph Miller, Roquinaldo Ferreira, Mariana Cândido, Jelmer Vos, Stacey Sommerdyk, and Vanessa Oliveira lent their expertise in the field of West Central African history. Alex Borucki, Alexandre Veira Ribeiro, Ana Lúcia Araújo, Carmen Alveal, Kalle Kananoja, Paulo Teodoro de Matos, and Warren Whatley helped me test and publicize some of my research findings in conferences, panels, and workshops in Brazil, Europe, and the United States. Conceição Neto, Fabrício Prado, Filipa Ribeiro da Silva, José Curto, and Paulo Silveira e Sousa shared valuable materials, references, and research tips. Phil Misevich, Nafees Khan, Olatunji Ojo, Badi Bukas-Yakabuul, Henry Lovejoy, Ugo Nwokeji, Yacine Daddi Adoun, and many others who go unnamed here (you know who you are), have always been a source of encouragement and intellectual motivation. English is not my primary language, but Suzan Eltis made sure the book was written as if penned by an English wordsmith.

I have been living abroad for a little over a decade now and, since my research is largely based outside my country of origin, I have had few opportunities to return and see my family. Although my life as a migrant is of course incomparable to that of thousands of Africans forced into the transatlantic slave trade, it allowed me to reflect on their experiences and on the lives of the people that they left behind. I am now acutely aware of not only the challenges of moving into a different culture, but also of the impact that the absence of a loved one has on those who stayed home. I am thus grateful for my family's understanding and support throughout these years. More difficult is to seek the understanding and thank the support of the person who followed me during this period with no guarantee of success. Livia, you left your family behind and abandoned an otherwise successful career to accompany me in this adventure. I am afraid I will never be able to repay you, but I will remain forever grateful for your sacrifice. This, my first book, is dedicated to you.

Abbreviations

AHI	Arquivo Histórico do Itamaraty, Rio de Janeiro, Brazil
AHNA	Arquivo Histórico Nacional de Angola, Luanda, Angola
AHU	Arquivo Histórico Ultramarino, Lisbon, Portugal
ANRJ	Arquivo Nacional, Rio de Janeiro, Brazil
BNA	British National Archives, Kew, England
BNRJ	Biblioteca Nacional, Rio de Janeiro, Brazil
Cod.	Codice
CU	Conselho Ultramarino, Lisbon, Portugal
Doc.	Document
FO	Foreign Office Series, London, England
SEMU	Secretaria de Estado da Marinha e Ultramar, Lisbon, Portugal

Introduction

In the 1840s, Nanga, a Kimbundu speaker from Libolo, near the coast of present-day Angola, was pawned by his mother. She used her son to free one of her brothers, who had been sold earlier for adultery, an offence in many parts of the region punishable by banishment, enslavement, or even death.[1] Africans in the region often pawned slaves or free family members as collateral, a way of securing quick credit to buy goods, pay debts, or invest in a business. The objective was to redeem the pawns within an agreed time period. In the interim, lenders could use the pawns for labor in several activities. If borrowers defaulted on their loans, pawned individuals, enslaved or free, could be further exchanged. Some clearly fell into the hands of creditors who foresaw selling them to traders rather than holding them as collateral.[2] This is what happened to Nanga. Although

---

[1] Details on Nanga's story come from Sigismund Wilhelm Koelle, *Polyglotta Africana*, ed. P. E. H. Hair and David Dalby (Graz: Akademische Druck, U. Verlagsanstalt, 1965), 15. On adultery as a crime and form of enslavement in West Central Africa see Roquinaldo Ferreira, "Slaving and Resistance to Slaving in West Central Africa." In *The Cambridge World History of Slavery*, ed. David Eltis and Stanley L. Engerman, vol. 3 (New York: Cambridge University Press, 2011), 121–22; Roquinaldo Amaral Ferreira, *Cross-Cultural Exchange in the Atlantic World: Angola and Brazil during the Era of the Slave Trade* (New York: Cambridge University Press, 2012), 198; Mariana P. Cândido, *An African Slaving Port and the Atlantic World: Benguela and Its Hinterland* (New York: Cambridge University Press, 2013), 230–32; Joseph C. Miller, *Way of Death: Merchant Capitalism and the Angolan Slave Trade, 1730–1830* (Madison: University of Wisconsin Press, 1988), 164.
[2] Toyin Falola and Paul E. Lovejoy, "Pawnship in Historical Perspective." In *Pawnship in Africa: Debt Bondage in Historical Perspective*, ed. Toyin Falola and Paul E. Lovejoy (Boulder: Westview Press, 1994); Paul E. Lovejoy and David Richardson, "Trust, Pawnship, and Atlantic History: The Institutional Foundations of the Old Calabar Slave Trade." *American Historical Review* 104, no. 2 (1999): 333–55; Paul E. Lovejoy and

his mother redeemed her sibling, she failed to reclaim her own son. Her creditors placed Nanga in the hands of Portuguese traders at Luanda who put him on a transatlantic slaver bound for Brazil.[3]

In the nineteenth century, the transatlantic slave trade was increasingly under attack. Despite the rising European demand for goods produced in the Americas with slave labor, such as cotton and sugar, slavery and the slave trade came to be seen as something that was morally wrong and should be suppressed.[4] Great Britain was no doubt the most important power in this process. Not only did it abolish its own slave trade in 1807, it encouraged other nations to follow suit by signing a series of bilateral agreements for the gradual suppression of the traffic. Britain established courts, some of them international, to adjudicate ships accused of illegal slave trading and deployed an antislave trade squadron to patrol the coasts of Africa and the Americas.[5] Nanga's story has a neat twist. A British man of war intercepted his vessel and took it for adjudication in Freetown, Sierra Leone. The court found the ship and its crew guilty of trading slaves and released all those enslaved.[6] Nanga, a free man, adopted the name John Smart and remained in Sierra Leone with a woman from his own country. Seven years after Nanga's liberation, Sigismund Koelle, a German missionary, took down his story and made it available for posterity as part of his *Polyglotta Africana*, primarily a study in African languages.[7]

Nanga did not share the fate of the majority of Africans forced into the transatlantic slave trade. He never worked on a plantation, in a mine, or in

David Richardson, "The Business of Slaving: Pawnship in Western Africa, c.1600–1810." *Journal of African History* 42, no. 1 (2001): 67–89.

[3] Koelle, *Polyglotta Africana*, 15.

[4] David Brion Davis, *Inhuman Bondage: The Rise and Fall of Slavery in the New World* (New York: Oxford University Press, 2006), 234–38; Seymour Drescher, *Abolition: A History of Slavery and Antislavery* (New York: Cambridge University Press, 2009), 208–09; David Eltis, *Economic Growth and the Ending of the Transatlantic Slave Trade* (New York: Oxford University Press, 1987), 23–26; James Walvin, *Crossings: Africa, the Americas, and the Atlantic Slave Trade* (London: Reaktion Books, 2013), 169–76.

[5] Eltis, *Economic Growth*, 81–101; Walvin, *Crossings*, 176–92.

[6] The "African Origins" portal, which provides users with access to all lists of Africans rescued from slave ships adjudicated at the courts of Freetown, has records of three individuals who fit Koelle's description of Nanga. Two sailed from Cabinda and one from Ambriz between 1843 and 1845. Although Nanga told Koelle that he had been handed to Portuguese slave traders at Luanda, he may have been transported from these other two ports because the Portuguese had prohibited the traffic from Luanda in 1836 and the British established a court at that port in 1845. David Eltis and Philip Misevich, "African Origins: Portal to Africans Liberated from Transatlantic Slave Vessels," Online database (2009), African ids 53559, 54216, and 175537, www.african-origins.org/.

[7] Koelle, *Polyglotta Africana*, 15.

the streets of a city in the Americas. He never felt the pain of having the family that he rebuilt at great cost torn apart as a result of a commercial transaction. He never spent the days wondering whether he or any of his descendants would ever regain freedom. Nonetheless, his journey from enslavement to shipment follows a trajectory similar to that by which millions of other Africans traveled to the Americas. This book focuses on that journey. From where did these Africans come? How were they transported? Who captured them? Why? What was the impact of the trade on their communities? More importantly, could anybody be enslaved or were there specific criteria determining who was eligible for enslavement? These questions lie at the heart of the whole enterprise and this book will explore them in light of the West Central African experience at the peak of its involvement in the traffic.

By focusing on the journey Africans took from the interior to the coast, this book contributes significantly to our understanding of the history of Africa and the African Diaspora. It traces for the first time the inland origins of the slaves carried off as the transatlantic slave trade reached its peak. Although most slaves transported to the Americas came from West Central Africa, historians have paid less attention to this region than to others involved in the trade. The book also sheds light on African motivation to participate in the traffic as well as on the ordeals that those caught up in this huge migration experienced. Finally, thanks to the sources examined and the maps they allowed us to create, historians of the African Diaspora will be better able to explore the African contribution to the making of the New World. In addition, descendants of Africans, at least those whose ancestors arrived in the last century of the trade, will be able to narrow their search for their ancestral homelands. The longevity of the transatlantic slave trade impacted the lives of millions of people. No single study will ever provide a full accounting of what happened, but an assessment of how the traffic unfolded in the African interior is fundamental to increasing our understanding of this tragic saga.

SLAVERY AND POLITICS

Scholars have often associated the huge number of slaves sold into the trade with major political developments in the interior of Africa, notably with processes of state formation and imperial expansion. They believe that the enslavement and subsequent sale of slaves required such great resources that only individuals who commanded significant numbers of followers could undertake such activities. J. D. Fage, for example, suggests that the slave trade tended to integrate, strengthen, and develop political authority, but to weaken or destroy more segmentary societies in Africa.[8] A. A. Boahen claims that the slave trade constituted the principal source of income for many rulers and military leaders, who had a monopoly over the sale and enslavement of individuals on the African coast.[9] Similarly, Patrick Manning argues that rulers, who succeeded in profiting and expanding at the expense of their neighbors, captured most of the slaves sold into the trade.[10] Finally, Martin Klein broadly endorses these positions by stressing that the trade required such large resources that rulers and raiding bands of professional warriors dominated the enslavement and sale of slaves across the Atlantic.[11]

In West Central Africa, the origins of slaves sold into the trade are frequently associated with the expansion of the Lunda Empire and the formation of the Imbangala Kingdom of Kasanje. On the basis of oral traditions collected in the mid-nineteenth century, in addition to Portuguese documentary evidence, Jan Vansina, David Birmingham, and Joseph Miller argue that the Lunda expansion began long before the eighteenth century. In addition, they claim Lunda dissidents, led by a man named Kinguri acting in accordance with Imbangala traditions, left their country after Luba hunters assumed control over the government. En route to a new environment, they encountered Portuguese soldiers, who were themselves at war with their neighbors on the coast of present-day Angola. Since the Portuguese were short of manpower, they welcomed the arrival of and recruited the newcomers, who proved to be great warriors. Further, these newcomers offered to exchange their prisoners of war for rare commodities imported from Europe, Asia, and the Americas. The Lunda expatriates saw this exchange as an opportunity to amass wealth and power. As a consequence, they continued to provide military support for the Portuguese. Over time, these Lunda named themselves Imbangala and founded a new state, the Kingdom of Kasanje, at the confluence of the Lucala and Kwango rivers. The Portuguese regarded

[8] J. D. Fage, "Slavery and the Slave Trade in the Context of West African History." *Journal of African History* 10, no. 3 (1969): 402.

[9] A. A. Boahen, "New Trends and Processes in Africa in the Nineteenth Century." In *General History of Africa*, ed. J. F. A. Ajayi, vol. 6 (London: Heinemann, 1989), 61.

[10] Patrick Manning, *Slavery and African Life: Occidental, Oriental, and African Slave Trades* (New York: Cambridge University Press, 1990), 132.

[11] Martin A. Klein, "The Impact of the Atlantic Slave Trade on the Societies of the Western Sudan." *Social Science History* 14, no. 2 (1990): 237.

this newly formed kingdom as the principal supplier of slaves shipped from West Central Africa.[12]

However, recent research suggests that the supply of slaves sold on the coast did not necessarily depend on processes of state formation and imperial expansion within Africa. David Northrup notes that the sale of slaves in the Bight of Biafra, a major source of slaves for the transatlantic trade, was conducted mostly without the participation of African rulers. He writes that decentralized societies such as the Efik, Igbo, and Ibibio dominated the slave trade in that region.[13] These societies were generally organized in clans or lineages headed by one or more individuals who had a vote in decisions affecting the entire society. Ugo Nwokeji argues that the Aro in particular, a subgroup of the Igbo, organized themselves as a "trade diaspora," which allowed them to maintain their own identity through festivals, homages, and patronage while at the same time facilitating their political and economic hegemony in the Bight of Biafra.[14] Walter Hawthorne and Andrew Hubbell also question the emphasis scholars have traditionally placed on the role of state formation and imperial expansion in the slave trade. In their view, scholars have underestimated the ability of decentralized societies to organize and participate actively in the supply of slaves from Africa as well as defend themselves from enslavers.[15] Hawthorne, whose work focuses specifically on the transatlantic trade, notes that, although decentralized, the rice-growing Balanta of present-day Guinea Bissau, supplied many slaves to the Americas, especially to northern Brazil. Similarly, David Eltis, observing

---

[12] This broadly summarizes a major debate Jan Vansina, David Birmingham, and Joseph Miller had in the pages of the *Journal of African History*. The principal references to this debate include Jan Vansina, "The Foundation of the Kingdom of Kasanje." *Journal of African History* 4, no. 3 (1963): 355–74; David Birmingham, "The Date and Significance of the Imbangala Invasion of Angola." *Journal of African History* 6, no. 2 (1965): 143–52; Jan Vansina, "More on the Invasions of Kongo and Angola by the Jaga and the Lunda." *Journal of African History* 7, no. 3 (1966): 421–29; Joseph C. Miller, "The Imbangala and the Chronology of Early Central African History." *Journal of African History* 13, no. 4 (1972): 549–74.

[13] David Northrup, *Trade without Rulers: Pre-Colonial Economic Development in South-Eastern Nigeria* (Oxford: Clarendon Press, 1978), 89–100.

[14] G. Ugo Nwokeji, *The Slave Trade and Culture in the Bight of Biafra: An African Society in the Atlantic World* (New York: Cambridge University Press, 2010), 17–21.

[15] Walter Hawthorne, "The Production of Slaves Where There Was No State: The Guinea-Bissau Region, 1450–1815." *Slavery and Abolition* 20, no. 2 (1999): 97–98; Andrew Hubbell, "A View of the Slave Trade from the Margin: Souroudougou in the Late Nineteenth-Century Slave Trade of the Niger Bend." *Journal of African History* 42, no. 1 (2001): 28. See also Martin A. Klein, "The Slave Trade and Decentralized Societies." *Journal of African History* 42, no. 1 (2001): 49.

a marked decline in the traffic from the Bight of Benin immediately after the Dahomean annexation of Allada and Ouidah in 1724 and 1727, suggests that processes of state formation and imperial expansion did not necessarily result in more slaves being sold into the trade.[16] Finally, Rebecca Shumway and Randy Sparks have argued more recently that the tendency of historians to focus on centralized states to the neglect of other populations has been detrimental to our knowledge of the history of the traffic from the Gold Coast.[17] As Shumway notes, "the coastal population was an essential component on how the Atlantic slave trade operated on the Gold Coast."[18]

Studies focused on the Lunda expansion itself cast doubt on the role of the slave trade in processes of state formation and imperial expansion in West Central Africa. They show that the Lunda expansion began much later than previously thought and may not have been responsible for the large number of slaves sold into the Atlantic. Based on an extensive study of kings' lists, Jean Luc Vellut claims that the Lunda expansion began in the late seventeenth century or at the beginning of the eighteenth century.[19] John Thornton dates the Lunda expansion from the same period, but he believes that it reached its maximum size, both geographically and demographically, only in 1852 with the death of Mwant Yav Nawej II, the first event recorded in Lunda history in contemporary documents.[20] Jeffrey Hoover, using linguistic data, argues that Imbangala traders introduced the figure of Kinguri into Lunda traditions, probably in the nineteenth century, to elevate the status of their own founding ancestors, who were not originally Lunda.[21] In other words, the frequently mentioned Lunda expansion, said to have begun long before the eighteenth century, may not have unfolded as previously believed. Jan Vansina, after revising his original position, went even further. Although he believes that the Lunda spread north of Angola,

---

[16] David Eltis, "The Volume and Structure of the Transatlantic Slave Trade: A Reassessment." *William and Mary Quarterly* 58, no. 1 (2001): 34.

[17] Rebecca Shumway, *The Fante and the Transatlantic Slave Trade* (Rochester: University of Rochester Press, 2011), 8; Randy J. Sparks, *Where the Negroes Are Masters: An African Port in the Era of the Slave Trade* (Cambridge: Harvard University Press, 2014).

[18] Shumway, *The Fante and the Transatlantic Slave Trade*, 8.

[19] Jean-Luc Vellut, "Notes sur le Lunda et la Frontière Luso-Africaine (1700–1900)." *Études d'Histoire Africaine* 3 (1972): 68.

[20] John K. Thornton, "The Chronology and Causes of Lunda Expansion to the West, c.1700–1852." *Zambia Journal of History* 1 (1981): 1.

[21] Jeffrey J. Hoover, "The Seduction of Ruweej: Reconstructing Ruund History (The Nuclear Lunda: Zaire, Angola, Zambia)" (Ph.D., Yale University, 1978), vol. 1, 213–14.

he claims that until 1846 there are no records of Lunda conquest to the south in what is now eastern Angola.[22] As a result, the slave trade would have offered little stimulus for Lunda expansion or the formation of other states in West Central Africa, including the Kingdom of Kasanje. As Vansina reflected upon the implications of this finding, "if the Kinguri story had only been subjected to critical appraisal from the outset, we historians would now be much more advanced than we are today."[23]

Recent studies on the history of slavery and the slave trade, however, are prompting some historians to reconsider the origins of the captives transported from West Central Africa. Instead of tracing these to places beyond the Kwango River, where the Lunda Empire was located, they are now increasingly indicating that these slaves came from regions much closer to the coast. José Curto, for instance, analyzing records of runaway slaves published in the *Boletim Oficial de Angola* between 1850 and 1876, shows that slaves living under Portuguese rule in Luanda and who were previously sold into the Atlantic hailed from a wide range of places, with the majority coming from the neighboring regions of Luanda and the Kwanza River.[24] Mariana Cândido, in an analysis of the slave trade from Benguela, in southern Angola, argues that the populations living near the coast were not immune to raids, kidnappings, and other forms of enslavement. "In contrast to a gradual movement inland," she writes, "the process of enslavement did not move only to the east, but also to the south, to the north, and finally bounced back to the west, towards the populations on the coast who lacked protection."[25] Similarly, Roquinaldo Ferreira, examining court records from eighteenth and nineteenth-century Luanda, observes that slaves who filed for freedom were generally individuals who had been captured in regions close to the coast, including areas under Portuguese influence. "African control over sources of slaves in the east," he argues, "exposed freeborn Africans living in the Luanda hinterland to enslavement."[26]

---

[22] Jan Vansina, "It Never Happened: Kinguri's Exodus and Its Consequences." *History in Africa* 25 (1998): 401.

[23] Ibid., 403. Vansina himself started this process. See Jan Vansina, *How Societies Are Born: Governance in West Central Africa before 1600* (Charlottesville: University of Virginia Press, 2004).

[24] José C. Curto, "*The Origin of Slaves in Angola: The Case of Runaways, 1850–1876*" (Seventh European Social Science and History Conference, Lisbon, 2008), 6–9.

[25] Mariana P. Cândido, *Fronteras de Esclavización: Esclavitud, Comercio e Identidad en Benguela, 1780–1850*, trans. María Capetillo Lozano (Mexico: El Colegio de México, 2011), 157–58.

[26] Ferreira, *Cross-Cultural Exchange*, 16.

Despite the work of these scholars, a detailed study of the origins of slaves leaving West Central Africa in the nineteenth century is still lacking, perpetuating the view that the Lunda were the region's main suppliers of slaves to the Americas. Joseph Miller, for instance, in his widely cited *Way of Death*, argues that in the nineteenth century the source of slaves shipped from Angola moved further east, as successive Lunda kings raided and plundered the populations living near the borders of their territories.[27] Achim von Oppen claims that the search for slaves to export was the principal motivation behind the eastward movement of the trading frontier.[28] Paul Lovejoy, in his well-known *Transformations of Slavery*, argues that the center of Lunda trade was the royal capital, "from where Lunda armies raided outwards, capturing slaves."[29] Jan Vansina, in spite of his revision, believes that the Lunda expansion north and the spreading of the Lunda influence in eastern Angola were undoubtedly linked to the slave trade.[30] Finally, John Thornton in his more recent volume, *A Cultural History of the Atlantic World*, argues "it is possible to see the expansion of the Lunda Empire from its base deep in central Africa (Shaba Province in the Democratic Republic of Congo) nearly 1,000 kilometers from the coast as a response to the development of the slave trade farther east."[31]

QUANTITATIVE VERSUS QUALITATIVE

This book uses new evidence and a fresh approach to revisit the debates over how people became enslaved and the location of their homelands. It examines a variety of sources, ranging from archival material, to published primary sources, and digital resources. Since the book focuses on a huge wave of migration, it draws significantly on quantitative methods to analyze the number of slaves transported, their demographic characteristics, and their geographic distribution. These methods were used less in the belief in their intrinsic superiority to qualitative methods of analysis,

---

[27] Miller, *Way of Death*, 146–47.

[28] Achim von Oppen, *Terms of Trade and Terms of Trust: The History and Contexts of Pre-Colonial Market Production around the Upper Zambezi and Kasai* (Münster: LIT Verlag, 1994), 59–61.

[29] Paul E. Lovejoy, *Transformations in Slavery: A History of Slavery in Africa*, 2nd edn. (New York: Cambridge University Press, 2000), 78 and 98.

[30] Vansina, "It Never Happened," 403.

[31] John K. Thornton, *A Cultural History of the Atlantic World, 1250–1820* (New York: Cambridge University Press, 2012), 85.

but rather because they were more adequate in view of the book's objectives, the types of sources examined, and the volume of information available. The latter, in fact, imposed a great barrier to earlier interpretations of the trade from West Central Africa. This approach, however, does not exclude qualitative methods. Indeed, in the following discussions of African motivation in participating in the trade, eligibility for enslavement, and especially the experiences of those captured and sold overseas, the qualitative approach takes precedence.

It is unfortunate that these two approaches have been set up in opposition to each other, as if they were somehow mutually exclusive. Cliometrics, or quantitative history, made a huge impact on the larger field following the publication of Philip Curtin's *The Atlantic Slave Trade* and Robert Fogel and Stanley Engerman's *Time on the Cross*.[32] Cliometricians contributed significantly to our knowledge of the history of slavery and the slave trade by providing us with an idea of how many people were transported from Africa, the ratio of slave to free in the Americas, and other details about the Middle Passage, family life, and labor routines in the New World. Such information is very helpful in contextualizing the experience of enslaved Africans and their descendants, but it does not reveal other aspects of their lives. Qualitative history has been around for a long time and often provides a rich account of the experiences of an individual, social group, or nation. Although it was partially eclipsed by the rise of cliometrics, qualitative history is now leading the field again thanks to the work of microhistorians such as Carlo Ginzburg and Natalie Zemon Davis. These authors have renewed academic interest in individual stories and how they can help us understand broader patterns of behavior and historical change.[33]

Some recent contributions to the field have echoed a remark Joseph Miller made long ago that numbers "have no meaning either in human terms or in perceiving the operational complexity and diversity of the trade."[34] Toby Green argues that "a quantitative emphasis distracts

---

[32] Philip D. Curtin, *The Atlantic Slave Trade: A Census* (Madison: University of Wisconsin Press, 1969); Robert William Fogel and Stanley L. Engerman, *Time on the Cross: The Economics of American Negro Slavery* (Boston: Little Brown, 1974).

[33] Carlo Ginzburg, *The Cheese and the Worms: The Cosmos of a Sixteenth-Century Miller*, trans. Anne Tedeschi and John Tedeschi (Baltimore: Johns Hopkins University Press, 1980); Natalie Zemon Davis, *The Return of Martin Guerre* (Cambridge: Harvard University Press, 1983).

[34] Joseph C. Miller, "The Slave Trade in Congo and Angola." In *The African Diaspora: Interpretative Essays*, ed. Martin L. Kilson and Robert I. Rotberg (London: Harvard University Press, 1976), 76.

attention from seeing how the advent of Atlantic slavery affected African societies, and from thinking through what the cultural, political and social consequences of this phenomenon were."[35] Mariana Cândido believes that "quantitative studies that analyze population exports, natural reproduction, and food production tend to neglect social transformations, such as the dependence of societies on slave labor."[36] Silke Strickrodt, while acknowledging that the quantitative approach "helps us to deal with broad trends and wide regions," argues "it is less useful for detailed analysis of minor ports."[37] Finally, Alice Bellagamba, Sandra Greene, and Martin Klein maintain that quantitative studies, whether they focus on Africa or the Americas, "are based on European and American shipping and customs records," and that "we need to hear how Africans understood and now remember that part of their own past associated with slavery and the slave trade." They claim "we need to listen to African voices."[38]

Although these are valid arguments, they often miss the point. Quantitative and qualitative methods are not mutually exclusive. In their attempts to reconstruct the past, historians must use both to develop their narratives. This book draws on quantitative sources such as shipping records, slave registers, and lists of liberated Africans to review broader patterns of the trade, while at the same time examining travel accounts, official correspondence, and testimonies of slave and freed individuals to shed light on the experiences of Africans pulled into the transatlantic traffic. A quarter century ago, Ginzburg argued for using both quantitative and qualitative tools with the latter "opening out into a series of case studies but never excluding, as we have said, serial [quantitative] research."[39] This project constitutes an application of that advice to the history of the later slave trade from West Central Africa.

[35] Toby Green, *The Rise of the Trans-Atlantic Slave Trade in Western Africa, 1300–1589* (New York: Cambridge University Press, 2012), 4–5.

[36] Cândido, *An African Slaving Port*, 14.

[37] Silke Strickrodt, *Afro-European Trade in the Atlantic World: The Western Slave Coast, c.1550-c.1885* (James Currey, 2015), 5.

[38] Alice Bellagamba, Sandra E. Greene, and Martin A. Klein, "Finding the African Voice." In *African Voices on Slavery and the Slave Trade*, ed. Alice Bellagamba, Sandra E. Greene, and Martin A. Klein (New York: Cambridge University Press, 2013), 2.

[39] Carlo Ginzburg and Carlo Poni, "The Name and the Game: Unequal Exchange and the Historiographic Marketplace." In *Microhistory and the Lost Peoples of Europe*, ed. Edward Muir and Guido Ruggiero, trans. Eren Branch (Baltimore: Johns Hopkins University Press, 1991), 7.

SOURCES AND ORGANIZATION

This book is organized into six chapters. Chapter 1 provides an assessment of the size and distribution of the flow of slaves leaving West Central Africa in the age of abolition, from the 1780s to the 1860s. The chapter draws on "Voyages: The Trans-Atlantic Slave Trade Database," to which I have contributed from my own considerable archival research.[40] I was not only one of the original contributors and builders of the core voyages database, but in this study I present new projections of slave departures that improve on those that currently display on the "Voyages" estimates page. It shows that the number of slaves shipped from West Central Africa increased between the late eighteenth and the first half of the nineteenth century as a result of the demand for primary commodities, such as sugar and cotton, in Europe and the suppression of the slave trade in the North Atlantic. Although scholars usually argue that the Lunda expansion triggered the massive number of slaves shipped from Angola in this period, my own analysis shows that the number of slaves shipped varied mostly as a result of events taking place across the Atlantic. Demand, rather than supply, drove the trade and most of its fluctuations.

Chapter 2 provides an analysis of the organization of the transatlantic slave trade from West Central Africa. It shows that the transportation and sale of slaves depended essentially on three categories of commercial agents: merchants, brokers, and traders. All three worked independently of the military power of both the Lunda and the Imbangala. Merchants oversaw the transatlantic phase of the business from assembling trade goods in Brazil, to the shipment of slaves from Angola. The second category, that of brokers, was a disparate group, made up of Portuguese and Brazilian subjects living in Angola. They comprised a mixed group that included descendants of Portuguese and Africans, in addition to rulers and subjects of various African polities located on the African coast. They brokered slaves brought from the interior for the commodities imported from overseas. The third group were traders, and served as middlemen between the brokers and slave suppliers in the interior of West Central Africa. They were mostly Africans, including the offspring of unions between Africans and Portuguese expatriates. Although a few individuals had multiple roles, the trade depended largely on these three separate groups.

[40] David Eltis et al., "Voyages: The Trans-Atlantic Slave Trade Database," Online database (2008), www.slavevoyages.org/.

Chapter 3 traces the inland origins of slaves leaving West Central Africa in the nineteenth century based on two sets of documents. The first consists of lists of liberated Africans compiled between 1832 and 1849 by the courts of mixed commission in Havana, Cuba, and Rio de Janeiro, Brazil. These lists were created to prevent the re-enslavement of Africans rescued from slave vessels by antislave trade naval cruisers. They provide details on 4,601 individuals, including their name, age, sex, height, and place of origin. The second set of documents is the slave registers of Angola compiled by Portuguese colonial officials in Luanda, Benguela, and Novo Redondo between 1854 and 1856. These registers, also used to prevent freed Africans from being re-enslaved, contain identical information to the lists of liberated Africans in Havana and Rio de Janeiro. The registers record details for 11,264 individuals. In addition to the records available in the "Voyages" database and the "African Origins" portal, these documents allow us to identify the ethnolinguistic origins of captives leaving West Central Africa.

Chapters 4, 5, and 6 seek to explain the transatlantic slave trade from an African perspective. Chapter 4 provides a demographic profile of the men, women, and children sold as slaves on the coast of Angola based on archival records in addition to data available in the "Voyages" database. It shows that the slave trade from Angola was largely shaped by African conceptions of gender and age. David Eltis and Stanley Engerman note that, in contrast to conventional wisdom, men were not the dominant demographic category in the transatlantic trade. Their work suggests that adult male slaves comprised much less than half of the total number of slaves carried across the Atlantic.[41] Herbert Klein and Ugo Nwokeji, among others, also argue that African conceptions of gender and age played a critical role in the slave trade. They show that slaves sold into the transatlantic trade varied according to gender and age, suggesting that African enslavers and traders had specific criteria for determining who remained a captive on the continent and who was sold on the coast.[42]

---

[41] David Eltis and Stanley L. Engerman, "Was the Slave Trade Dominated by Men?" *Journal of Interdisciplinary History* 23, no. 2 (1992): 240–46.

[42] Herbert S. Klein, "African Women in the Atlantic Slave Trade." In *Women and Slavery in Africa*, ed. Claire C. Robertson and Martin A. Klein (Madison: University of Wisconsin Press, 1983), 35–37; G. Ugo Nwokeji, "African Conceptions of Gender and the Slave Traffic." *William and Mary Quarterly* 58, no. 1 (2001): 52; Claire C. Robertson and Martin A. Klein, "Women's Importance in African Slave Systems." In *Women and Slavery in Africa*, ed. Claire C. Robertson and Martin A. Klein (Madison: University of Wisconsin Press, 1983), 3–5; Joseph C. Miller, "Women as Slaves and Owners of Slaves: Experiences from Africa, the Indian Ocean World, and the Early Atlantic." In *Women*

The slave trade from Angola was no exception; it followed similar patterns to those of other regions of slave embarkation.

Chapter 5 provides an analysis of African motives for enslaving other Africans and selling them into the trade, based on slave prices in Luanda, the principal port of embarkation in Angola. It shows that Africans who enslaved and sold other Africans into the trade were motivated primarily by economic factors. Philip Curtin suggested that Africans were politically motivated to sell other Africans into the slave trade. He argued that the number of slaves embarked from the coast between the Senegal and Gambia rivers did not correspond to the demand for slaves overseas, since an increase in price did not result in more slaves being shipped. He attributed the variation in the number of slaves carried from Senegambia to the political situation in the region's hinterland, which was often characterized by widespread violence and warfare.[43] Curtin's argument clearly favored the association of the slave trade with processes of state formation and imperial expansion, directly connecting the two. However, Philip Le Veen, David Richardson, and David Eltis, among others, challenged this position based on several price series of slaves shipped from different African regions. Their work clearly shows the supply of slaves on the coast responded to variations in demand as measured by price.[44] In West Central Africa, the available evidence indicates that the supply of slaves also responded to variations in price, suggesting that Africans were economically motivated to participate in the trade. This finding further indicates that state formation and imperial expansion were not the sole reasons Africans participated in the trade.

The commodities for which Africans traded slaves also shed light on their motives to participate in the traffic. David Richardson and George Metcalf argue that African patterns of consumption shed new light on

and Slavery: Africa, the Indian Ocean, and the Medieval North Atlantic, ed. Gwyn Campbell, Suzanne Miers, and Joseph C. Miller, vol. 1 (Athens: Ohio University Press, 2007), 4–11; Paul E. Lovejoy, "Internal Markets or an Atlantic-Sahara Divide? How Women Fit into the Slave Trade of West Africa." In *Women and Slavery: Africa, the Indian Ocean, and the Medieval North Atlantic*, ed. Gwyn Campbell, Suzanne Miers, and Joseph C. Miller, vol. 1 (Athens: Ohio University Press, 2007), 259–61.

[43] Philip D. Curtin, *Economic Change in Precolonial Africa: Senegambia in the Era of the Slave Trade* (Madison: University of Wisconsin Press, 1975), vol. 1, 156–68.

[44] E. Philip Le Veen, "The African Slave Supply Response." *African Studies Review* 18, no. 1 (1975): 9; David Richardson, "Prices of Slaves in West and West Central Africa: Toward an Annual Series, 1698–1807." *Bulletin of Economic Research* 43, no. 1 (1991): 43–48; Eltis, *Economic Growth*, 15 and 182–83.

what motivated Africans to enslave other Africans and sell them into the transatlantic slave trade.[45] Hence, in addition to price series, Chapter 5 analyzes lists of imports at Luanda for several years between 1785 and 1864. These lists show that Africans traded slaves for a wide variety of commodities imported from Europe, Asia, and the Americas. Although weapons formed a significant percentage of the commodities for which slaves were traded, textiles and alcoholic beverages were in fact of greater value. The fact that Africans imported more trade than war commodities indicates that economic gains were the primary motivation for their participation in the traffic. The slave trade was not dominated just by political or military developments in the interior of Africa.

Finally, Chapter 6 analyzes both primary and secondary sources dealing with specific cases of enslavement in the interior of Angola to examine further the question of who was eligible for enslavement and sale across the Atlantic. Because the slave trade has been commonly associated with processes of state formation and imperial expansion, scholars have tended to see slaves shipped from Africa merely as victims of war. Here, I explore other possibilities. Africans could also become slaves through trickery, judicial proceedings, or even voluntary enslavement. Causes of the last phenomenon included catastrophic events such as famine and drought. The chapter focuses primarily on African perceptions of who was eligible for enslavement, as defined by the victims' sex, age, identity, social status, and form of enslavement, among other categories.[46] It provides an analysis of different processes of enslavement to assess what induced Africans to enslave and sell other Africans into the transatlantic slave trade. David Eltis and Nathan Huggins, for example, argue that identity was a crucial element in determining who remained captive on the continent and who was sold into Atlantic markets.[47] Robin Law draws attention to the judicial nature of African slavery, stressing differences between legal and

---

[45] David Richardson, "West African Consumption Patterns and Their Influence on the Eighteenth Century English Slave Trade." In *The Uncommon Market: Essays in the Economic History of the Atlantic Slave Trade*, ed. Henry A. Gemery and Jan S. Hogendorn (New York: Academic Press, 1979), 304–05; George Metcalf, "A Microcosm of Why Africans Sold Slaves: Akan Consumption Patterns in the 1770s." *Journal of African History* 28, no. 3 (1987): 377–78.

[46] Sean Stilwell, *Slavery and Slaving in African History* (New York: Cambridge University Press, 2014), 9.

[47] David Eltis, *The Rise of African Slavery in the Americas* (New York: Cambridge University Press, 2000), 57–61; Nathan Irvin Huggins, *Black Odyssey: The Afro-American Ordeal in Slavery* (New York: Pantheon Books, 1977), 20.

illegal enslavement in the interior of the continent.[48] Others have argued that external pressures, such as the demand for slaves on the coast, transformed the way Africans viewed slavery, making what they previously considered illegal enslavement only too common.[49]

The slave trade from West Central Africa was one of the largest and longest waves of coerced migration in history. Many scholars have long believed that the majority of slaves sold on the coast came from the continent's deep interior, as victims of wars waged by the Lunda Empire. However, this book throws doubt on this position and explores alternative interpretations for the peak years of the trade. Moreover, it will provide members of the African Diaspora with new information about their ancestors. As hard as it may seem for us to accept, Africans sold on the coast were enslaved by other Africans in various ways and shipped by traders linked to a complex commercial network created to carry millions of men, women, and children as slaves across the Atlantic. Clearly, economics motivated Africans to enslave and sell other Africans, but these individuals acted according to their own dictates and mores to determine who was and was not eligible for enslavement. Angola and other countries of present-day West Central Africa still bear the legacies of this past, which have offered an important obstacle in the formation of national identities in the region.[50] In the final analysis, these conventions fitted well with the overall operation of the transatlantic slave trade and made West Central Africa the principal source of slaves for the Americas well into the nineteenth century.

---

[48] Robin Law, "Legal and Illegal Enslavement in West Africa, in the Context of the Trans-Atlantic Slave Trade." In *Ghana in Africa and the World: Essays in Honor of Adu Boahen*, ed. Toyin Falola (Trenton: Africa World Press, 2003), 513–14.

[49] Lovejoy, *Transformations in Slavery*, 10–12; Linda Heywood, "Slavery and Its Transformation in the Kingdom of Kongo, 1491–1800." *Journal of African History* 50, no. 1 (2009): 1–22; Cândido, *An African Slaving Port*, 13–17; Ferreira, *Cross-Cultural Exchange*, 96–98.

[50] Marcia C. Schenck and Mariana P. Cândido, "Uncomfortable Pasts: Talking about Slavery in Angola." In *African Heritage and Memories of Slavery in Brazil and the South Atlantic World*, ed. Ana Lúcia Araújo (Amherst: Cambria Press, 2015), 213–52. Alternative views are available in Linda M. Heywood, *Contested Power in Angola, 1840s to the Present* (Rochester: University of Rochester Press, 2000), xiii–xvi; Marissa Jean Moorman, *Intonations: A Social History of Music and Nation in Luanda, Angola, from 1945 to Recent Times* (Athens: Ohio University Press, 2008), 2–3; Justin Pearce, *Political Identity and Conflict in Central Angola, 1975–2002* (New York: Cambridge University Press, 2015), 5–17.

I

The Atlantic Slave Trade in the Century of Abolition

In the late eighteenth century, the slave trade from West Central Africa entered a new age of social, political, economic, and ultimately ideological change. Economic growth and industrialization in Europe, particularly in Britain, increased the demand for primary commodities imported from the Americas, such as sugar, cotton, rice, and tobacco. These were produced with slave labor brought from Africa and, as the demand for these items increased, so did the demand for slaves carried across the Atlantic. Ironically, although slavery was widespread in the Americas, some Europeans had begun to question the morality of an institution that deprived some individuals of their liberty for the benefit of others.[1] Moreover, they became increasingly persuaded that slave labor was inferior to free labor because slaves lacked the incentive to work.[2] The French Revolution and the 1791 slave rebellion in Saint Domingue, present-day Haiti, further questioned slavery, contributing to the spread of the abolitionist movement in the Atlantic world.[3] As a consequence, at the beginning of the nineteenth century, the slave trade declined as some nations began to retreat from the business. In 1807, both the US Congress and the British Parliament prohibited their citizens from participating in the trade and, soon after, the British initiated a campaign to suppress the entire

---

[1] Davis, *Inhuman Bondage*, 231–49.

[2] Seymour Drescher, *The Mighty Experiment: Free Labor versus Slavery in British Emancipation* (New York: Oxford University Press, 2002), 9–23. The main source for this argument is Adam Smith, *An Inquiry into the Nature and Causes of the Wealth of Nations* (London: W. Strahan and T. Cadell, 1776), vol. 1, 471–72.

[3] Davis, *Inhuman Bondage*, 160–61.

trade from Africa, which continued throughout the balance of the nineteenth century.[4]

This new era of antislavery sentiment had a profound impact on the trade from West Central Africa. Despite British efforts to suppress it, the number of slaves embarked from the region remained high, as the center of gravity shifted from the North to the South Atlantic. During the eighteenth century, the slave trade expanded largely because of the demand for labor in the British and French Caribbean. British and French traders were the principal suppliers of slaves for the Caribbean. They purchased the majority of their slaves on the coast of West Africa, north of the Equator. However, as these nations withdrew from the business at the beginning of the nineteenth century, that traffic declined. Other nations sought to tap the sources of slaves previously dominated by British and French traders, notably Portugal, Spain, and Brazil. In order to prevent this from happening, Britain signed treaties with each of these countries that restricted or banned their involvement in the traffic. Thus, in 1810 Britain and Portugal signed a treaty for the gradual suppression of the trade, especially from ports outside Portuguese jurisdiction in Africa.[5] In 1815, an Anglo-Portuguese treaty prohibited Portuguese traders carrying slaves north of the Equator.[6] Independent from Portugal since 1822, Brazil tacitly agreed to the terms of this 1815 treaty, and Brazilian traders too were banned from purchasing slaves from African regions located north of the line.[7] In 1817, Britain signed a similar treaty with Spain, except the prohibition was to apply to the whole of the Atlantic. In 1826, it signed a further treaty with Brazil, establishing outright abolition of the slave trade within three years following ratification in 1827.[8] Moreover, Britain sent warships to patrol the coast of West Africa to intercept vessels violating these agreements. The antislavery conventions established

---

[4] Roger Anstey, *The Atlantic Slave Trade and British Abolition, 1760–1810* (Atlantic Highlands: Humanities Press, 1975), 396–98; Paul Finkelman, "Regulating the African Slave Trade," *Civil War History* 54, no. 4 (2008): 379.

[5] Leslie Bethell, *The Abolition of the Brazilian Slave Trade: Britain, Brazil and the Slave Trade Question, 1807–1869* (Cambridge: Cambridge University Press, 1970), 8–9; João Pedro Marques, *Os Sons do Silêncio: O Portugal de Oitocentos e a Abolição do Tráfico de Escravos* (Lisbon: Imprensa de Ciências Sociais, 1999), 93–94.

[6] Bethell, *The Abolition*, 13–14; Marques, *Os Sons do Silêncio*, 103–04.

[7] Bethell, *The Abolition*, 13–14.

[8] David R. Murray, *Odious Commerce: Britain, Spain, and the Abolition of the Cuban Slave Trade* (New York: Cambridge University Press, 1980), 70–71; Bethell, *The Abolition*, 60–61; Marques, *Os Sons do Silêncio*, 153–54.

mixed commission courts around the Atlantic to adjudicate vessels accused of illegal trading.[9] As the British increased their efforts to suppress the traffic in the North Atlantic, the number of captives in the South Atlantic continued to rise well into the nineteenth century, making West Central Africa the major source of slaves for the Americas.

Some major figures in the field believe that in the nineteenth century a rising demand for labor in the Americas pushed the sources of slaves shipped from West Central Africa deeper into the region's interior. Joseph Miller has argued that the shifting origins of slaves formed what he called "slaving frontiers." He claims that since the sixteenth century these frontiers moved gradually from the coast to the interior of West Central Africa. In the nineteenth century, Miller maintains, these frontiers had reached the populations living beyond the valley of the Kwango River, forcing thousands of Africans into slavery.[10] Paul Lovejoy also believes the nineteenth century saw the trade drawing on slaves from the interior of West Central Africa. He posits that the new demand for slaves in the Americas required many Lunda and Luba warlords to search for slaves deep in the interior of West Central Africa.[11] Patrick Manning claims the journey of a slave coffle, a train of captives chained together, from the region's interior doubled in length as the trade expanded, resulting in a sharp decline in the inland populations.[12]

A close analysis, however, shows there is insufficient evidence to support the idea of a nineteenth-century expansion of such frontiers. Although the treaties signed with Portugal, Spain, and Brazil did initially cause an expansion of the Iberian slave trade from West Central Africa, the withdrawal of other nations from the business partly offset this expansion. Iberian traders spread their activities along the coast of West Central Africa because they tapped into the sources of slaves previously dominated by their competitors. Moreover, since Brazil and the Spanish colonies depended largely on slave labor, they simply had no other options but to spread their activities along the African coast, especially to regions where they had a long tradition of trading slaves, such as in West Africa. Despite the treaties, Iberian governments often turned a blind eye to the activities of their traders. Brazil, perhaps, is a notorious case. In 1831, the

---

[9] Leslie Bethell, "The Mixed Commissions for the Suppression of the Transatlantic Slave Trade in the Nineteenth Century." *Journal of African History* 7, no. 1 (1966): 79–83; Eltis, *Economic Growth*, 85–103.
[10] Miller, *Way of Death*, 140–46 and Map 5.1.
[11] Lovejoy, *Transformations in Slavery*, 149.   [12] Manning, *Slavery and African Life*, 70.

government reassured Britain of its commitment to suppress the traffic by enacting its own law to abolish the trade, in spite of which Brazilian traders continued their activities.[13] Since the law prohibited trafficking in both hemispheres, traders no longer felt restricted to West Central Africa and expanded their operations, albeit illegally, to other African regions, including areas as far as Southeast Africa. Therefore, the size of the Iberian trade was insufficient to move the slaving frontiers further into the interior of West Central Africa. At least in this respect, the trade between the late eighteenth and the mid-nineteenth century followed a pattern of continuity rather than expansion. This pattern can be better explained with the help of "Voyages: The Trans-Atlantic Slave Trade Database."[14]

DEMAND

The most complete database of slaving voyages available, "Voyages" contains information on almost 2 million slaves shipped from West Central Africa between 1781 and 1867, the last year a transatlantic slave venture was reported to have left the region.[15] "Voyages" provides not only a database of shipping records but also estimates of all slaves shipped that can be broken down by national carriers and regions of embarkation and disembarkation. These estimates were built using information from the database itself and secondary sources to supplement periods for which the database lacks hard voyage information. The "Voyages" estimates page shows that approximately 2.8 million Africans embarked as slaves from the coast of West Central Africa between 1781 and 1867, 29 percent more than the number of slaves according to shipping records alone. This estimate, however, can be further refined.

"Voyages" draws on records of maritime activity in the Americas. After the prohibition of the slave trade in the North Atlantic, many slave traders from Bahia, in Northeast Brazil, applied to the Portuguese and later Brazilian authorities for licenses to purchase slaves at Cabinda or Molembo, on the coast of West Central Africa, instead of their traditional ports of slave embarkation at the Bight of Benin, in West Africa.

---

[13] Bethell, *The Abolition*, 62–72; Brazil, *Collecção das Leis do Império do Brazil de 1831: Actos do Poder Legislativo* (Rio de Janeiro: Typographia Nacional, 1875), 182.

[14] Eltis et al., "Voyages."

[15] David Eltis, "The Nineteenth Century Transatlantic Slave Trade: An Annual Time Series of Imports into the Americas Broken Down by Region," *Hispanic American Historical Review* 67, no. 1 (1987): 128–29.

Nevertheless, most of them continued to trade in the Bight of Benin and used the licenses to deceive British naval officers should the latter intercept them while carrying a slave cargo loaded north of the Equator.[16] As a result, from 1816 until 1830, when the complete ban came into force this bias in the sources was transferred to the shipping records available in "Voyages." David Eltis was the only historian to address this problem by reallocating to the Bight of Benin all slaves originally recorded to have been shipped from the ports north of the Congo River to Bahia.[17] It is now possible to address this issue with more precision.

The "Voyages" database allows users to fine tune their search for data. In order to improve the accuracy of the estimates, the share of slaves carried in Portuguese and Brazilian vessels from Cabinda and Molembo to Bahia between 1816 and 1830 can be discounted from the remaining ports and subtracted from the total number of slaves carried from West Central Africa. The database shows that in the 15 years before 1816 Bahia purchased only 2,237 slaves from Cabinda, while between 1816 and 1830, this number increased to 41,059. Further, it shows that Bahia did not purchase a single slave from Molembo in the 15 years before 1816, but between 1816 and 1830, there are records indicating some 46,333 slaves leaving Molembo for Bahia. As the 1815 treaty may have indeed forced some Bahian traders to purchase slaves in West Central Africa, it seems plausible that, between 1816 and 1830, only a fraction of the slaves recorded in the database actually embarked from Cabinda and Molembo to Bahia. Hence, the number of slaves leaving these ports for Bahia between 1816 and 1830 in the estimates was reduced to approximately 63 percent of the observable totals. This percentage represents the midpoint between the share of the number of slaves carried from West Central Africa to Bahia from 1801 to 1815 and those from 1816 to 1830. Similarly, the number of slaves shipped from Cabinda and Molembo in the database was reduced to 63 percent to correct for the overrepresentation of these ports in the total estimated number of slaves embarked from West Central Africa in these 15 years on the "Voyages" estimate page. Although this percentage may look high, the

---

[16] Alexandre Vieira Ribeiro, "O Tráfico Atlântico de Escravos e a Praça Mercantil de Salvador, c.1680–1830" (M.A., Universidade Federal do Rio de Janeiro, 2005), 58, 61, and 137; Pierre Verger, *Fluxo e Refluxo: O Tráfico de Escravos entre o Golfo de Benin e a Bahia de Todos os Santos dos Séculos XVII a XIX* (São Paulo: Corrupio, 1987), 414–19.

[17] David Eltis, "Slave Departures from Africa, 1811–1867: An Annual Time Series," *African Economic History*, no. 15 (1986): 146.

TABLE 1.1 *Slaves leaving West Central Africa, 1781–1867*

Periods	Number of slaves embarked	Average of slaves embarked per year
1781–1807	974,190	36,081
1808–1830	913,884	39,734
1831–1850	730,474	36,524
1851–1867	156,779	9,222
All Years	2,775,327	31,900

Sources: David Eltis et al., "Voyages: The Trans-Atlantic Slave Trade Database," Online database, 2008, www.slavevoyages.org/ and Daniel B. Domingues da Silva, "The Atlantic Slave Trade from Angola: A Port-by-Port Estimate of Slaves Embarked, 1701–1867," *International Journal of African Historical Studies* 46, no. 1 (2013): 121–22.

overall impact on "Voyages" estimated number of slaves transported from the region between 1781 and 1867 is less than one percent. Table 1.1 summarizes the results of this procedure.[18]

Table 1.1 shows the number of slaves shipped from West Central Africa between the late eighteenth and the mid-nineteenth century using four key periods. The first begins in the 1780s, with the expansion of the demand for slaves in the Americas and ends in 1807, with the abolition of the British slave trade. The second period begins in 1808, with the transference of the Portuguese court to Rio de Janeiro, in Southeast Brazil, and the opening of Brazilian ports for direct trade with friendly nations, especially Britain. This period ends in 1830, with the suppression of the slave trade to Brazil following the 1826 Anglo-Brazilian treaty. This was a critical period in the trade, since the center of gravity shifted from the North to the South Atlantic, where West Central Africa is located. The third period begins in the following year, when the trade from the region became illegal, and ends in 1850, when Brazil did in fact close its ports to all vessels carrying slaves from Africa. Finally, the fourth period represents the period of decline of the trade, between 1851 and 1867, the last year in which there are records of slaves being shipped from the coast of West Central Africa.

Although the traffic varied widely within each of these periods, the outflow of slaves from West Central Africa remained relatively constant

---

[18] Additional information on the adjustment of "Voyages" figures is available in Daniel B. Domingues da Silva, "The Atlantic Slave Trade from Angola: A Port-by-Port Estimate of Slaves Embarked, 1701–1867," *International Journal of African Historical Studies* 46, no. 1 (2013): 107–22.

from the late eighteenth until the mid-nineteenth century. In the first period, ships belonging to various nationalities embarked an average of 36,080 slaves per year. This figure increased approximately 9 percent in the following period, to 39,735 per year, as a result of suppression of the trade in the North Atlantic. However, in the third period, the average number of slaves embarked declined to levels approximating those found prior to the abolition of the British trade. Between 1831 and 1850, the average number of slaves shipped from West Central Africa declined to 36,525 per year. The traffic in the region declined significantly only after the abolition of the Brazilian trade in 1850, when the average number shipped from West Central Africa fell a precipitous 75 percent to about 9,220 slaves per year. It is apparent that from the late eighteenth to the mid-nineteenth century West Central Africa served as a steady source of slaves for the Americas.

The trade from West Central Africa varied mostly as a result of the demand for labor in the Americas and British efforts to suppress the transatlantic trade. In the late eighteenth century, demand from the Americas had increased the competition for slaves along the coast of West Central Africa. The Portuguese, the principal traders in this region, had been there since the sixteenth century and controlled two outlets, Luanda and Benguela. British and French traders, by contrast, used to purchase most of their slaves in West Africa, but as the demand for slaves across the Atlantic increased after 1700, they had extended their activities to points north of the Congo River. Unlike the Portuguese, however, they obtained most of their captives at ports controlled by independent African polities trading out of Cabinda, Molembo, Loango, and other ports around the mouth of the Congo River. In the late eighteenth century, the presence of British and French slavers in the region increased so much that the Portuguese, located further south, began to fear for their own supplies. In 1782, for example, Manoel da Silva Ribeiro Fernandes, a trader in the service of the Portuguese colonial government, sailed for the ports north of Luanda and reported that the French conducted a lively trade at Cabinda and Loango.[19] In 1793, the Portuguese governor of Angola, Manoel de Almeida e Vasconcelos, noted that the British trade at Ambriz had significantly reduced the supply of slaves at Luanda from the north of Angola.[20]

---

[19] "Relação de uma viagem à costa ao norte de Luanda por Manoel da Silva Ribeiro Fernandes ao Senhor Ajudante de Ordens Pedro José Corrêa Quevedo," 15 August 1782, AHU, CU, Angola, box 65 doc. 64.

[20] Manoel de Almeida e Vasconcelos to Martinho de Melo e Castro, 25 April 1793, AHU, CU, Angola, box 78 doc. 57.

Nonetheless, from the last decade of the eighteenth to the first decade of the nineteenth century, the competition for slaves in West Central Africa tended to decline as a result of, first, the Haitian Revolution and, second, the abolition of the British slave trade. In 1791, the slaves of Saint Domingue, a French colony in the Caribbean, rebelled. The rebellion spread throughout the island, reaching an unprecedented scale, and culminated in rebel independence in 1804. Saint Domingue was renamed Haiti, the first modern state founded by people of African ancestry in the Americas and the second independent nation in the continent. Before the rebellion, Saint Domingue was the main producer of tropical produce in the Americas and served as the principal destination for slaves embarked in French vessels from the coast of West Central Africa.[21] With the independence of Haiti, the French slave trade virtually collapsed, significantly reducing the number of slaves shipped in French vessels from West Central Africa. As the "Voyages" estimates indicate, in the ten years preceding the slave rebellion, French traders shipped about 128,840 from the coast of West Central Africa but, in the ten years following the rebellion, this figure declined to 32,615, almost all of whom arrived between 1791 and 1793. Particularly after 1793, the Haitian Revolution reduced the competition for slaves on the coast of West Central Africa.

The abolition of the British slave trade in 1807 further reduced the international competition for slaves on the region's coast. After the Haitian Revolution, the British were the only real competition for the Portuguese. They expanded their slaving activities along the coast of West Central Africa by shipping many of the captives previously carried in French vessels. The estimates show that in the ten years preceding the slave rebellion in Saint Domingue, British traders shipped 16,710 slaves from the coast of West Central Africa, but in the following ten years this figure increased to 115,720. The British slave trade increased as a direct result of the Haitian Revolution and the subsequent collapse of its French counterpart. However, with the abolition of the trade in 1807, British

---

[21] C. L. R. James, *The Black Jacobins: Toussaint Louverture and the San Domingo Revolution*, 2nd edn. (New York: Vintage Books, 1963), 224–35; Eugene D. Genovese, *From Rebellion to Revolution: Afro-American Slave Revolts in the Making of the Modern World* (Baton Rouge: Louisiana State University Press, 1979), 84–97; David Geggus, "The French and Haitian Revolutions, and Resistance to Slavery: An Overview," *Revue Française d'Histoire d'Outre-Mer* 76, no. 282–83 (1989): 107–24; Carolyn Fick, *The Making of Haiti: The Saint-Domingue Revolution from Below* (Knoxville: University of Tennessee Press, 1990), 1–2; Laurent Dubois, *Avengers of the New World: The Story of the Haitian Revolution* (Cambridge: Belknap Press of Harvard University Press, 2004), 1–2 and 95–97.

slaving activities along the coast of West Central Africa came to a complete halt. Overall, the international competition for slaves in the region declined significantly, resulting in a new phase in the exodus of captives from West Central Africa.

After the abolition of the British slave trade, Iberian carriers established a major presence in the region. Iberian carriers included vessels belonging to Portugal and Spain, as well as Iberian America – Cuba, Brazil, Puerto Rico, and Uruguay. However, between 1808 and 1830, Portuguese and Brazilian traders carried off the majority of slaves from West Central Africa. In 1808, the Prince Regent Dom João VI transferred the Portuguese court to Rio de Janeiro to escape the Napoleonic invasion of Lisbon led by General Jean Andoche Junot.[22] After arriving in Brazil, Dom João opened Brazilian ports for the first time to international trade, particularly with the British, who had escorted the Portuguese royal family across the Atlantic.[23] The transfer of the Portuguese court and the opening of the Brazilian ports increased the population of Rio de Janeiro significantly. Census data for Rio de Janeiro shows that the city's population increased 14 percent in this period, from 46,944 in 1803 to 54,255 in 1808.[24] As the city's inhabitants depended largely on slave labor, this increase also stimulated the expansion of the slave trade from West Central Africa.

The major source of increased demand for the region's slaves was, however, the growth of Brazilian commercial agriculture. From the late eighteenth century, Brazilian agriculture benefited from the decline of gold production in Goiás, Minas Gerais, and Mato Grosso, three captaincies situated in the interior of Brazil. Gold had been the principal commodity exported from Brazil, but production in these captaincies gradually declined, from an average of 1,072 *arrobas* produced at its peak period

---

[22] Alan K. Manchester, "The Transfer of the Portuguese Court to Rio de Janeiro." In *Conflict and Continuity in Brazilian Society*, ed. Henry H. Keith and S. F. Edwards (Columbia: University of South Carolina Press, 1969), 148–63; Kirsten Schultz, "The Transfer of the Portuguese Court and Ideas of Empire," *Portuguese Studies Review* 15, no. 1–2 (2007): 367–91; Jerry Adelman, *Sovereignty and Revolution in the Iberian Atlantic* (Princeton: Princeton University Press, 2006), 222–38; Gabriel Paquette, *Imperial Portugal in the Age of Atlantic Revolutions: The Luso-Brazilian World, c. 1770–1850* (New York: Cambridge University Press, 2013), 85–95.

[23] Paulo Bonavides and Roberto Amaral, *Textos Políticos da História do Brasil*, 3rd edn. (Brasília: Senado Federal, 2002), vol. 1, 410–11.

[24] Dauril Alden, "Late Colonial Brazil, 1750–1808." In *The Cambridge History of Latin America*, ed. Leslie Bethell, vol. 2 (New York: Cambridge University Press, 1984), 605, Table 3; Mary C. Karasch, *Slave Life in Rio de Janeiro, 1808–1850* (Princeton: Princeton University Press, 1987), 61, Table 3.1.

between 1750 and 1754 to about 299 *arrobas* between 1795 and 1799.[25] Many individuals sought to invest in other activities such as the production of sugar, rice, and cotton. Sugar producers in Brazil, in particular, also benefited from the Haitian Revolution, which had ruined their competitors in Saint Domingue. Sugar exports from Bahia, for example, increased from about 480,000 *arrobas* in 1788 to 746,600 *arrobas* in 1798. Sugar exports from Pernambuco also increased, from about 275,000 *arrobas* in 1790 to 560,000 in 1807. Similarly, sugar exports from Rio de Janeiro expanded from 200,000 *arrobas* in 1790 to 487,200 in 1800.[26] As gold exports from the Brazilian interior declined, the traditional centers of sugar production in Brazil ensured that demand for West Central African captives remained high.

The expansion of Brazilian agricultural exports was not limited to sugar. Exports of rice and cotton, for example, also increased during the late eighteenth and early nineteenth centuries. The majority of rice and cotton exported from Brazil was produced in the captaincies of Maranhão and Pará, located in the Amazon Basin, mainly with African slave labor imported from Upper Guinea. Rice was produced mostly for consumption in Portugal, while cotton was grown for export to the larger European market. By 1781, rice exports from Pará and Maranhão, as well as from Rio de Janeiro, were more than enough to allow Portugal to ban the entry of all foreign rice.[27] Cotton production in Pará and Maranhão also increased significantly, spreading quickly to other captaincies. In 1799, for example, the Bishop of Olinda, a meticulous observer of the Brazilian economy at that time, noted that in Pernambuco cotton exports "almost equaled the value of sugar and all other products combined."[28] As a result, between 1780 and 1800, Brazil emerged as a major cotton supplier for the Lancashire factories during the Industrial Revolution in England, ranking after the British West Indies and the Mediterranean, and before the United States. [29]

[25] Virgílio Noya Pinto, *O Ouro Brasileiro e o Comércio Anglo-Português: Uma Contribuição aos Estudos da Economia Atlântica no Século XVIII*, 2nd edn. (São Paulo: Companhia Editora Nacional, 1979), 114. Pinto calculates the weight of one *arroba* of gold at approximately 14.7 kilograms.

[26] Alden, "Late Colonial Brazil," 627–31.

[27] Ibid., 641; Manuel Nunes Dias, *Fomento e Mercantilismo: A Companhia Geral do Grão Pará e Maranhão (1755–1778)* (Belém: Universidade Federal do Pará, 1970), vols. 1, 431–52.

[28] Cited in Alden, "Late Colonial Brazil," 637.

[29] Thomas Ellison, *The Cotton Trade of Great Britain* (London: Effingham Wilson, 1886), 86; William Henry Johnson, *Cotton and Its Production* (London: Macmillan, 1926), 190–91.

Table 1.2 confirms that Brazil was the principal market for slaves embarked from West Central Africa. Brazil alone served as the destination for about 74 percent of all slaves shipped between the late eighteenth and the mid-nineteenth century. The remaining slaves were carried to different areas of the Caribbean, mainland North America, and British enclaves in Africa, to which naval cruisers escorted the slave vessels they had detained. The Africans rescued by British naval forces were generally liberated at either a mixed commission or a Vice-Admiralty court established in Sierra Leone, West Africa, for the adjudication of cases involving vessels accused of illegal slave trading. These individuals were rarely repatriated. In most cases, they settled down in Sierra Leone, merged with the local population, or joined the British navy.[30] The majority of slaves shipped from West Central Africa disembarked in Rio de Janeiro, Southeast Brazil. Table 1.2 shows that over 1.4 million slaves were shipped to Southeast Brazil alone between 1781 and 1867. Pernambuco was the second principal market for slaves, the destination for about 312,200 slaves embarked from the region. Bahia, in third place, received approximately 243,100 slaves, and the captaincies of Pará and Maranhão, in Amazonia, took about 47,700 slaves shipped from West Central Africa to Brazil. In short, from the late eighteenth until the mid-nineteenth century, Brazil had a strong connection to West Central Africa, serving as the principal market not only for the region's slaves, but also for captives carried off from all African regions, including Southeast Africa.

Those slaves shipped from West Central Africa were employed in several regions in the interior of Brazil. Studies focusing on the Brazilian internal trade are in their infancy, but the first indications are that slaves disembarked in Brazil from Africa were distributed to several places. Between 1760 and 1779, about 30 percent of all slaves landed at Bahia were transported to regions far into the interior of Brazil.[31] The majority of this group went, as before, to the former gold districts of Minas Gerais, which received 18 percent of all slaves shipped to the interior of Brazil.[32] However, in the nineteenth century, Maranhão became the major destination for all slaves sold in Bahia. Between 1811 and 1820, for example, about 30 percent of all captives leaving Bahia, both Africans and Creoles, went to Maranhão.[33] Slaves arriving in Rio de Janeiro were also sold

[30] Daniel B. Domingues da Silva et al., "The Diaspora of Africans Liberated from Slave Ships in the Nineteenth Century." *Journal of African History* 55, no. 3 (2014): 349–64.
[31] Ribeiro, "O Tráfico Atlântico," 101.   [32] Ibid., 107.   [33] Ibid., 115.

TABLE 1.2 *Slaves leaving West Central Africa by region of disembarkation (in thousands), 1781–1867*

Regions	Sub-regions	1781–1807	1808–1830	1831–1850	1851–1867	Total
Brazil	Amazonia	25.0	21.4	1.3	-	47.7
	Bahia	94.1	127.0	20.9	1.1	243.1
	Pernambuco	103.6	144.8	63.8	0.0	312.2
	SE Brazil	336.6	514.8	565.6	3.1	1,420.1
Other		11.9	15.8	6.4	-	34.1
British Caribbean		142.8	4.6	2.5	-	149.9
French Caribbean		173.3	2.4	-	-	175.7
Spanish Caribbean		26.7	78.6	48.2	135.3	288.8
Other		60.2	4.5	21.7	17.2	103.6
All regions		974.2	913.9	730.5	156.8	2,775.4

Note: Other regions include mainland North America, the Dutch Caribbean, the Danish West Indies, and Africa.
Source: Same as Table 1.1.

to several regions in the interior of Brazil. Between 1819 and 1830, approximately 43 percent of Rio de Janeiro landings were redirected from the city to other Brazilian markets.[34] The majority of them were sent to Minas Gerais, which received 59 percent of the total shipped from Rio de Janeiro. By this time, Minas Gerais had become a major producer of food for the internal market.[35] A further 24 percent went mostly to São Paulo, in Southeast Brazil, where they were employed in sugar and coffee plantations.[36] The majority of the remainder, about 10 percent, went to Rio Grande do Sul, in southern Brazil, where they were used in various activities but particularly in jerked beef production.[37]

The opening of the Brazilian ports to foreign shipping, especially British, resulted in lower transportation costs for Brazilian plantation produce. This, in turn, stimulated the Brazilian slave trade from West Central Africa. *Lloyd's Register of Shipping* shows that, after the British

[34] Roberto Guedes and João Luís Fragoso, "Alegrias e Artimanhas de uma Fonte Seriada: Os Códices 390, 421, 424 e 425: Despachos de Escravos e Passaportes da Intendência de Polícia da Corte, 1819–1833." In *Tráfico Interno de Escravos e Relações Comerciais no Centro-Sul do Brasil, Séculos XVIII e XIX*, ed. IPEA (Brasília: Instituto de Pesquisa Econômica Aplicada, 2000), calculated from table 3.
[35] Ibid., calculated from table 4; Amilcar Martins Filho and Roberto B. Martins, "Slavery in a Non-Export Economy: Nineteenth Century Minas Gerais Revisited," *Hispanic American Historical Review* 63, no. 3 (1983): 556–65.
[36] Guedes and Fragoso, "Alegrias e Artimanhas," calculated from table 4.   [37] Ibid.

abolished their slave trade, they redeployed their slaving fleet to the commodity trade in the tropics. Since these vessels were originally designed to sail in the warm waters of Africa, their hulls were covered with copper sheets, which not only better protected them from sea worms, but also improved their speed and durability.[38] British ex-slavers sailed for several places in the Caribbean and South America, such as Antigua, Bahamas, Cuba, Dominica, Jamaica, and Peru. However, at the beginning of the nineteenth century, Brazil served as the single major destination for all British ex-slavers. *Lloyd's Register of Shipping* indicates that 33 percent of all voyages undertaken by British ex-slavers between 1808 and 1811 went to Brazil.[39] Although West Central Africa represented just one, albeit the major, source of slaves for Brazil, slaves brought from this region probably produced a significant percentage of the commodities that these British ex-slavers carried to Europe. The opening of the Brazilian ports resulted in lower costs for Brazilian commerce and a higher demand for slaves.

The British connection to the slave trade from West Central Africa was not limited to the transportation of produce cultivated by the region's slaves in Brazil. The spread of British credit following the opening of the Brazilian ports to international trade also fueled the trade from West Central Africa. David Eltis examined the British consular and naval correspondence together with an analysis of the trade goods that Cuban and Brazilian slave traders used to purchase their slaves and shows that British subjects contributed significantly to the post-1807 traffic. Eltis states that they "owned, managed, and manned slaving adventures; purchased newly imported Africans in the Americas; supplied ships, equipment, insurance, and most important of all trade goods and credit to foreign slave traders."[40] British firms could wait up to two years to receive returns on their investments. This was particularly useful to Brazilian traders, given the scarcity of credit available in most financial centers in Brazil.[41]

---

[38] Peter M. Solar and Klas Rönnbäck, "Copper Sheathing and the British Slave Trade." *Economic History Review* Early view (2014): 1–3, doi:10.1111/ehr.12085.

[39] David M. Williams, "Abolition and the Re-Deployment of the Slave Fleet, 1807–11." *Journal of Transport History* 11, no. 2 (1973): 106–11.

[40] David Eltis, "The British Contribution to the Nineteenth Century Trans-Atlantic Slave Trade." *Economic History Review* 32, no. 2 (1979): 211.

[41] Ibid., 220; David Eltis, "The British Trans-Atlantic Slave Trade after 1807." *Maritime History* 4, no. 1 (1974): 8–9; Eltis, *Economic Growth*, 58–59; Miller, *Way of Death*, 505–08.

SUPPLY

Iberian carriers dominated the trade from West Central Africa following the bilateral treaties Britain signed with Portugal in 1810 and 1815, and with Spain in 1817. Figure 1.1 shows that Iberian traders increased their activities along the coast of West Central Africa in the aftermath of the treaties' ratification. They sought to abolish the trade gradually, starting first, in the Portuguese case, with the prohibition of the traffic from ports outside Portuguese control in Africa and then with the suppression of the trade north of the Equator, although in the case of the 1817 Anglo-Spanish treaty this ban was to extend to the whole of the Atlantic (north and south) from May 1820. Many Iberian traders, who had been purchasing slaves on the coast north of the Equator, now began to search for alternative sources of slaves south of the Equator. This shift increased the Portuguese trade from West Central Africa significantly. The number of slaves transported in Iberian vessels from the region increased from an average of 26,090 per year between 1806 and 1815 to an average of 43,340 per year between 1816 and 1825.

A large number of these slaves were embarked from ports controlled by several independent African polities situated north of Luanda. These ports had been selling most of their slaves to the British and the French. However, with the abolition of the British trade and the Haitian Revolution, Iberian carriers extended their slaving activities to these ports, especially after 1810, when many traders who did not have commercial connections at the Portuguese outlets, such as Luanda and Benguela, began to purchase slaves from ports mainly north of the Congo River, now vacated by British and French carriers. Additionally, Portuguese slave traders based in Brazil found it more economical to purchase slaves at African-controlled ports rather than Luanda and Benguela, because Africans collected lower taxes on slaves embarked than their Portuguese competitors further south.[42] "Voyages" indicates that after 1810 Iberian carriers shipped almost all their Angolan slaves from ports north of Luanda, even after adjusting for the bias available in the sources documenting the slave trade from Cabinda and Molembo to Bahia.

After the prohibition of the Portuguese trade north of the Equator and the total ban of Spanish slaving activities, the supply of captives from

---

[42] Roquinaldo Amaral Ferreira, *Dos Sertões ao Atlântico: Tráfico Ilegal de Escravos e Comércio Lícito em Angola, 1830–1860* (M.A., Universidade Federal do Rio de Janeiro, 1996), 86–89.

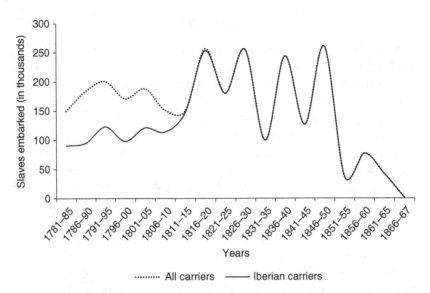

FIGURE 1.1 Slaves leaving West Central Africa by national carriers, 1781–1867
Source: Same as Table 1.1.

Angola fluctuated in response to British efforts to suppress the trade. Figure 1.1 shows that the trade from West Central Africa peaked three times after 1815. Each of these peaks was related to the British attempts to suppress the traffic. The first was between 1826 and 1830. In 1826, an Anglo-Brazilian treaty determined that Brazil would abolish the transatlantic slave trade three years after the 1827 ratification, making the Brazilian slave trade illegal after 1830.[43] Although Brazil agreed to the terms of the treaty, it effectively never closed its ports to the slave trade until the mid-nineteenth century. In anticipation of the 1830 ban, however, traders increased their activities in West Central Africa. Many of them invested heavily in the traffic. The number of slaves shipped from West Central Africa increased from about 180,380 embarked between 1821 and 1825 to 254,860 between 1826 and 1830.

Between 1836 and 1840, trade from the region peaked for a second time as a result of two important events in Europe. The first was the formal abolition of the Portuguese slave trade. In 1836, the Portuguese government enacted a law prohibiting the trade from all Portuguese

---

[43] Bethell, *The Abolition*, 60–61; Bonavides and Amaral, *Textos Políticos*, vol. 1, 833–35.

possessions in Africa, including Luanda and Benguela.[44] However, at that time the government lacked the means to enforce the law, and once again many traders increased their activities before its expected implementation in Luanda and Benguela. The second event was a British measure: the passage of Lord Palmerston's bill in 1839. When this bill became law it allowed the British navy to capture any vessel flying Portuguese colors suspected of trading slaves on the African coast and take it before a British domestic court.[45] The act was a clear violation of international law, but it signaled to traders that their active days were coming to an end. Many traders again rushed to West Central Africa, increasing the number of slaves shipped from the region from approximately 99,660 between 1830 and 1835 to 243,800 slaves between 1836 and 1840.

None of these measures was entirely effective, as there is a yet a third peak in the West Central African traffic, this time between 1846 and 1850, when the British changed their focus from the Portuguese to the Brazilian slave trade. In 1844, the British and Portuguese established a mixed commission court as well as a naval station at Luanda, from where they could better patrol the coast of West Central Africa.[46] In the following year, the British Parliament approved Lord Aberdeen's act, a measure similar to the 1839 legislation but applicable to Brazilian vessels as well as those carrying no registration papers and without any apparent national affiliation.[47] Once more, the British navy could seize such vessels and have them condemned in British courts. Additionally, in 1850 British naval interventions at two Brazilian ports had a huge impact throughout the country.[48] These actions were a major violation of Brazilian sovereignty, and they served as a final call for Brazilian authorities to pass and enforce new legislation against the slave trade. These measures prevented Iberian traders from using traditional ports of embarkation and led them to expand their activities north and south of Luanda. As a result, the number of slaves shipped from West Central Africa increased from about 126,600 between 1841 and 1845 to 260,400 between 1846 and 1850.

---

[44] Marques, *Os Sons do Silêncio*, 203–14; Roquinaldo Ferreira, "The Suppression of the Slave Trade and Slave Departures from Angola, 1830s–1860s." *História Unisinos* 15, no. 1 (2011): 4.

[45] Bethell, *The Abolition*, 156–64.

[46] Bethell, "The Mixed Commissions," 79; Samuël Coghe, "The Problem of Freedom in a Mid-Nineteenth Century Atlantic Slave Society: The Liberated Africans of the Anglo-Portuguese Mixed Commission in Luanda (1844–1870)." *Slavery and Abolition* 33, no. 3 (2012): 481–83; Ferreira, "The Suppression," 10–11.

[47] Bethell, *The Abolition*, 259–66.   [48] Eltis, *Economic Growth*, 215–16.

The supply of slaves from the region also varied in response to important events in the Atlantic. Figure 1.2 shows the estimated numbers
shipped from West Central Africa by place of embarkation. In the late
eighteenth century, places north of Luanda shipped the majority of the
slaves carried from West Central Africa. These ports included Ambriz,
Cabinda, Loango, Molembo, and the mouth of the Congo River, in
addition to smaller places like Kilongo and Mayumba. Independent
African polities such as the kingdoms of Kongo, Kakongo, Loango, and
Ngoyo controlled these ports and had sold most of their slaves to non-
Iberian slave traders. British and French slavers in particular conducted
such a lively trade in these ports that the Portuguese tried to halt this
commerce by taking possession of them. In 1783, for example, the
Portuguese occupied Cabinda and built a small fort on the coast to prevent
the sale of slaves to foreign traders. However, in the following year,
a French squadron arrived at Cabinda and formed an alliance with the
local rulers that forced the Portuguese to destroy their fort and leave the
area.[49] In 1788, the Portuguese in Luanda made another attempt to reduce
the competition for slaves by waging a war against the Marquis of
Musulu, a dissident of the Kingdom of Kongo. The Marquis controlled
Ambriz, an important outlet for British slave traders. In an attempt to
intercept this commerce from the interior, the Portuguese built a fort at the
mouth of the Loge River. In view of what had happened in Cabinda,
however, the colonial office in Lisbon ordered the governor of Angola to
recall his forces and destroy the fort two years after the war.[50] The ports

[49] Governmental Board of Angola to Martinho de Melo e Castro, 11 July 1783, AHU, CU,
      Angola, box 66 doc. 68, 69, 70 and 74; Pedro Álvares de Andrade to Martinho de Melo
      e Castro, 12 February 1784, AHU, CU, Angola, box 68 doc. 29; Pedro Álvares de
      Andrade to Martinho de Melo e Castro, 24 March 1784, AHU, CU, Angola, box 68
      doc. 54; António Máximo de Sousa Magalhães to Martinho de Melo e Castro,
      8 October 1784, AHU, CU, Angola, box 69 doc. 34.
[50] Manoel de Almeida e Vasconcelos to Martinho de Melo e Castro, 23 April 1791, AHU,
      CU, Angola, box 76 doc. 18; Manoel de Almeida e Vasconcelos to Martinho de Melo
      e Castro, 31 December 1791, AHU, CU, Angola, box 76 doc. 102; Manoel de Almeida
      e Vasconcelos to Martinho de Melo e Castro, 17 March 1792, AHU, CU, Angola, box 77
      doc. 31. See also David Birmingham, *Trade and Conflict in Angola: The Mbundu and
      Their Neighbours under the Influence of the Portuguese, 1483–1790* (Oxford: Clarendon
      Press, 1966), 157–58; Jan Vansina, *Kingdoms of the Savanna: A History of Central
      African States until European Occupation* (Madison: University of Wisconsin Press,
      1966), 182 and 191; Phyllis M. Martin, *The External Trade of the Loango Coast,
      1576–1870: The Effects of Changing Commercial Relations on the Vili Kingdom of
      Loango* (Oxford: Clarendon Press, 1972), 137–38; Anne Hilton, *The Kingdom of
      Kongo* (New York: Clarendon Press, 1985), 211.

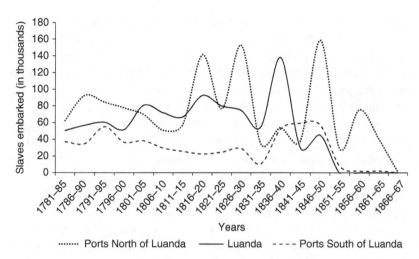

FIGURE 1.2 Slaves leaving West Central Africa by port of embarkation, 1781–1867
Source: Daniel B. Domingues da Silva, "The Atlantic Slave Trade from Angola: A Port-by-Port Estimate of Slaves Embarked, 1701–1867." *International Journal of African Historical Studies* 46, no. 1 (2013): 121–22.

north of Luanda thus remained open for international commerce throughout the late eighteenth century.

Although African-controlled ports were open to all comers, the number of slaves shipped from ports north of Luanda declined in the late eighteenth century in the face of the transatlantic developments described above. The British expansion was not sufficient to offset the decline, and when they pulled out of the business, further decline occurred north of Luanda. The estimates show that the number of slaves shipped from these ports by all carriers fell in the five years immediately after the slave rebellion in Saint Domingue from 92,650 to 84,500. Between 1801 and 1805, with the independence of Haiti, this number fell further to approximately 69,500, and then to 50,590 after abolition of the British slave trade, a figure barely half the number shipped before the 1791 rebellion.

In contrast, traffic from Luanda increased during the late eighteenth century. Luanda was the single largest port of slave embarkation on the African coast. It shipped about 34 percent of West Central Africa's slaves between 1781 and 1867. The Portuguese had dominated this port since the sixteenth century, except for a brief interlude of Dutch occupation from 1641 to 1648. In the late eighteenth century, the number of slaves shipped from Luanda increased as Brazilian plantations, supplied by Portuguese traders, took advantage of events in the wider Atlantic. Luanda and the northern ports shared some internal supply routes. As the activities of the British and French declined, many of the slaves that were previously sold through these ports were diverted for sale at Luanda. The estimates show that, compared to the late eighteenth century, the trade from Luanda increased significantly at the beginning of the nineteenth century. Between 1801 and 1810, the number of slaves shipped from Luanda increased approximately 27 percent from the previous decade.

South of Luanda, on the other hand, slave departures declined steadily from the late eighteenth century until the mid-1830s. Benguela and Novo Redondo were the departure points in this region. Benguela alone shipped the majority of slaves from these ports. Lesser ports to the south of Luanda included Benguela Velha, Quicombo, Salinas, and the mouth of the Kwanza River, which traders used occasionally as clandestine embarkation sites during the era of suppression. Unlike departures from Luanda and points north, the majority of captives leaving from such ports came from the central plateau of present-day Angola, an area dominated by several African polities, sometimes in conflict with one another. These included the kingdoms of Kakonda, Mbailundu, Viye, and Wambu. Although wars between African powers generally produced large numbers of slaves, the conflicts in the Angolan highlands did not have the same effect, as the trend line for the southern ports in Figure 1.2 clearly shows.

In any event, in the nineteenth century the supply of slaves on the coast of West Central Africa varied greatly with efforts to suppress the transatlantic trade. Figure 1.2 shows that soon after the tightening of restrictions on the trade north of the Equator, the number of slaves leaving from both Luanda and the northern ports increased. Portuguese traders carried off the majority of these. Many of these traders may never have previously purchased slaves in this part of the continent. They had probably traded slaves in regions north of the Equator, such as the Bights of Benin and Biafra. However, as the pressure on the trade in those areas increased, they had to purchase slaves in other regions, such as West Central Africa or Southeast Africa. For many, the African-controlled ports north of Luanda emerged as an ideal alternative as British and French competitors left this part of the coast. In addition, Luanda and Benguela merchants had few connections in the northern ports and, as already noted, taxes were lower there. As late as 1847, the British commissioner at Luanda noted "the abandonment of the port of Luanda for that of Ambriz, the resort now of almost all the foreign vessels, is partly accounted for ... by their having no duties to pay at the latter."[51] It is not surprising that the numbers carried off from the long coast north of Luanda swelled after 1816.

Brazilian independence and the already mentioned Anglo-Brazilian treaty of 1826 added impetus to the increased flows of captives in the north. Following independence in 1822, many Brazilian traders sought to avoid Portuguese ports. Revenues generated at Luanda and the southern ports, still part of the Portuguese Empire, declined.[52] Rumors that a fleet commanded by Lord Cochrane, in the service of the Brazilian government, was departing from Pernambuco to capture Luanda led Portuguese authorities there to strengthen their defenses.[53] Given the political conflict between Portugal and Brazil, many traders turned to African-controlled outlets north of Luanda. As the Anglo-Brazilian treaty of 1826 took effect, traders rushed to the northern ports in order to purchase slaves before Brazil closed its ports to those arriving from Africa.

After 1830, the distribution of departures across West Central Africa shifted once again. Numbers leaving north of Luanda declined, while exports from Luanda and the ports south of Luanda increased. In 1825, Portugal recognized Brazilian independence in return for Brazilian compensation for Portuguese financial losses and undertakings not to support the independence of any other Portuguese colony.[54] This agreement favored traders, because it allowed them to resume their activities at Portuguese ports on the African coast. Many dealers based in Brazil, notably in Bahia and Rio de Janeiro, developed commercial relations with their counterparts based in Luanda and Benguela, further increasing the number of slaves shipped from these ports at the beginning of the 1830s.[55] However, the expansion of the trade from Luanda and the ports south of it was short-lived. In 1836, the Portuguese government banned

[51] H.M.'s Commissioners to Viscount Palmerston, 14 February 1848, in Great Britain, *Irish University Press Series of British Parliamentary Papers: Slave Trade* (Shannon: Irish University Press, 1968), vol. 36, 105.

[52] José Joaquim Lopes de Lima, *Ensaios sobre a Statistica das Possessões Portuguezas* (Lisbon: Imprensa Nacional, 1844), vol. 3, 165–68.

[53] Nicolau de Abreu Castelo Branco to Count of Sub-Serra, 23 February 1825, AHU, CU, Angola, box 147 doc. 34. See also Boris Fausto, *História do Brasil*, 8th edn. (São Paulo: Editora da Universidade de São Paulo, 2000), 144.

[54] Bonavides and Amaral, *Textos Políticos*, vol. 1, 812–15.

[55] Ferreira, "Dos Sertões ao Atlântico," 82–85; Mariana P. Cândido, "Merchants and the Business of the Slave Trade in Benguela C. 1750–1850," *African Economic History* 35 (2007): 4–11; Mariana P. Cândido, "Trans-Atlantic Links: The Benguela-Bahia Connections, 1700–1850." In *Paths of the Atlantic Slave Trade: Interactions, Identities, and Images*, ed. Ana Lúcia Araújo (Amherst: Cambria Press, 2011), 239–72;

trading from its possessions in Africa.[56] Additionally, British policymakers began to pursue the suppression of the transatlantic trade more aggressively, following the passage of the previously mentioned Palmerston and Aberdeen acts of 1839 and 1845, respectively, as well as the establishment of a mixed commission court at Luanda.[57] Furthermore, Britain, in addition to France, Portugal, and the United States, increased naval patrols off the African coast.[58] As a result, the number of slaves shipped from Luanda and the ports south of Luanda declined in the 1840s.

Even so, as long as Brazil remained open for the trade and Africans continued to supply slaves, captive departures from West Central Africa remained high. Between 1846 and 1850, the region's trade reached its highest level in the nineteenth century. Approximately 260,000 enslaved Africans were sold into the transatlantic trade from West Central Africa in that period alone. The majority of them embarked at the African-controlled ports north of Luanda. Despite aggressive legislation and naval reinforcements, the trade declined significantly only after 1850, when Brazil finally closed its ports to all vessels carrying slaves from Africa.[59] Following the abolition of the Brazilian trade, some traders continued to sail to West Central Africa to purchase slaves, but most of these captives were now destined for Cuba, the principal market for the last victims of the transatlantic trade. The numbers shipped after 1850 never came close to matching those taken to Brazil prior to that year.

CONCLUSION

From the late eighteenth until the mid-nineteenth century, West Central Africa was a major source of slaves for the Americas. The slave rebellion in Saint Domingue and the abolition of the British trade decreased the number of slaves shipped from the region. However, with the growing restrictions on the trade north of the Equator, average numbers shipped from West Central Africa recovered to levels matching those of the years

---

Mariana P. Cândido, "South Atlantic Exchanges: The Role of Brazilian-Born Agents in Benguela, 1650–1850." *Luso-Brazilian Review* 50, no. 1 (2013): 66–71.

[56] Marques, *Os Sons do Silêncio*, 203–14; Ferreira, "The Suppression," 4.

[57] Bethell, *The Abolition*, 156–64; Bethell, "The Mixed Commissions," 79; Coghe, "The Problem of Freedom in a Mid-Nineteenth Century Atlantic Slave Society: The Liberated Africans of the Anglo-Portuguese Mixed Commission in Luanda (1844–1870)."

[58] Eltis, *Economic Growth*, 94–95.

[59] Bonavides and Amaral, *Textos Políticos*, vol. 2, 212–14.

when British and French traders were still engaged in the traffic. In this period, Iberian carriers expanded their activities on the West Central African coast by tapping sources north of Luanda. The expansion of Brazilian commercial agriculture, the transference of the Portuguese court to Rio de Janeiro, the opening of the Brazilian ports to international trade, and the spread of British capital in Brazilian markets all contributed to the expansion of the Iberian trade along the coast of West Central Africa. As a consequence, the numbers shipped remained high well into the nineteenth century.

Changing opinion about the morality and viability of slavery in Europe and the Americas had a profound impact on the slave trade from West Central Africa. At first glance, it appears that this shift was particularly and paradoxically negative for the region, given that when suppression of the trade focused initially on West Africa regions further south emerged as the principal source of captives for the Americas. That said, the slave rebellion in Saint Domingue and the abolition of the British trade spared the region's population from the effects of an even more rapidly expanding trade. Had the French regained Saint Domingue from the insurgents and the British remained active in the trade, the numbers shipped would probably have been higher than they actually were. In that case, the demand for slaves might indeed have expanded the slaving frontiers deep into the interior of West Central Africa, as many scholars have argued. However, these events remained in the realm of a counterfactual world. The slave rebellion of Saint Domingue, the abolition of the British trade, and the campaign for the suppression of the transatlantic trade in large measure checked the expansion of the Iberian trade. The impact of the traffic on the interior of West Central Africa was less extensive than scholars have generally believed, as will be seen in the following chapters.

2

The Commercial Organization of the Slave Trade

In the nineteenth century, a complex network of merchants, brokers, and traders governed the trade from West Central Africa. While they controlled much of the human input into the traffic, they did so within a framework that was shaped by environmental factors in the Atlantic. Merchants based in Portugal and Brazil organized most of the shipments to the Americas. They bankrolled these voyages individually or in partnership with others, including ship captains. Merchants purchased their captives from brokers located along the coast of West Central Africa. These brokers controlled the supply of human cargo on the coast but depended in turn on traders who transported captives from the interior to the ports. Although these categories are analyzed individually, they frequently overlapped. Brokers, for example, often tried to break into the shipping business and finance transatlantic voyages themselves. Traders, on the other hand, had to work hard to acquire enough contacts and resources to operate as brokers on the coast of West Central Africa. Nevertheless, these categories will be examined independently of each other to provide a better understanding of how slaves left the region in the final decades of the traffic.

OCEANIC PATTERNS

Let us first consider patterns of wind and sea currents that shaped the direction of the slave trade. Both wind and sea currents flow in the same direction throughout the year, changing little from one season to the next.[1]

---

[1] Luiz Felipe de Alencastro, *O Trato dos Viventes: Formação do Brasil no Atlântico Sul* (São Paulo: Companhia das Letras, 2000), 57–63; Alfred W. Crosby, *Ecological Imperialism:*

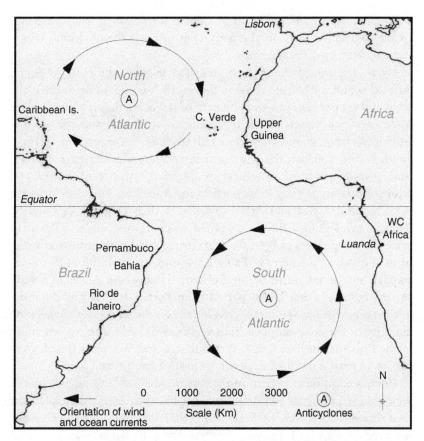

FIGURE 2.1 Wind and sea currents of the North and South Atlantic
Source: Adapted with permission from Daniel B. Domingues da Silva, "The Atlantic Slave Trade to Maranhão, 1680–1846: Volume, Routes and Organization." *Slavery and Abolition* 29, no. 4 (2008): 486.

However, the Atlantic gyres, to use the correct term, differ north and south of the Equator. Figure 2.1 shows these movements in schematic perspective. In the North Atlantic, the wind and sea currents move clockwise like a giant wheel, while in the South Atlantic they move counterclockwise. The gyres on either side of the Atlantic are separated by the doldrums, which are calm

The Biological Expansion of Europe (New York: Cambridge University Press, 1986), 104–32; Daniel B. Domingues da Silva, "The Atlantic Slave Trade to Maranhão, 1680–1846: Volume, Routes and Organisation." *Slavery and Abolition* 29, no. 4 (2008): 485–87; Miller, *Way of Death*, 318–24.

waters flowing around the Equator. Captains, navigating from one hemisphere to another, had no alternative but to cross the doldrums, which certainly increased voyage times.

Gyres determined the trade routes, and those in the North Atlantic differed significantly from those in the South Atlantic. In the former, the wind and sea patterns saw the shipment of slaves via the classic triangular trade in which vessels sailed from Europe to Africa and then to the Americas, from where they returned to their homeports in Europe. South of the Equator, the wind and sea currents facilitated a bilateral trading system, in which vessels departed from the Americas to Africa, and returned directly to their homeports in the Americas. The trade between West Central Africa and Brazil provides a clear example of how the Atlantic gyres shaped the routes of the trade. Portuguese and Brazilian vessels loading slaves in West Central Africa sailed both north and south of the Equator. However, as Table 2.1 shows, the majority of the slaves shipped to regions north of the Equator, in this case Amazonia, were carried in vessels that had departed from Portugal. This was the more challenging venture, as it meant crossing the doldrums. The overwhelming majority of the slaves shipped from West Central Africa to regions south of the Equator, such as Bahia, Pernambuco, and Southeast Brazil, were carried in vessels that had departed from Brazilian ports.

Compared to other regions in the Americas, South Atlantic patterns of wind and sea currents allowed merchants based in Brazil to supply their own regions with slaves. Table 2.1 shows that approximately 89 percent of the captives shipped from West Central Africa to Bahia were carried in vessels that had departed from Bahia. This pattern is also evident in other Brazilian regions situated south of the Equator. In Pernambuco, the ratio was 82 percent and Southeast Brazil 95 percent. Vessels leaving from any of these regions sailed southward propelled by the Brazilian current running along the coast of Brazil until they were able to catch the West Wind Drift that would take them across the Atlantic. When they sighted the African coast, they sailed northward along the coast of West Central Africa propelled by the Benguela current until they reached their destination in Africa. To return, vessels re-entered the Benguela current sailing northward until they were able to access the South Equatorial current that would carry them to Brazil. When they reached the Brazilian coast, they sailed southward propelled by the Brazilian current until arriving at their final destination.

The voyage between West Central Africa and Brazil was one of the shortest in the transatlantic trade. Vessels leaving that region for Pernambuco between the late eighteenth and the mid-nineteenth century

TABLE 2.1 *Percentage of slaves leaving West Central Africa distributed by region of departure and home port of the vessels that carried them, 1781–1867*

Regions where slaving venture organized	Regions of disembarkation			
	Amazonia	Bahia	Pernambuco	SE Brazil
Portugal	54.6	1.7	6.8	2.6
Amazonia	8.2	0.0	0.0	0.0
Bahia	10.1	88.8	2.2	1.5
Pernambuco	12.2	1.8	81.7	1.0
SE Brazil	15.0	7.5	8.6	94.6
Others	0.0	0.2	0.7	0.3
Totals	100.0	100.0	100.0	100.0

Note: Others in regions of departure include Cuba, Rio de la Plata, India, Southeast Africa, and unspecified regions in Brazil.
Sources: David Eltis et al., "Voyages," and Domingues da Silva, "The Atlantic Slave Trade from Angola," 121–22.

crossed the Atlantic on average in 33 days. A crossing to Bahia took a little over a month, 34 days on average, and to Southeast Brazil it took about 40 days.[2] These ships were among the largest carriers in the trade. The number of slaves carried per vessel from West Central Africa to Pernambuco averaged 376; to Bahia, 349; and to Southeast Brazil, 435.[3] In comparison, British ships loading slaves in the same region between 1781 and 1808 took about 55 days to cross the Atlantic and carried only 289 Africans on average.[4] French ships sailing in the same period as the British took somewhat longer, 60 days, to cross the ocean, but carried almost as many slaves, 361, as Brazilian-bound vessels.[5] Although Portuguese and Brazilian ships carried such large numbers of slaves, the

[2] Calculated based on a sample of 255 records of voyages of ships leaving West Central Africa to Bahia, 62 to Pernambuco and 1,117 to Southeast Brazil between 1781 and 1867 available in the "Voyages" database.
[3] Calculated based on a sample of 364 records of voyages of ships leaving West Central Africa to Bahia, 543 to Pernambuco and 2,226 to Southeast Brazil between 1781 and 1867 available in the "Voyages" database.
[4] The length of voyage for British vessels was calculated based on a sample of 163 records of voyages, while the average number of slaves transported was based on a sample of 579 records available in the "Voyages" database.
[5] The length of voyage for French vessels was calculated based on a sample of 219 records of voyages, while the average number of slaves transported was based on a sample of 367 records available in the "Voyages" database.

mortality rate during the voyage was surprisingly low. From the late eighteenth century until the end of the trade, deaths at sea averaged about 6 percent of the total number of slaves shipped to Bahia and about 7 percent to Pernambuco and Southeast Brazil.[6] In the British trade between 1781 and 1808, the equivalent figure was lower, 3 percent, but from 1788 the British trade was subject to Parliamentary legislation. The French, in the same period, experienced much higher rates, 11 percent.[7] The fact that French ships often carried a large number of captives and had to cross the doldrums to reach their destination might account for the time difference as well as the higher mortality rate. Clearly, then, the patterns of wind and sea currents in the South Atlantic provided Brazilian merchants with an advantage over their European counterparts.

The connections between Brazil and West Central Africa were not governed purely by environmental factors. Cultural and economic ties developed between the regions. In 1630, when the Dutch invaded Pernambuco, they discovered that the majority of slaves used in the Portuguese sugar plantations came from Angola, in West Central Africa. Johannes de Laet, drawing on Portuguese records collected after the occupation, noted that "from Angola alone in the years 1620, 21, 22, 23, being four years, to the Captaincy of Pernambuco have been disembarked 15,430 Blacks."[8] The Dutch, like most Europeans at that time, regarded the sugar industry of Pernambuco as highly profitable, and they attempted to maintain slave trading routes that the Portuguese had established. In 1641, the Dutch captured Luanda, which then, as later, served as the major port of embarkation and the capital of the Portuguese government in Angola.[9]

---

[6] Calculated based on a sample of 222 records of voyages of ships leaving West Central Africa to Bahia, 39 to Pernambuco and 1,177 to Southeast Brazil between 1781 and 1867 available in the "Voyages" database.

[7] The mortality rate for slaves transported from West Central Africa in British vessels was calculated based on a sample of 113 records of voyages, while that for slaves transported in French vessels was calculated based on a sample of 76 records.

[8] Joannes de Laet, *Iaerlijck Verhael van de Verrichtingen der Geoctroyeerde West-Indische Compagnie in derthien Boecken. Tweede Deel: Boek IV-VII (1627–1630)*, ed. S. P. L'Honoré Naber ('s-Gravenhage: Martinus Nijhoff, 1932), 139. I would like to thank Rik van Welie for this reference.

[9] Alencastro, *O Trato dos Viventes*, 210–15; C. R. Boxer, "Salvador Correia de Sá E Benevides and the Reconquest of Angola in 1648." *Hispanic American Historical Review* 28, no. 4 (1948): 489–92; C. R. Boxer, *Salvador de Sá and the Struggle for Brazil and Angola, 1602–1686* (London: University of London Press, 1952), 240–42; Ralph Delgado, *História de Angola* (Lisbon: Banco de Angola, 1970), vol. 2, 215–24.

However, the Dutch occupation of Luanda was short-lived. In 1648, Salvador Corrêa de Sá e Benevides recaptured Luanda with a fleet assembled in Rio de Janeiro. Corrêa de Sá was governor of Rio de Janeiro, where he owned land and slaves. After retaking Luanda, he reorganized the Portuguese colony in Angola, appointing members of his expedition to key offices in the government.[10] This process created bonds between Brazil and West Central Africa. Appointing Brazilian officers, such as João Fernandes Vieira and André de Vidal Negreiros, to positions in the government of Angola further strengthened the transatlantic ties. Both men had distinguished themselves in the 1650s during the reconquest of Pernambuco.[11] They were among the longest serving governors in Angola. Governors of Angola were generally appointed for three-year terms, but João Fernandes Vieira served for about four years, between 1658 and 1661, and Negreiros served for almost six years immediately after him.[12]

The discovery of gold in the interior of Brazil in the 1690s had a similar impact on the ties between Brazil and West Central Africa. Rising gold production attracted large numbers of Portuguese immigrants to Brazil.[13] They settled not only in the mining centers but also on the coast, especially in Bahia, Pernambuco, and Rio de Janeiro, which served as the main ports of entry to the gold producing areas. Moreover, they expected to tap some of the wealth coming in and out of the interior by engaging in trading activities in these regions. In Pernambuco, the arrival of these immigrants resulted in serious conflicts with the local community because gold exports had increased the price of commodities imported from abroad, including slaves.[14] Sugar planters, for example, became increasingly indebted to traders who had migrated from Portugal. However, in Bahia and Rio de Janeiro the local community was able to accommodate the

---

[10] Carlos Dias Coimbra, ed., *Livro de Patentes do Tempo do Sr. Salvador Correia de Sá e Benevides* (Luanda: Instituto de Investigação Científica de Angola, 1958), passim.

[11] Alencastro, *O Trato dos Viventes*, 221–38; Boxer, "Salvador Correia de Sá," 1948, 504–11; Boxer, *Salvador Correia de Sá*, 1952, 261–69; Delgado, *História de Angola*, vol. 2, 376–93; Evaldo Cabral de Mello, *Olinda Restaurada: Guerra e Açúcar no Nordeste, 1630–1654* (Rio de Janeiro: Editora Forense-Universitária, 1975), 171–208.

[12] "Catálogo dos Governadores do Reino de Angola," *Arquivos de Angola*, 1, 3, no. 34–36 (1937): 275–84; Elias Alexandre da Silva Corrêa, *História de Angola*, ed. Manuel Múrias (Lisbon: Editorial Ática, 1937), vol. 1, 275–84.

[13] C. R. Boxer, *The Golden Age of Brazil, 1695–1750: Growing Pains of a Colonial Society* (Berkeley: University of California, 1962), 35–36; Pinto, *O Ouro Brasileiro*, 51–53.

[14] Evaldo Cabral de Mello, *A Fronda dos Mazombos: Nobres Contra Mascates, Pernambuco, 1666–1715* (São Paulo: Companhia das Letras, 1995), 177–80.

newcomers with less friction. Planters in Bahia and Rio regarded the arrival of Portuguese immigrants as an opportunity to build commercial alliances and raise the status of their families by creating direct links with the metropolis. The immigrants saw the planters as an important means of getting access to local power and prestige, and they began to marry daughters of planter families.[15] A strong community of local merchants emerged in Bahia and Rio de Janeiro, which increasingly dominated the West Central African trade.

In the mid-eighteenth century, the Portuguese government tried to limit the power that Brazilian merchants exercised over the trade from West Central Africa. In 1755 and 1759, the Portuguese Prime Minister, Sebastião José de Carvalho e Melo, created two trading companies based in Lisbon; the Companhia Geral de Comércio do Grão Pará e Maranhão and the Companhia Geral de Comércio de Pernambuco e Paraíba. The minister granted the two companies a monopoly over all maritime trade, including the slave trade, to the northern captaincies of Brazil as well as to Pernambuco and its neighboring captaincies, Alagoas, Paraíba, Rio Grande do Norte, and Ceará.[16] In Bahia, the government also tried to curtail the control of local merchants over the trade by abolishing the *Mesa do Bem Comum*, the trading board of the Bahian merchants.[17]

---

[15] Rae Jean Flory, "Bahian Society in the Mid-Colonial Period: The Sugar Planters, Tobacco Growers, Merchants and Artisans of Salvador and the Recôncavo, 1680–1725" (Ph.D., University of Texas, 1978), 98–109; João Luís Ribeiro Fragoso, "A Nobreza da República: Notas sobre a Formação da Primeira Elite Senhorial do Rio de Janeiro (Séculos XVI e XVII)." *Topoi*, no. 1 (2000): 58–60; John Norman Kennedy, "Bahian Elites, 1750–1822." *Hispanic American Historical Review* 53, no. 3 (1973): 423–24; Antônio Carlos Jucá Sampaio, "Famílias e Negócios: A Formação da Comunidade Mercantil Carioca na Primeira Metade do Setecentos." In *Conquistadores e Negociantes: Histórias de Elites no Antigo Regime nos Trópicos. América Lusa, Séculos XVI a XVIII,* ed. João Luís Ribeiro Fragoso, Antônio Carlos Jucá de Sampaio, and Carla Maria de Carvalho de Almeida (Rio de Janeiro: Civilização Brasileira, 2007), 234–60; David Grant Smith, "The Mercantile Class of Portugal and Brazil in the Seventeenth Century: A Socioeconomic Study of the Merchants of Lisbon and Bahia, 1620–1690" (Ph.D., University of Texas, 1975), 288–90 and 400–02.

[16] António Carreira, *As Companhias Pombalinas de Navegação, Comércio e Tráfico de Escravos entre a Costa Africana e o Nordeste Brasileiro* (Bissau: Centro de Estudos da Guiné Portuguesa, 1969), 31–33 and 249–52; Dias, *Fomento e Mercantilismo*, vol. 1, 207–25; José Ribeiro Júnior, *Colonização e Monopólio no Nordeste Brasileiro: A Companhia Geral de Pernambuco e Paraíba (1759–1780)* (São Paulo: HUCITEC, 1976), 82–83.

[17] Alexandre Vieira Ribeiro, "A Cidade de Salvador: Estrutura Econômica, Comércio de Escravos e Grupo Mercantil (c.1750–c.1800)" (Doctorate, Universidade Federal do Rio de Janeiro, 2009), 375–77; Verger, *Fluxo e Refluxo*, 105–08.

A further government initiative reformed the taxes on slaves shipped from its Angolan colony in 1758. Although this revision was couched in the language of free trade, it in fact provided the state with more control over the commerce. Before 1758, slaves shipped from Angola were taxed on the basis of a *peça da Índia*, a unit equivalent to a prime adult slave of a certain height. Children, disabled individuals, and adults shorter than the designated height had been considered as a fraction of a *peça da Índia* for purposes of tax collection.[18] However, following the 1758 reform, officials began to collect taxes on each individual embarked, rather than on the basis of *peça da Índia*, effectively an increase in taxes. The reform also integrated taxes previously levied separately, with the *peças de Índia* combined with the *preferências*, a 2,000 *réis* fee collected for each slave embarked on ships carrying *efeitos próprios*, merchandize belonging to the ship owners, whose captains wished to go to the front of the departure queue.[19] The *preferências* was first established in 1684, but not every merchant was required to pay it.[20] The 1758 tax reform abolished this practice, but it obliged every captain clearing from Luanda to pay an additional fee with no discernable benefit.

The Portuguese government also tried to erode Brazilian control over the trade by promoting individuals loyal to Lisbon to major offices in the government of Angola. In 1764, Francisco Inocêncio de Sousa Coutinho became governor in Angola and introduced a series of initiatives, including the development of the wax and ivory trade, aimed at reducing the colony's dependence on human trafficking. Additionally, he was responsible for the first attempt to build a European iron factory in the interior of Angola in a place called Nova Oeiras, between the Lucala and Luina rivers, another attempt at diversifying the colony's economy. Sousa Coutinho governed Angola for almost eight years, between 1764 and 1772.[21] His successors were also loyal to the central administration in

---

[18] Curtin, *The Atlantic Slave Trade*, 22–23; Enriqueta Vila Vilar, *Hispanoamerica y el Comercio de Esclavos* (Seville: Escuela de Estudios Hispano-Americanos, 1977), 189–90. Curtin implied that only male slaves could be considered *peças da Índia*, but the documents cited by Vila Vilar clearly state that female slaves could also be considered *peças da Índia*.

[19] Dom José I, "Ley para Ser Livre, e Franco o Commercio de Angola, e dos Portos, e Sertões Adjacentes," *Arquivos de Angola*, 1, 2, no. 13–15 (1936): 532–33; Dom José I, "Ley sobre a Arecadação dos Direitos dos Escravos, e Marfim, que Sahirem do Reino de Angola, e Pórtos da sua Dependencia," *Arquivos de Angola*, 1, 2, no. 13–15 (1936): 538–39.

[20] Dom Pedro II, "Ley sobre as Arqueações dos Navios que Carregarem Escravos, 28 de Março de 1684," *Arquivos de Angola*, 1, 2, no. 11–12 (1936): 315.

[21] da Silva Corrêa, *História de Angola*, vol. 2, 29–44; "Catálogo dos Governadores do Reino de Angola," 526–31; Ana Madalena Trigo de Sousa, "Uma Tentativa de Fomento

Lisbon, and were relatively successful in maintaining Sousa Coutinho's initiatives. Miguel António de Melo, for example, governor between 1797 and 1802, founded another iron factory at Trombeta in the present-day province of Cuanza Norte.[22] Despite these efforts, merchants based in Bahia, Pernambuco, and Rio de Janeiro still exercised major control over the trade from West Central Africa, as the demand for labor in those regions increased over time.

MERCHANTS

Brazilian merchants organized shipments from West Central Africa through individual enterprises or in partnership with others. The "Voyages" database provides an indication of the frequency with which they engaged in the trade by listing the names of individuals and partnerships that sponsored slaving voyages across the Atlantic. The data are particularly rich for the period from the late eighteenth century until 1830, when the trade to Brazil became illegal. The database names those who financed slaving ventures for 43 percent of all voyages to Bahia between 1781 and 1830; 64 percent of those to Pernambuco; and 52 percent to Southeast Brazil. In the Bahia sample, there are 130 individuals who sponsored slaving voyages in this period, 21 of whom were ship captains. In addition to these individuals, the Bahia sample contains references to 24 partnerships listed under the names of individual dealers.[23] The Pernambuco sample identifies 23 partnerships plus 105 merchants, 20 of these were also captains. Finally, the sample for Southeast Brazil includes 196 merchants, 35 of whom were captains, in addition to 18 partnerships, as well as identifying individual entrepreneurs.

The trade between West Central Africa and Brazil generated some degree of concentration of ownership but probably not enough to suggest significant restrictions on competition. Table 2.2 shows that the traffic was largely centered in the hands of a few individuals and partnerships. In Bahia, three merchants financed ten or more voyages to West Central

Industrial na Angola Setecentista: A 'Fábrica do Ferro' de Nova Oeiras (1766–1772)." *Africana Studia* 10 (2007): 293–305.

[22] Miguel António de Melo to Rodrigo de Sousa Coutinho, 18 March 1800, in *Arquivos de Angola* ser. 1, vol. 4, nos. 52–54 (1939): 295–300; Miguel António de Melo to Rodrigo de Sousa Coutinho, 5 April 1800, in *Arquivos de Angola* ser. 1, vol. 4, nos. 52–54 (1939): 307–08.

[23] These records appear in the database with a star (*) next to the name of the partnership representative.

TABLE 2.2 *Concentration of ownership of vessels embarking slaves at West Central Africa, 1781–1867*

Regions	Range of voyages	Number of merchants	Percentage of merchants	Number of voyages	Percentage of voyages
Bahia	1 to 3	138	89.6	187	60.9
	4 to 6	8	5.2	41	13.4
	7 to 9	5	3.2	35	11.4
	10 +	3	1.9	44	14.3
	Total	154	100	307	100
Pernambuco	1 to 3	109	85.2	146	42.2
	4 to 6	6	4.7	30	8.7
	7 to 9	7	5.5	58	16.8
	10 +	6	4.7	112	32.4
	Total	128	100	346	100
SE Brazil	1 to 3	161	75.2	218	24.1
	4 to 6	21	9.8	101	11.2
	7 to 9	9	4.2	65	7.2
	10 +	23	10.7	520	57.5
	Total	214	100	904	100

Source: Same as Table 2.1.

Africa. They comprised about 2 percent of all traders, but their names appear associated with 44 voyages, or about 14 percent of all voyages leaving West Central Africa. In Pernambuco, 6 merchants, representing about 5 percent of all dealers, appear associated with 112 voyages, or approximately 32 percent of all voyages. Finally, in Southeast Brazil the slave trade from West Central Africa was also considerably concentrated, with 23 merchants and companies financing 10 or more voyages. They constituted about 11 percent of all traders, and their names were associated with 520 voyages, or about 57 percent of all those involved in the West Central Africa-Southeast Brazil branch of the traffic.

Small investors, defined here as financing on average one to three voyages, formed the majority of such individuals and played an important role in the South Atlantic slave trade. Although we view it as immoral today, public acceptance of slavery and the slave trade at that time was such that anyone who had some capital available could invest in the business without any loss of moral standing. In Bahia, small investors numbered 138 individuals, or about 89 percent of all merchants, and their names appear associated with 187 voyages, or approximately 61 percent of all voyages. In Pernambuco, 109 individuals invested in one to three voyages, close to 85 percent of all merchants, but they financed 146 voyages, or about 42 percent of the total. In Southeast Brazil, the participation of small investors was less important than in Bahia and Pernambuco, but here there were nevertheless 161 of them, approximately 75 percent of all dealers, associated with a mere 218 or 24 percent of all voyages.

In the period of the legal trade, before 1831, the activities of the larger merchants are easier to trace than those of small investors. Slave traders who participated frequently in the traffic were usually members of the social, political, and economic elite of Brazil. Detailed records of their lives survive in the archives, which historians have used to reconstruct some individual careers. These big traders generally had prestigious titles granted by institutions like the *Ordem de Cristo* or Order of Christ.[24] They also had a seat at the administration of related institutions like the *Santa Casa da Misericórdia*, an important source of credit in many cities in Portugal and Brazil.[25] These individuals included men such as Elias Coelho Sintra in Pernambuco, Pedro Rodrigues Bandeira in Bahia, and the well-known Elias Antônio Lopes in Rio de Janeiro, who donated the palace at the Quinta da Boa Vista, where the Portuguese royal family resided between 1808 and 1821.[26] The activities of the many small investors are more difficult to unearth, because they left few records of their lives. Although the names of hundreds of them survive, historians have not been able to collect sufficient information to establish profiles of these individuals. Nevertheless, their numbers clearly show that they viewed the activity as an opportunity to increase their wealth.

After 1830, the activities of traders in general are more difficult to trace because the traffic to Brazil was illegal. Individuals continued to finance slaving voyages by forming partnerships for specific voyages. However, the

---

[24] Manolo Florentino, *Em Costas Negras: Uma História do Tráfico Atlântico de Escravos entre a África e o Rio de Janeiro, Séculos XVIII e XIX* (São Paulo: Companhia das Letras, 1997), 204–08; Alexandre Vieira Ribeiro, "O Comércio de Escravos e a Elite Baiana no Período Colonial." In *Conquistadores e Negociantes: Histórias de Elites no Antigo Regime nos Trópicos. América Lusa, Séculos XVI a XVIII*, ed. João Luís Ribeiro Fragoso, Carla Maria de Carvalho de Almeida, and Antônio Carlos Jucá de Sampaio (Rio de Janeiro: Civilização Brasileira, 2007), 332–34.

[25] Flory, "Bahian Society in the Mid-Colonial Period," 262; Ribeiro, "O Comércio de Escravos," 333–34.

[26] Marcus J. M. de Carvalho, *Liberdade: Rotinas e Rupturas do Escravismo no Recife, 1822–1850* (Recife: Universidade Federal de Pernambuco, 2002), 118; Florentino, *Em Costas Negras*, 207; Ribeiro, "O Comércio de Escravos," 330–31.

prominence achieved by some merchants suggests that during these years the trade was becoming increasingly concentrated in the hands of those who had developed the necessary contacts required to bypass the authorities and introduce slaves to Brazil. Such merchants included Joaquim Pereira Marinho in Bahia, Gabriel José Antônio in Pernambuco, and Manoel Pinto da Fonseca in Rio de Janeiro, who promoted their major trading status in order to remind the Brazilian slave-owning class of their services.[27] Public acceptance of slavery and the associated trade was such that traders had no need to conceal their activities. Dependency on the trade gave merchants access to important centers of decision-making in national politics.[28] Additionally, it allowed them to mix with the Brazilian aristocracy, largely consisting of planters and slave owners.[29] Major traders had considerable standing in Brazilian society.

Although these merchants organized the logistics of the trade and took much of the credit for the successful disembarkation of slaves, they were not acting alone. They relied on an extensive commercial network that linked not only Brazil, Portugal, and West Central Africa, but also involved the United States and Great Britain. Until the beginning of the nineteenth century, much of the merchandise used to purchase slaves was produced in Portugal and Brazil. Some of it included textiles imported from the Portuguese colonies in Asia. Merchants in Brazilian ports then assembled these commodities into appropriately mixed cargoes and exchanged them for slaves in West Central Africa. After the opening of the Brazilian ports to international trade in 1808, Brazilian traders increasingly used British goods, particularly textiles, to buy slaves because African consumers considered British textiles superior to those of the Portuguese.[30] Additionally, the Industrial Revolution in Britain reduced the production costs of manufactured goods, which was reflected in their price in the international market.[31] In 1810, reduced customs duties levied on British commodities imported into Brazil further increased their attractiveness in relation to locally produced goods and other imports.[32] Slave merchants based in Brazil began to rely on British traders for trade goods intended for Africa.

[27] Carvalho, *Liberdade*, 118; Mary C. Karasch, "The Brazilian Slavers and the Illegal Slave Trade, 1836–1851" (M.A., University of Wisconsin, 1967), 12–15; Cristina Ferreira Lyrio Ximenes, "Joaquim Pereira Marinho: Perfil de um Contrabandista de Escravos na Bahia, 1828–1887" (M.A., Universidade Federal da Bahia, 1999), 1–21.
[28] Karasch, "The Brazilian Slavers," 14–15.   [29] Ibid.
[30] Miller, *Way of Death*, 349; Karasch, "The Brazilian Slavers," 27–35.
[31] Eltis, *Economic Growth*, 47.   [32] Fausto, *História do Brasil*, 122–24.

After 1830, the organization of the trade from West Central Africa became increasingly internationalized. Roquinaldo Ferreira notes that as the British increased their efforts to abolish the slave trade, merchants expanded their trading networks to places outside Brazil, especially to Cuba and the United States.[33] From there, they organized slaving expeditions free from interference by the Brazilian authorities as well as the British navy. These merchants contracted with Portuguese and Spanish traders located in these countries to obtain vessels, goods, false documents, as well as the American flag to use on at least the outbound portion of their slaving expeditions.[34] American registration papers, in particular, served as an important factor in the illegal trade because, in contrast to the Brazilian government, the United States did not grant the British the right to search their vessels until 1862.[35]

Merchants based in Brazil were not the only businessmen using international networks to organize slaving expeditions. Planters in the southern United States willing to re-open the transatlantic trade also tapped these networks to organize clandestine voyages. Charles Lamar from Georgia provides perhaps the most striking example. In 1858, Lamar made a deal with Captain William Corrie. They purchased a racing yacht built in Long Island, fitted it with the help of Portuguese traffickers based in New York, and sent it to West Central Africa.[36] The *Wanderer* embarked 350 slaves at Ambriz and 47 days later it arrived at Jekyll Island, Georgia.[37] The slaves brought in the yacht were quickly sold to planters in Georgia, South Carolina, and Florida.[38] Eventually, the American authorities discovered Lamar's intrigue and arrested him and his associates in Georgia. They were charged with piracy and slave trading, but were not convicted. Lamar's slaving expedition was one of the last successful disembarkations of slaves from Africa in the United States, but it illustrates that after 1830 the organization of the West Central African trade extended far beyond Brazil.

---

[33] Ferreira, "Dos Sertões ao Atlântico," 100–03.

[34] Eltis, "The British Trans Atlantic Slave Trade after 1807," 9; Eltis, *Economic Growth*, 134 and 157; Karasch, "The Brazilian Slavers," 27–35; Miller, *Way of Death*, 505–09.

[35] Ferreira, "Dos Sertões ao Atlântico," 176.

[36] Erik Calonius, *The Wanderer: The Last American Slave Ship and the Conspiracy That Set Its Sails* (New York: St. Martin's Press, 2006), 45–52 and 66–82.

[37] Eltis et al., "Voyages," voyage id 4974. See also Emory University, Robert W. Woodruff Library, Manuscripts, Archives and Rare Book Library, Mss 172, Wanderer (Ship) Records, Logbook of the yacht "Wanderer."

[38] Calonius, *The Wanderer*, 125–33; Tom Henderson Wells, *The Slave Ship Wanderer* (Athens: University of Georgia Press, 1967), 24–29.

The Portuguese connection to the trade between Cuba and West Central Africa was more important than that to the United States. William Gervase Clarence-Smith has long called attention to the participation of Portuguese merchants in this business. He shows Cuban slave traders often relied on the commercial expertise of Portuguese merchants in order to obtain false documents, colors, and provisions to carry slaves from West Central Africa as well as other regions controlled by the Portuguese. He further notes that Cuban dependence on Portuguese trading networks stemmed not only from a need for commercial expertise but also from a "lack of internationally recognized and occupied colonial possessions in Sub-Saharan Africa."[39] More recently, Roquinaldo Ferreira has pointed out that Portuguese merchants based in Angola played a key role in the supply of slaves to Cuba during the illegal period of the traffic. Merchants such as António Severino de Avellar and Guilherme José da Silva Correia, also known as Guilherme do Zaire, lived in Luanda but usually assisted Cuban vessels to load slaves at ports located north of Luanda, especially at Ambriz and at the mouth of the Congo River.[40] The Cuban trade from West Central Africa increased significantly in this period, from an annual average of 1,400 captives embarked in the 1840s to 10,200 in the 1850s.[41] The demand for labor on the Cuban sugar plantations was the principal factor behind this increase, but the Portuguese commercial networks facilitated the process.

BROKERS

The trade from West Central Africa depended on merchants established on the region's coast. Some of them were Africans who acted as brokers or middlemen responsible for purchasing slaves in the interior and selling them to transatlantic traders. At embarkation ports such as Cabinda, Molembo, and Loango, rulers regulated the supply of slaves by nominating a representative to collect taxes before granting traders the right to trade. These individuals could not enforce a monopoly, and they seldom left their capitals unattended to interfere in commercial affairs on the coast. In return for captives, rulers wanted a mix of foreign commodities, such as firearms, gunpowder, textiles, and alcohol. They distributed these

[39] William Gervase Clarence-Smith, "The Portuguese Contribution to the Cuban Slave and Coolie Trades in the Nineteenth Century." *Slavery and Abolition* 5, no. 1 (1984): 26–27.
[40] Ferreira, "Dos Sertões ao Atlântico," 100–06.
[41] Calculated from Domingues da Silva, "The Atlantic Slave Trade from Angola," 121–22.

goods to loyal followers to consolidate their own power, but also advanced them on credit to traders supplying slaves from the interior to the coast.[42] In this way, they maintained a nexus of commercial power on the coast, as a counter to the interior, where the centers of political life were generally located.

The agents of African rulers on the coast held titles directly connected to their functions. In Loango, they were known as *mafuco* or *mafouk* and in Cabinda and Molembo as *mambuco* or *mambouk*, meaning customs officer responsible specifically for Atlantic commerce. These agents were usually the first people traders met when they arrived at these northern ports. They collected taxes from traders either at their vessels or in tents on the shore. The negotiations were usually lengthy, and involved displays of power, with no little amount of rum consumed on both sides, generally underwritten by traders from Europe and the Americas. Once an agreement was reached with the tax collectors, however, the former set up shop on the shore and began to negotiate with anyone interested in selling slaves.[43] Such negotiations could take a long time, but they usually involved lower transaction costs for traders than their initial encounters with royal officials. The price paid for slaves was negotiated with each seller separately.[44]

The trade at ports dominated by decentralized states was similar to that at ports controlled by centralized states, except in two respects. At the former, rituals and processions commonly preceded commercial exchanges. Additionally, the transatlantic merchants usually bartered one-on-one with the community leaders, rather than their representatives. In 1782, for example, Manoel da Silva Ribeiro Fernandes sailed to the ports north of Luanda and described his encounter with a prince of Nsoyo, a former province of the old Kingdom of Kongo, which by that time was no longer the imperial structure of previous centuries. His description provides a vivid account of how decentralized societies conducted the slave trade.

The prince came with about three hundred men carrying drums, flutes, and lugubrious instruments as well as firearms; most of them were no longer working and neither had gunpowder of quality. Others were carrying wooden clubs, knives, cassava roots, and corn stalks. They were all wearing dresses made of straws. The prince looked like a woman, wearing the same dress as the princess

[42] Miller, *Way of Death*, 40–70 and 94–103.
[43] Martin, *The External Trade*, 97–99; Miller, *Way of Death*, 184–85.
[44] Martin, *The External Trade*, 100–03; Miller, *Way of Death*, 175–80.

when I met her, and the headdress of a grenadier, in addition to a large sword on his side, and a Crucifix of the Lord in his hands. He then entered the Church between six blacks holding knives, marched through the sacristy, passed around a gate in front of the altar, knelt before the principal chapel [...] shouted and all the people in front of the Church's door entered, knelt, and began to sing a song. After they finished, the prince left the sacristy, marched around the Church, re-entered the sacristy, and then left the building through its main door towards a square, where he ordered two chairs to be placed, distant a fathom from each other, one for him and another for me. He then sat and summoned me. I sat and dealt directly with him.[45]

From the late eighteenth to the mid-nineteenth century, a number of families with historic connections to the trade dominated the supply of slaves at the principal embarkation points north of Luanda. Phyllis Martin notes that this was the case at Cabinda, in the Kingdom of Ngoyo. Some of these families had famous ancestors or connections to the royal court at Mbanza Ngoyo. Others, such as the Franque family at Cabinda, gained prominence because of wealth garnered during the trade.[46] The family's founder, Kokelo, was a servant of a French trader who had died at Cabinda and left his possessions to his African employee. Kokelo continued to participate in the trade, rising from a minor figure in the community to a successful broker and merchant.[47] His descendants followed him into the business and expanded the family's influence. Perhaps, the most important example was Francisco Franque, who at the age of eight was sent to be educated in Brazil. At the beginning of the nineteenth century, he returned to Cabinda and assumed the family's business just as Dutch, French, and British traders withdrew from the port. Francisco Franque, of course, remained in business on the basis of his connection with Bahia and Rio de Janeiro, and the Franque family became one of the principal slave suppliers on the whole West Central African coast.[48]

The supply of captives at the Portuguese ports of embarkation was different. At Luanda, Benguela, and Novo Redondo, individuals from many different backgrounds predominated. Some of them were Portuguese expatriates while others were Luso-African Creoles, that is, descendants of unions of Portuguese expatriates and Africans. Traders originally from Brazil also operated at these ports, working as

---

[45] "Relação de uma viagem à costa ao norte de Luanda por Manoel da Silva Ribeiro Fernandes ao Senhor Ajudante de Ordens Pedro José Corrêa Quevedo," 15 August 1782, AHU, CU, Angola, cx. 65 doc. 64.
[46] Phyllis M. Martin, "Family Strategies in Nineteenth Century Cabinda." *Journal of African History* 28, no. 1 (1987): 71.
[47] Ibid.   [48] Ibid., 73.

representatives of trading houses at Bahia, Pernambuco, and Rio de Janeiro. Finally, some were Africans who spoke Portuguese and adopted European fashion and customs. Perhaps the most notable example was Dona Ana Joaquina dos Santos e Silva, a woman who emerged in the nineteenth century as one of the wealthiest merchants in Luanda.[49] Some sources claim her father was a Portuguese trader and her mother a mixed race woman from Luanda, but others suggest that she was born an African slave.[50] Either way, these individuals collectively made up a tiny percentage of the resident population in the Portuguese ports. Census records from Benguela, for example, show that merchants comprised less than 2 percent of the total population living in the port between 1796 and 1815.[51] However, since the trade was the principal economic activity in Benguela, they were also the wealthiest residents.

The central administration in Lisbon regulated the trade from Portuguese Angola. It established customs houses at the principal ports called *feitorias* or *alfândegas*, where colonial officials supervised both the disembarkation of merchandise brought from abroad and the embarkation of slaves to the Americas. These bureaucrats were also responsible for collecting taxes levied on slave departures.[52] The 1758 tax law, as we have seen, allowed vessels carrying *efeitos próprios* to load slaves and depart as soon as they were ready, instead of leaving according to the order of arrival. The new regulation also specified age-specific taxes. Adult slaves, males or females, were taxed 8,700 *réis*, small children 4,350 *réis*, and

---

[49] Carlos Alberto Lopes Cardoso, "Dona Ana Joaquina dos Santos Silva: Industrial Angolana da Segunda Metade do Século XIX." *Boletim Cultural da Câmara Municipal de Luanda* 37 (1972): 5; Júlio de Castro Lopo, "Uma Rica Dona de Luanda." *Portucale*, 2, 3, no. 16–17 (1948): 126–27.

[50] Douglas L. Wheeler, "Angolan Woman of Means: D. Ana Joaquina Dos Santos E Silva, Mid-Nineteenth Century Luso-African Merchant-Capitalist of Luanda." *Santa Barbara Portuguese Studies Review* 3 (1996): 284–85.

[51] "Mapa das Pessoas Livres e Escravos ... " 15 June 1796, AHU, CU, Angola, box 83 doc. 66; "Mapa das Pessoas Livres e Escravos ... " 1797, AHU, CU, Angola, box 85 doc. 28; "Ocupação dos Habitantes da Paróquia de São Felipe de Benguela," 1809, AHU, CU, Angola, box 121 doc. 32; "Ocupação dos Habitantes da Paróquia de São Felipe de Benguela," 1810, AHU, CU, Angola box 121A doc. 36; "Ocupação dos Habitantes da Paróquia de São Felipe de Benguela," 1815, AHU, CU, Angola, box 131 doc. 45. Mariana Cândido believes that the merchant community of Benguela comprised between 3 and 17 percent of the total population of this port, but her calculations clearly included traders operating between Benguela and the interior. See Cândido, "Merchants," 9.

[52] António Miguel de Mello, "Regimento da Alfandega da Cidade de São Paulo d'Assumpção Capital do Reino de Angola, 21 de Outubro de 1799." *Arquivos de Angola*, 1, 2, no. 11–12 (1936): 410–14.

nursing infants were tax free, if embarked with their mothers.[53] This system of tax collection remained in effect until 1836, when the Portuguese prohibited all transatlantic trading from their African possessions. With the traffic banned, traders increasingly moved their activities to African-controlled or clandestine ports north and south of Luanda.

Portuguese export duties were collected from merchants rather than captains of slave vessels. The trade from West Central Africa was an expensive and risky business, with profits ranging from as little as 3 to 90 percent of the original investment.[54] Capital always seems to have been scarce, and the purchase of slaves in the interior was made possible only via merchandise advanced on credit, ultimately extended from overseas. The factor driving this arrangement was the fact that African traders in the interior demanded payment at the moment of the exchange. As a consequence, merchants in Portuguese Angola became indebted to their counterparts in Portugal and Brazil.[55] Yet they bore most of the risks until slaves were sold in the Americas. Above all, these merchants had more to lose from deaths of captives in transit than their counterparts in Portugal or Brazil, on whose ships they dispatched their captives.

High risks meant only a few individuals would become major slave merchants. A successful career in Portuguese Angola required several years of experience in trading slaves. The service records of Anselmo da Fonseca Coutinho provide insight into just how much experience a slave merchant had to have before he or she became a major supplier. In 1806, the Governor and Captain General of Angola, Fernando António de Noronha, submitted these records to the Portuguese Regent Prince, showing Coutinho's contribution to the colony's royal revenue. They included two lists of his trading activities spanning a period of almost 40 years, from 1768 until 1806, and comprise the most extensive record available of slaves shipped by a single merchant based in Luanda.[56] More important,

---

[53] Dom José I, "Ley sobre a Arecadação," 537–38.

[54] Eltis, *Economic Growth*, 152–62; Florentino, *Em Costas Negras*, 154–70.

[55] Miller, *Way of Death*, 298–300; José Carlos Venâncio, *A Economia de Luanda e Hinterland no Século XVIII: Um Estudo de Sociologia Histórica* (Lisbon: Editorial Estampa, 1996), 175–78.

[56] "Certidão de António José Manzoni de Castro," 31 May 1796, enclosed in the "Petição de Anselmo da Fonseca Coutinho," s.d., AHU, CU, Angola, box 115 doc. 45 and "Certidão de António Martiniano José da Silva e Sousa," 10 March 1806, enclosed in the "Petição de Anselmo da Fonseca Coutinho," s.d., AHU, CU, Angola, box 115 doc. 45. A detailed analysis of these records is available in Daniel B. Domingues da Silva, "The Supply of Slaves from Luanda, 1768–1806: Records of Anselmo Da Fonseca Coutinho." *African Economic History* 38 (2010): 53–76.

they provide a rare opportunity to trace the career of a successful merchant.

Anselmo da Fonseca Coutinho, son of António da Fonseca Coutinho, Knight of the Order of Christ, was born in Luanda.[57] Little is known about Coutinho's early years at this point, but as an adult he was clearly ambitious and climbed to the top of Luanda's social ladder by accumulating titles and high military rank. In 1784, the Portuguese Queen Dona Maria confirmed Coutinho as Colonel of the Auxiliary Troops of Massangano, in the interior of Angola.[58] Two years later, the queen made him knight of her own house and granted him a symbolic stipend of 600 *réis* per month.[59] Coutinho was then promoted to Colonel of the Militia of Luanda. In 1799, he followed in his father's footsteps and became Knight of the Order of Christ, the most distinguished title in the Portuguese Empire.[60] He was able to apply for this title thanks to his older sister, Dona Ana Maria, heiress to her father's estate. She had transferred the remuneration and recognition of all services performed by their father for the Crown to her brother, who had supported her throughout her life.[61] Finally, sometime between 1807 and 1810, Governor and Captain General of Angola António Saldanha da Gama promoted Coutinho to commander of the Militia of Luanda.[62]

Clearly the governors of Angola had a favorable opinion of him. The Baron of Moçâmedes (1784–1790), for instance, referred to him as "the most trustworthy merchant in Luanda."[63] Manoel de Almeida e Vasconcelos (1790–1797) called Coutinho "one of the most condign vassals of His Majesty," and Fernando António de Noronha (1802–1806) said that Coutinho was a "credit worthy and useful inhabitant of Angola."[64] All these comments resulted from Coutinho's commercial power and political influence. In fact, between 1768 and 1806 Coutinho

---

[57] "Atestação de Manoel de Almeida e Vasconcelos," 7 February 1793, AHU, CU, Angola, box 115 doc. 45. "Instrumento em Pública Forma Sobrescrito por Felipe Benício e Rosa Mascarenhas," 8 June 1795, AHU, CU, Angola, box 115 doc. 45.

[58] ANTT, Registo Geral de Mercês, Dona Maria I, Book 16, f. 126.   [59] Idem.

[60] ANTT, Registo Geral de Mercês, Dona Maria I, Book 29, ff. 224v and 243.

[61] "Instrumento em Pública Forma Sobrescrito por Felipe Benício e Rosa Mascarenhas," 8 June 1795, AHU, CU, Angola, box 115 doc. 45.

[62] João de Oliveira Barbosa to Conde das Galvêas, 2 December 1810, AHU, CU, Angola, box 121A doc. 31.

[63] "Atestação do Barão de Moçâmedes," 6 October 1790, AHU, CU, Angola, box 115 doc. 45.

[64] "Atestação de Manuel de Almeida Vasconcelos," 2 January 1796, AHU, CU, Angola, box 115 doc. 45. "Atestação de Fernando António de Noronha," 27 February 1806, AHU, CU, Angola, box 115 doc. 45.

alone embarked about 5 percent of all slaves shipped from Luanda. As the slave trade was the principal economic activity of this port, this ratio impressed the highest authorities in Angola.[65]

Coutinho's records suggest that the career of a successful merchant took many years to build capital and access internal sources of slaves. Table 2.3 shows the number of slaves shipped by him over a period of approximately 40 years, drawn from the two previously cited lists copied from the customs books of Luanda. It indicates that he took almost half of this 40-year period to become a major merchant, shipping slaves only occasionally during the first 12 years of activity. He became a first class merchant only after 1785, when he was able to load a couple of vessels per year with captives, assuming 350 as the average carrying capacity of each vessel. The first list of shipments has no dates of embarkation, but both followed the books' chronological order, allowing distribution of Coutinho's shipments according to the opening and closing dates of each. Although the first book is dated 9 May 1767, the first list begins in the following year, presumably when he shipped his first slaves, and ends 31 May 1796. The second list continues from this date until 10 March 1806.

Coutinho's records also shed light on the commercial strategies that Luandan merchants employed. As with all slave traders, their profits were vulnerable to shipboard mortality, so they devised ways to reduce this risk. One means was to assign their slaves to several vessels. Luanda was a busy slaving port with a large number of vessels arriving and leaving annually. The frequency of vessels calling at the port allowed merchants to allocate small shipments of slaves in several different vessels. Stanley Engerman and others have noted that mortality at sea was unevenly distributed. Most vessels had very low mortality, but a few had high numbers of deaths.[66] Coutinho's strategy reduced the risk of losing an entire cargo at sea in the event a venture was captured, destroyed, sunk, or subject to an epidemic. It also allowed Luandan merchants to dispose quickly of a highly vulnerable commodity. Slaves often arrived from the journey to the coast exhausted, undernourished, and, as a consequence, susceptible to disease. Their condition tended to deteriorate further while on the coast, as merchants often had too many slaves on their properties. Crowded barracoons increased the risks of malnourishment and

---

[65] Domingues da Silva, "The Supply of Slaves from Luanda," 55.

[66] Stanley L. Engerman et al., "Transoceanic Mortality: The Slave Trade in Comparative Perspective." *William and Mary Quarterly* 58, no. 1 (2001): 100–02.

TABLE 2.3 *Number of slaves shipped by Anselmo da Fonseca Coutinho,*
1768–1806

Lists	Periods	Number of years	Number of slaves	Number of slaves per year
1	1 January 1768 to 11 January 1780	12.0	478	40
	12 January 1780 to 4 February 1785	5.1	733	145
	5 February 1785 to 31 May 1796	11.3	7,933	701
2	31 May 1796 to 16 October 1798	2.4	1,865	787
	17 October 1798 to 10 March 1806	7.4	5,833	789
	Total	38.2	16,842	441

Source: Reproduced with permission from Daniel B. Domingues da Silva, "The Supply of Slaves from Luanda, 1768–1806: Records of Anselmo da Fonseca Coutinho." *African Economic History* 38 (2010): 60.

contagious diseases. This reality put a premium on selling slaves as soon as possible. Table 2.4 shows the size of Coutinho's shipments between 1768 and 1806. It indicates that this major merchant typically shipped his slaves in small numbers per vessel. In fact, he rarely shipped a full cargo of slaves at any one time. The majority of his shipments consisted of no more than 50 slaves per vessel, but in fact almost half of all his shipments, 48 percent, ranged between one and ten slaves only. No doubt other merchants followed a similar strategy.

Partnering with other merchants, not only in Europe and the Americas but also in Africa, also reduced risk. Such business arrangements meant that individuals invested less capital in a voyage than they would if they undertook the entire enterprise alone. Table 2.5 shows the structure of ownership of the slaves Coutinho dispatched between 1768 and 1806. It indicates that almost 60 percent of his shipments were made in partnership with others. He sent approximately 30 percent of the slaves on his own account in addition to 10 percent on behalf of others. However, the table also indicates that partnerships became possible only after a merchant had gained experience and developed a sound reputation. At the beginning of his career, from 1768 through 1785, Coutinho owned outright the majority of the slaves he embarked. This long period

TABLE 2.4 *Size of Coutinho's slave shipments,*
1768–1806

Size of shipments	Number of vessels
1–50	207
51–100	10
101–150	2
151–200	7
201–250	5
251–300	4
301–350	3
351 over	17
Total	255

Source: Reproduced with permission from Domingues da Silva, "The Supply of Slaves from Luanda," 63.

TABLE 2.5 *Structure of ownership in Coutinho's shipment of slaves (in row percentages), 1768–1806*

List	Approximate years of shipment	On Coutinho's account	In partnership	On behalf of others
1	1768–1780	90.4	9.6	-
	1780–1785	78.2	21.8	-
	1785–1796	33.8	66.2	-
2	1796–1798	16.5	43.1	40.4
	1798–1806	24.0	61.3	14.8
	Total	32.2	58.4	9.4

Source: Reproduced with permission from Domingues da Silva, "The Supply of Slaves from Luanda," 64.

of apprenticeship eventually provided him with sufficient experience and resources to attract other merchants as partners. As his career evolved successfully, his joint ventures widened to include shipments made on behalf of others. Since slaves were at risk of dying before they reached markets in the Americas, well-established merchants in Luanda were willing at times to offer their services as agents for others in the business.

Luandan and Benguelan merchants understood that owning the vessels that shipped their goods reduced their exposure to risk. To increase their control over the itineraries of voyages and the conditions under which slaves were carried, they often tried to break into the shipping business after accumulating sufficient resources. Coutinho's records show that he owned three vessels, which he used both to ship slaves and to rent out to the government: the corvette *Rainha dos Anjos*, the brigantine *Flor do Mar*, and the smack *Santo António e Almas*.[67] Coutinho used the first two in the slave trade, although in 1799 he loaned the second for a military expedition to Benguela organized by Governor and Captain General of Angola Miguel António de Melo. Coutinho frequently reserved the smack *Santo António e Almas* for state activities, but at some point in the government of Miguel António de Melo (1797–1802) French privateers captured the corvette *Rainha dos Anjos* while it was delivering slaves to Rio de Janeiro. Coutinho responded by asking the governor to release his smack from the royal service so he could use it in the trade.

Luandan merchants like Coutinho were, of course, responsible for the well-being of their slaves until the moment of embarkation. During the period of the legal trade, they kept them in *quintais*, that is, in enclosures on their properties at the major ports, where the supply of water and food was frequently a major concern.[68] Luanda had only one well, in addition to the city cisterns at the fort of São Miguel and the Public Granary of Luanda. It was located at some distance from the coast, in the neighborhood of Maianga. Moreover, it was not very reliable because of brackish water and the pressure of high demand.[69] During periods of water shortage, colonial officials entertained the idea of building a canal that would connect Luanda to the Kwanza River, but this never materialized.[70] As a consequence, merchants had to import potable water from the Bengo River, about 20 kilometers north of Luanda. African traders dominated this thriving trade in water from the Bengo. They loaded barrels with the precious liquid, transported them along the coast in canoes, and distributed them to Luandan residents. Unfortunately, slave merchants sometimes stored these barrels in poor conditions, so the water became contaminated.[71] Slaves contracted diarrhea and dysentery, two of the principal causes of death in the trade. Eltis, Lewis, and McIntyre

[67] "Carta de Ofício de Miguel António de Melo," 9 May 1799, AHU, CU, Angola, box 115 doc. 45. "Petição de Anselmo da Fonseca Coutinho a Miguel António de Melo," s.d., AHU, CU, Angola, box 115 doc. 45. The Voyages Database provides information on only two records of slaving voyages with Coutinho's name as owner; one for an unnamed ship, which set sail in 1799, and the other for the *Bergantim Flor do Mar*, which sailed between 1810 and 1811. Eltis et al., "Voyages," voyage id 46,313 and 49,898.

[68] Ferreira, "Dos Sertões ao Atlântico," 66–70; Miller, *Way of Death*, 390.

[69] Miller, *Way of Death*, 395–96; Venâncio, *A Economia de Luanda*, 60–61.

[70] See, for example, José de Oliveira Barbosa to Conde das Galvêas, 31 July 1813, AHU, CU, Angola, box 125 doc. 46.

[71] Miller, *Way of Death*, 396–97; Venâncio, *A Economia de Luanda*, 61.

calculated trader losses from mortality and morbidity in the British commerce and discovered that they "contributed to more than 40 percent of the price difference between slaves in Africa and healthy slaves in the Caribbean."[72]

Food was another major concern. Until the mid-eighteenth century, most slave provisions were produced on Jesuit farms near Luanda or brought from Brazil.[73] However, with the expulsion of the Jesuits from the Portuguese Empire in 1759, Africans and Luso-Africans became increasingly responsible for food supplies.[74] In Luanda, for example, African and Luso-African food producers sold their grains at the Public Granary of Luanda, founded in 1764 by Governor Sousa Coutinho.[75] The term "grains" is used loosely here, given that they included cassava, maize, and beans, but they were produced mostly in *arimos* or farms near Luanda, located along the Bengo, Icolo, Zenza, and Dande rivers.[76] In 1844, Commander Lopes de Lima noted that this region "could well be called the granary of Luanda."[77] Although Luanda was situated near rich sources of grains, that did not save the city from periodic shortages. As Jill Dias and Joseph Miller have observed, Angola suffered prolonged periods of drought and famine.[78] In 1792, one of these famines was so severe that the governor was compelled to allow food producers in Luanda to sell cassava flour at the Public Granary according to the market price as opposed to the price established by the government.[79] In 1841, another period of severe drought struck the city, followed by an invasion of locusts originating north of Luanda. George Tams, a German physician who had

[72] David Eltis, Frank D. Lewis, and Kimberly McIntyre, "Accounting for the Traffic in Africans: Transport Costs on Slaving Voyages." *Journal of Economic History* 70, no. 4 (2010): 950.
[73] Arlindo Manuel Caldeira, "Angola and the Seventeenth-Century South Atlantic Slave Trade." In *Networks and Trans-Cultural Exchange: Slave Trading in the South Atlantic, 1590–1867*, ed. David Richardson and Filipa Ribeiro da Silva (Leiden: Brill, 2014), 136–37; Venâncio, *A Economia de Luanda*, 83–88.
[74] Miller, *Way of Death*, 270–71, 297–98, and 351–55.
[75] "Catálogo dos Governadores do Reino de Angola," 527; Miller, *Way of Death*, 352; da Silva Corrêa, *História de Angola*, vol. 2, 31; Venâncio, *A Economia de Luanda*, 65.
[76] Aida Freudenthal, *Arimos e Fazendas: A Transição Agrária em Angola, 1850–1880* (Luanda: Chá de Caxinde, 2005), 149–65.
[77] Lopes de Lima, *Ensaios*, vol. 3, 194.
[78] Jill R. Dias, "Famine and Disease in the History of Angola, c.1830–1930." *Journal of African History* 22, no. 3 (1981): 350–59; Joseph C. Miller, "The Significance of Drought, Disease and Famine in the Agriculturally Marginal Zones of West-Central Africa." *Journal of African History* 23, no. 1 (1982): 20–22.
[79] Manoel de Almeida e Vasconcelos, 5 October 1792, AHU, CU, Angola, cod. 1634, 11.

traveled to Portuguese Angola in that year, witnessed this event and noted that it "was the second swarm that had threatened Luanda within six years; the preceding one took the same direction, and evidently sought the more luxuriant regions to the south."[80] Severe periods of famine usually followed such invasions, exacting a huge toll on slaves awaiting passage to the Americas.

Problems with supplies could trigger contagious diseases, especially smallpox, often associated with the large number of men, women, and children held in the slave yards. In 1782, the Portuguese government addressed this issue by creating quarantine stations at the principal ports of disembarkation in the Americas.[81] At the point of boarding, however, this problem remained largely unaddressed. In 1804, Governor Noronha considered inoculating slaves to prevent the spread of smallpox in Luanda and reduce slave mortality at sea. Inoculation had been introduced in the West in 1721, but Governor Noronha's idea came from a recommendation made by the Secretary of the Overseas Council in Lisbon as well as the Portuguese Regent Prince based on an experiment conducted on a French vessel, which reputedly lost only one captive at sea after transporting 250 inoculated slaves. The governor ordered the city physician to replicate the experiment in Luanda, but there is no evidence that he did so.[82] In 1814, the Governor of Benguela, João de Alvelos Leiria, faced with a city overcrowded with slaves, informed his superior at Luanda that he allowed vessels to embark more slaves than their legal capacity. "There are 1,400 slaves in this situation," he wrote, "with many more arriving from the interior, but we can already feel the consequences with the spread of smallpox and hunger."[83] The threat of epidemics was constant.

---

[80] Georg Tams, *Visit to the Portuguese Possessions in South-Western Africa* (London: T. C. Newby, 1845), vol. 2, 39.

[81] Jaime Rodrigues, *De Costa a Costa: Escravos, Marinheiros e Intermediários do Tráfico Negreiro de Angola ao Rio de Janeiro, 1780–1860* (São Paulo: Companhia das Letras, 2005), 284.

[82] Fernando António de Noronha to Visconde de Anadia, 2 August 1804, AHU, CU, Angola, box 110 doc. 33. See also Cary P. Gross and Kent A. Sepkowitz, "The Myth of the Medical Breakthrough: Smallpox, Vaccination, and Jenner Reconsidered." *International Journal of Infectious Diseases* 3, no. 1 (1 July 1998): 55–56; Eugenia W. Herbert, "Smallpox Inoculation in Africa." *Journal of African History* 16, no. 4 (1975): 552–53; Dauril Alden and Joseph C. Miller, "Out of Africa: The Slave Trade and the Transmission of Smallpox to Brazil, 1560–1831." *Journal of Interdisciplinary History* 18, no. 2 (1987): 195–200.

[83] João de Alvelos Leiria to José de Oliveira Barbosa, 19 October 1814, AHU, CU, Angola, box 129 doc. 63. See also João de Alvelos Leiria to José de Oliveira Barbosa,

During the period of the illegal trade, traffickers in Portuguese Angola faced an additional challenge. As noted in the previous chapter, in 1836 Portugal prohibited the embarkation of slaves from all of its African possessions. A few years later, in 1844, the British increased their antislave trade patrols off West Central Africa, and the Portuguese allowed them to establish a naval station as well as a mixed commission court at Luanda. Slave merchants responded by moving their operations to clandestine areas away from the traditional ports of embarkation, such as Kilongo, Mayumba, and Penedo, situated north of Luanda, and Quicombo, Salinas, Benguela Velha, and the mouth of the Kwanza River, to the south of the city. The exact location of some of these places, for example, Alecuba, Ambona, Bomara, Cape Mole, and Grenada Point, remains unclear.

After 1836, slave merchants could no longer rely on their *quintais*, official sources of provisions, and other infrastructure that had previously formed the basis of their operations. They now had to transport slaves rapidly to more remote locations prearranged with captains of slave vessels, where slaves were held in barracoons, a word meaning shelter or warehouse derived from the Portuguese *barracão* or the Spanish *barracón*.[84] These barracoons were built at some distance from the shore in order to conceal their presence from antislave trade cruisers patrolling the coast.[85] Some of the merchants engaged in the illegal slave trade went to great lengths to secure a successful dispatch, even shipping slaves at night. George Tams met Arsênio Pompeu Pompílio de Carpo, one of the most renowned Luandan slave merchants active during the period of the illegal trade, and described his strategy to bypass the authorities.

A rapid mode of traveling was indispensable to Mr. Arsênio, for he was often obliged to take very long journeys on horseback during the night, when his personal presence was suddenly required at the place where his slaves were embarked. Considerable and repeated losses had induced him to adopt the plan of embarking the slaves during the night at a distance from Luanda. One morning,

---

26 October 1814, AHU, CU, Angola, box 129 doc. 63; João de Alvelos Leiria to António de Araújo de Azevedo, 18 November 1814, AHU, CU, Angola, box 129 doc. 63; and "Abaixo Assinado dos Negociantes de Benguela," s.d., AHU, CU, Angola, box 129 doc. 63.

[84] "Merriam-Webster Dictionary Online," 2011, barracoon, www.merriam-webster.com/.

[85] Ferreira, "Dos Sertões ao Atlântico," 38–42. Joseph Miller equates the barracoons of the illegal period of the slave trade from Angola to the *quintais* of the legal period. See Miller, *Way of Death*, 387–401.

when I paid him a professional visit on account of a chronic disorder of the liver, to which he had become subject by his long residence in different parts of Brazil, he told me that; although he was so ill, he had ridden sixteen leagues during the preceding night, in order to be present at the embarkation of his slaves to the south of the Dande River.[86]

TRADERS

Traders from the interior who supplied Arsênio and his fellow merchants were mostly Africans or Luso-Africans. Merchants and colonial officials on the coast called them by different terms that changed over time but usually derived from the regions where they purchased slaves or the community from which the traders themselves originated. One of the earliest terms used to designate these traders was *pombeiros*, from the Kikongo *pumbu*. In the sixteenth and seventeenth centuries, many slaves came from regions near Malebo Pool, which Kikongo speakers called *Pumbu*. The coastal merchants incorporated the word *Pumbu* into their vocabulary as *pombo*, and began calling all traders travelling between the interior and the coast *pombeiros*.[87] This term was still widely used in the eighteenth and nineteenth centuries, even though Malebo Pool was no longer an important source of slaves.

Another term commonly applied to traders was *ambaquista*, which emerged in the eighteenth century and was widely used in the nineteenth, when traders operating from Ambaca began to dominate the supply chain. Ambaca was a major slave trading post located about 220 kilometers southeast of Luanda. Traders operating at this post usually obtained slaves in the immediate hinterland of Luanda, between the rivers Dande and Kwanza. However, in the nineteenth century, there are references to *ambaquistas* trading in regions as far south as the central plateau of Angola.[88] Eventually, *aviados, volantes, ambulantes, sertanejos, feirantes, quimbares*, or *kimbares* also became synonyms for *pombeiros*.[89]

---

[86] Tams, *Visit to the Portuguese Possessions*, vol. 1, 251–52.

[87] Willy Bal, "Portugais Pombeiro, Commerçant Ambulant du 'Sertão.'" *Annali dell'Istituto Universitario Orientalis, Naples* 7 (1965): 148–51; Birmingham, *Trade and Conflict*, 17, note 1; Cândido, *Fronteras de Esclavización*, 66–72; Miller, *Way of Death*, 189–90.

[88] Ferreira, "Dos Sertões ao Atlântico," 215–16; Beatrix Heintze, *Pioneiros Africanos: Caravanas de Carregadores na África Centro-Ocidental entre 1850 e 1890*, trans. Marina Santos (Lisbon: Caminho, 2002), 229–59; Miller, *Way of Death*, 644.

[89] Bal, "Portugais Pombeiro," 152–61; Manolo Florentino, "The Slave Trade, Colonial Markets, and Slave Families in Rio de Janeiro, Brazil, ca.1790–ca.1830." In *Extending*

Initially, each term referred to a specific aspect of the trade, but by the nineteenth century they were all used to designate traders operating in the interior.

Traders operating between the interior and the coast numbered in the hundreds, if not the thousands. In 1809, the census returns of Benguela show that there were about 412 "traders who traveled to the interior with commodities of merchants from this port."[90] This number would have been much larger if the caravan porters, who normally lived outside the city limits, had been included in the count. The average size of the caravans is unclear, but it must have varied significantly. Joseph Miller says that *pombeiros* usually organized small-scale caravans with five or eight porters at most, but "twenty to one hundred slaves would not have been an uncommon range of sizes for commercial expeditions in the eighteenth century."[91] In the nineteenth century, the size of caravans increased to accommodate the overseas demand for products in addition to slaves. Miller believes that in this period the largest caravans included about 1,000 porters.[92] Isabel Castro Henriques argues that such caravans averaged about 1,500 people.[93] Maria Emília Madeira Santos claims that they "always had over a thousand people but many included three thousand or more."[94] This last view seems implausible, at least for the slave trade era, as the comment primarily reflects produce trade in the late nineteenth century.

The recruitment of porters also varied significantly. Traders from Kasanje and Lunda typically recruited them from within their own families, viewing the caravan trade as a family enterprise.[95] Africans and Luso-Africans from Portuguese Angola typically used porters from the various chiefdoms under Portuguese suzerainty. These chiefdoms were obliged as vassals to provide the Portuguese ports of slave embarkation with a certain

---

the Frontiers: Essays on the New Transatlantic Slave Trade Database, ed. David Eltis and David Richardson (New Haven: Yale University Press, 2008), 283–84; Jan Vansina, "Ambaca Society and the Slave Trade c.1760–1845." *Journal of African History* 46, no. 1 (2005): 8–9.

[90] "Ocupações dos Habitantes da Paróquia de São Felipe de Benguela," 1809, AHU, CU, Angola, box 121 doc. 32. A copy of this document is also available in AHU, CU, Angola, box 121A doc. 32.

[91] Miller, *Way of Death*, 191.   [92] Ibid.

[93] Isabel Castro Henriques, *Percursos da Modernidade em Angola: Dinâmicas Comerciais e Transformações Sociais no Século XIX*, trans. Alfredo Margarido (Lisbon: Instituto de Investigação Científica Tropical, 1997), 408.

[94] Maria Emília Madeira Santos, *Nos Caminhos de África: Serventia e Posse (Angola, Século XIX)* (Lisbon: Instituto de Investigação Científica Tropical, 1998), 18.

[95] Henriques, *Percursos da Modernidade*, 405–06.

number of porters to carry commodities in caravans between the coast and the interior.[96] These porters received little or no payment, and were often abused by caravan leaders. In 1839, the Portuguese government in Lisbon attempted to prohibit the use of involuntary porters, but traders continued to use coercion to recruit from chiefdoms under Portuguese nominal rule. Many chiefs barred recruitment in their own territories because they viewed the work as humiliating or wanted to exploit such labor for their own benefit. Roquinaldo Ferreira notes that some chiefs used porters in their own caravans, while others took bribes from their subjects in exchange for exemption from this service.[97] It is unclear whether these porters also worked as slave drivers on the march to the coast but, since some chiefs also engaged in the trade and many of them view the activity as a family enterprise, this is not implausible.

Merchandise from the coast was exchanged for slaves at different places in the interior, according to where the best prices or trading terms could be found. Traders usually purchased slaves directly from African suppliers, but in the eighteenth century the Portuguese colonial government designated a number of *feiras*, or fairs, where traders were supposed to exchange wares for slaves. Most of these fairs were located in the Kingdom of Kasanje, with which the Portuguese entertained regular diplomatic relations.[98] The Portuguese government created these fairs to undermine the effects of the *reviro*, a commercial strategy that traders in the interior used to maximize their purchasing power. It comprised the *Pombeiros* using Portuguese commodities they had obtained in Luanda to purchase captives that they then sold to British and French traders operating north of Luanda. They subsequently returned to the interior taking with them the British and French goods that Africans apparently preferred. Once in the interior, they were able to obtain more slaves than the first transaction had yielded. The *reviro* thus allowed *pombeiros* to accumulate significant resources, which may have rivaled those of the coastal merchants based in Luanda.[99]

---

[96] Carlos Couto, *Os Capitães-Mores em Angola no Século XVIII: Subsídios para o Estudo da sua Actuação* (Luanda: Instituto de Investigação Científica de Angola, 1972), 245–56; Ferreira, "Dos Sertões ao Atlântico," 195–97 and 213–20; Beatrix Heintze, "Luso-African Feudalism in Angola? The Vassal Treaties of the Sixteenth to the Eighteenth Century." *Revista Portuguesa de História* 18 (1980): 123–24.

[97] Ferreira, "Dos Sertões ao Atlântico," 214–20.

[98] Cândido, *An African Slaving Port*, 185 and 189; Ferreira, *Cross-Cultural Exchange*, 47–53; Henriques, *Percursos da Modernidade*, 109–15; Miller, *Way of Death*, 582–89; Venâncio, *A Economia de Luanda*, 156–62.

[99] Ferreira, "Dos Sertões ao Atlântico," 198; Miller, *Way of Death*, 276–79.

A trading board based at Luanda, called *Junta de Comércio*, was responsible for organizing slave fairs in the interior of Angola, which were intended to prevent practices such as the *reviro*. The board appointed both directors and clerks to check the items exchanged for slaves and it had the effect of limiting the activities of *pombeiros*. Furthermore, it provided merchants on the coast with a clearer idea of the destination of their commodities and the number of slaves for which they were exchanged.[100] The slave fairs remained important supply centers until the beginning of the nineteenth century. Moreover, when the British and French withdrew, traders in the interior could no longer use the *reviro* to maximize their purchasing power. The *pombeiros* then gradually abandoned the fairs and resorted to trading directly with African suppliers in the interior.

SEASONAL VARIATIONS

Assessments of the supply of slaves from the interior to the coast must take into account the seasons and the agricultural calendar of the populations living inland from the coast. Generally, historians have argued that seasonal variations in the slave trade occurred as a function of the demand for labor in the Americas. They have viewed the crop cycle of the slave plantations in the Americas as shaping the seasonal variations in the trade to the Americas.[101] However, records of vessels arriving at Luanda compiled by Portuguese customs officials between 1736 and 1808 suggest a different interpretation.[102] They show that the slave trade varied

---

[100] Ferreira, "Dos Sertões ao Atlântico," 199; Miller, *Way of Death*, 586–89; Venâncio, *A Economia de Luanda*, 156–57.

[101] Stephen D. Behrendt, "Ecology, Seasonality, and the Transatlantic Slave Trade." In *Soundings in Atlantic History: Latent Structures and Intellectual Currents, 1500–1830*, ed. Bernard Bailyn and Patricia L. Denault (Cambridge: Harvard University Press, 2009), 45–47; Florentino, *Em Costas Negras*, 60–63; Herbert S. Klein, "The Portuguese Slave Trade From Angola in the Eighteenth Century." *Journal of Economic History* 32, no. 4 (1972): 900. In another version of Klein's article, he acknowledges that the number of slaves shipped from Angola varied significantly throughout the year, but dismissed the climatic evidence as having any influence on this variation. "While the rainy season can be said to have been of some influence, it does not appear to be the predominant factor." He then attributes the seasonal variation of the Portuguese slave trade from Angola to American demands. One should note, however, that gold was the principal commodity exported from Portuguese America during the mid-eighteenth century, and output did not vary by season. See Herbert S. Klein, *The Middle Passage: Comparative Studies in the Atlantic Slave Trade* (Princeton: Princeton University Press, 1978), 33–34.

[102] These records are described in detail in Klein, "The Portuguese Slave Trade from Angola," 894–905; Klein, *The Middle Passage*, 23–37; Corcino Medeiro dos Santos,

according to the climate, as well as the agricultural calendar of the populations living in the interior. These records include the name of the vessels and date of their arrival at Luanda. The creators of the "Voyages" database integrated similar data from the Americas. Combined, these data allow us to calculate the number of slaves leaving Luanda monthly between the eighteenth and nineteenth centuries.

West Central Africans categorized seasons according to variations in rainfall, which served as an important indication of the optimal time to plant, harvest, and process food. In addition, rainfall determined the most suitable periods to wage wars and organize long-distance trade expeditions. However, given the variations in topography and latitude from one region to another, climate figures covering large areas are meaningless for a calculation of shipment variations in the slave trade. Figure 2.2 shows that the patterns of rainfall in Angola vary significantly between the coast and the interior. As Jill Dias noted, precipitation levels increase in a southwesterly direction, from the central plateau toward the coast, reaching an extreme near Moçâmedes.[103] Given the irregular distribution of rainfall throughout the territory, the number of slaves shipped from Luanda has to be measured against the levels of rainfall in their regions of provenance.

As will be seen in the following chapter, most slaves leaving Luanda came from regions within 400 kilometers of the coast. The majority were Kimbundu and Kikongo farmers, who planted many of their crops along the main rivers of the region, such as the Kwanza to the south and the Bengo and Dande to the north. However, because they did not use irrigation, they depended heavily on the rain. Fortunately, patterns of rainfall in this region are dependable compared to other places, monthly change over the year being within 15 and 25 percent of the country's annual average. Malanje is located within the region of provenance of the majority of the slaves shipped from Luanda. Unfortunately, precipitation data for the interior of Angola in the nineteenth century is unavailable, but meteorologists have recorded levels of precipitation there for 396 months between 1951 and 1984.[104] These data can be compared to the number of slaves shipped to derive an idea of the seasonal variations in the trade from

"Relações de Angola com o Rio de Janeiro (1736–1808)." *Estudos Históricos*, no. 12 (1973): 5–66.

[103] Dias, "Famine and Disease," 350.
[104] Robert Hoare, "WorldClimate: Weather and Climate Data Worldwide," Online database, (1996), www.worldclimate.com/.

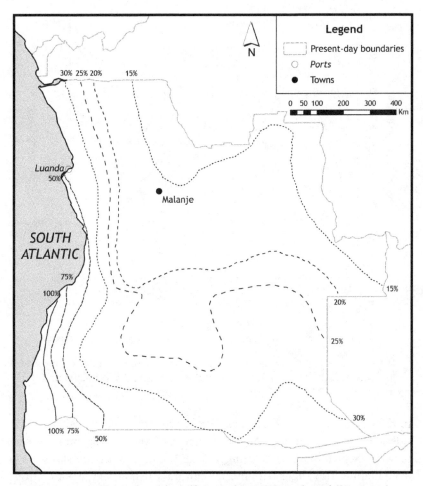

FIGURE 2.2 Lines of equal coefficient of variability of rainfall in Angola
Source: Dario X. de Queirós, *Variabilidade das Chuvas em Angola* (Luanda:
Serviço Meteorológico de Angola, 1955). Based on Jill Dias, "Famine and Disease
in the History of Angola, c.1830–1930." *Journal of African History* 22, no. 3
(1981): 351.

Luanda under the reasonable assumption that climatic patterns in the
region did not change massively over the previous century.

Figure 2.3 shows that the number of captives leaving Luanda peaked
during the middle of the year, between May and August. This corresponds
with the region's driest season of the year, known as *cacimbo*, when a total
of 47,200 slaves on average were dispatched between 1736 and 1808.

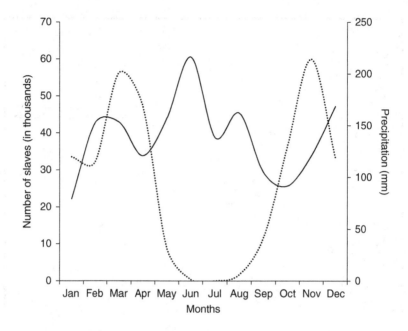

FIGURE 2.3 Seasonal variations in the slave trade from Luanda, 1736–1808
Sources: Eltis et al., "Voyages" and Robert Hoare, "WorldClimate."

In the other seasons, the average number of slaves embarked was considerably lower; 35,400 between January and April, and 34,000 between September and December. The seasonality of the slave trade from Luanda also aligns with the agricultural calendar of the populations living in the hinterland. Italian Capuchins, who traveled widely throughout Kimbundu and Kikongo territories during the seventeenth century, noted that Africans in this region experienced two agricultural cycles. The first began at the end of January, with the cultivation of the land, and ended with the harvest in late April. The second cycle started in September, after the long, dry season, and ended in December. The Capuchins further noted that between May and August Africans neither sowed nor harvested.[105]

[105] Mário José Maestri Filho, *A Agricultura Africana nos Séculos XVI e XVII no Litoral Angolano* (Porto Alegre: Universidade Federal do Rio Grande do Sul, 1978), 52–56; Adriano Parreira, *Economia e Sociedade em Angola na Época da Rainha Jinga, Século XVII* (Lisbon: Estampa, 1990), 29–31.

As we might expect, traders in Portugal and Brazil increased the number of vessels available for the trade during May to August, keeping the number of slaves transported per vessel steady throughout the year. The records available in the "Voyages" database show that between 1736 and 1808 371 vessels embarked slaves at Luanda between January and April, 499 between May and August, and 348 between September and December. In other words, the number of vessels loading slaves between May and August was at least 26 percent higher than in the other months. Mean numbers of slaves held steady with 382 per ship between January and April, 378 between May and August, and 391 between September and December.

The constant flow of slaves leaving Luanda provided the Brazilian plantations and mines with a regular supply of coerced labor throughout the year. The sugar plantations greatly benefited from this steady supply of slaves because of the lengthy agricultural cycle. As Stuart Schwartz observed, the pace of labor on Brazilian sugar plantations continued incessantly for about eight to nine months, beginning in late July or August and ending in May of the following year.[106] Since the trade from Luanda peaked just before the beginning of the harvesting season, it would appear that it was oriented to provide these plantations with a fresh contingent of labor from Africa. However, given the diversification of Brazilian exports at this time, sugar was clearly not the only force driving the demand for slaves. Rice, cotton, and tobacco were also produced with slave labor but were not necessarily grown and processed at the same time as sugar cane.[107] Rice production, for example, started in September or October with the fields' clearing. Planting and weeding continued in the following months until the harvest season started from the end of May through July.[108] Cotton production followed more or less the same cycle as that of rice. The production of tobacco, however, lasted about a year: four months for cultivation, starting in March, April, or May, and from six to eight months for harvesting and processing, commencing in July, August, or September.[109] Moreover, during the eighteenth century, gold

[106] Stuart B. Schwartz, *Sugar Plantations in the Formation of Brazilian Society, Bahia, 1550–1835* (New York: Cambridge University Press, 1985), 100–01.
[107] Alden, "Late Colonial Brazil," 627–53; José Jobson de A. Arruda, *O Brasil no Comércio Colonial* (São Paulo: Editora Ática, 1980), 604–30.
[108] Walter Hawthorne, *From Africa to Brazil: Culture, Identity, and an Atlantic Slave Trade, 1600–1830* (New York: Cambridge University Press, 2010), 155–63.
[109] Jean Baptiste Nardi, *O Fumo Brasileiro no Período Colonial: Lavoura, Comércio e Administração* (São Paulo: Brasiliense, 1996), 52–53.

rather than sugar was the principal commodity exported from Brazil, and gold was not produced in cycles.[110] The service industry, another important sector of the Brazilian economy, also employed large numbers of slaves, especially in the cities, and it operated independently of the calendar on the sugar plantations.[111] Finally, Portuguese policies aimed at controlling inflation and protecting monopolistic rights also shaped the traffic.[112] Overall, these factors combined indicate that the seasonal fluctuations were more important on the Angolan than on the Brazilian side of the transatlantic slave market.

CONCLUSION

Merchants, brokers, and traders played a central role in the transatlantic trade from West Central Africa. They bought ships, imported commodities, and mobilized many other resources to secure transportation of slaves from the interior of West Central Africa to the Americas, especially Brazil. They came from different backgrounds but had shared interests: the accumulation of wealth, power, and prestige. To achieve their goals, they employed several commercial strategies aimed at reducing risks and maximizing profits. Some of these strategies included partnerships and the transportation of small numbers of slaves in different vessels. Traders had to factor in environmental issues that determined certain aspects of the trade. The most relevant were no doubt the gyres of the South Atlantic and patterns of rainfall in the African interior. Additionally, as the trade became increasingly illegal, they had to devise ways to avoid antislave trade cruisers patrolling the coasts of Africa and the Americas. Despite these limitations, merchants, brokers, and traders successfully carried out their activities well into the nineteenth century.

---

[110] Pinto, *O Ouro Brasileiro*, 112–17; A. J. R. Russell-Wood, "Colonial Brazil: The Gold Cycle, c.1690–1750." In *The Cambridge History of Latin America*, ed. Leslie Bethell, vol. 2 (New York: Cambridge University Press, 1984), 593–600.

[111] Alden, "Late Colonial Brazil," 606–07.

[112] In this sense, the law of 1684 and the tax reform of 1758 are particularly important. One should also note the period of activity of the trading companies of Grão Pará and Maranhão, and Pernambuco and Paraíba, which had the monopoly of the slave trade to these areas between the 1750s and 1770s. See the discussion above.

3

The Origins of Slaves Leaving West Central Africa

Although West Central Africa was the principal source of slaves to the Americas during the nineteenth century, the inland origins of these Africans have not been clear. Scholars such as Joseph Miller, Jan Vansina, and John Thornton, among others, have in general suggested that these slaves came from deep in the interior of West Central Africa. These historians argue that the demand for slaves in the Americas stimulated the expansion of the slaving frontier to the border of present-day Angola with the Democratic Republic of the Congo. Further, they maintain that the majority of slaves shipped were prisoners of wars waged by the Lunda Empire. Lunda kings viewed the trade as an opportunity to expand their power by exchanging captives for foreign commodities, which they used to cement alliances, raise armies, and annex neighboring territories.

However, lists of liberated Africans from Cuba and Brazil, in addition to slave registers made by Portuguese colonial officials in Angola, reveal a different pattern. Analysis of these new sources indicates that in the nineteenth century slaves came from several places, with the majority coming from regions much closer to the coast than previously thought. Moreover, these records suggest that slaves and enslavers were not unknown to one another. They came from different ethnic groups but often spoke the same language and shared similar values. Additionally, these records show that the impact of the trade on the African populations was more localized than commonly assumed, with the majority of those shipped originating from a few specific areas near the ports of embarkation. These findings challenge the view of West Central Africa as a region ravaged by wars and crossed by caravans transporting huge numbers of people from distant lands. They also indicate that slaves sold into the Atlantic not only comprised outsiders, but also people who were born and raised as members of the same communities that enslaved them.

Scholarly knowledge of the origins of the slaves shipped from West Central Africa derives largely from oral traditions collected in the second half of the nineteenth century. These traditions suggest a group of Lunda dissidents left their country at the beginning of the sixteenth century after Luba hunters took control of their territory, located at the Upper Kasai River. These Lunda dissidents moved west, joining forces with people they met en route and with whom they founded new polities such as the Imbangala Kingdom of Kasanje, located at the confluence of the rivers Kwango and Lui. Inevitably, some of these encounters were violent, and the thousands who became prisoners of war were made available for sale to transatlantic slave traders. African rulers soon realized the gains to be made from the sale of slaves on the coast of West Central Africa. The trade provided them with rare commodities such as guns, textiles, and alcohol that they used to expand their power throughout the region's interior.[1]

According to current thinking, in the nineteenth century this practice of exchanging foreign merchandise for prisoners of war continued with disastrous consequences for the populations of West Central Africa. Africans searched for slaves in regions further and further away from the coast. Joseph Miller has stated:

Because the richest returns from converting goods into people came from spreading textiles and imports widely into areas where they remained rare, or from employing guns to capture slaves in the regions farthest from home, the transformation of the African political economies acquired an expansive geographical momentum that drove its violence off toward the east. From the earliest period of slave exporting in western central Africa, the political revolutions thus moved toward the interior, leaving behind them a growing commercialized area under new regimes oriented toward the Atlantic trade.[2]

Miller concludes that in the nineteenth century the slave trade had spread to the deep interior of West Central Africa, bringing dramatically disruptive changes to those living in this region.

---

[1] This paragraph summarizes a long debate about the foundation of the kingdoms of West Central Africa. Important references to this debate include Vansina, "The Foundation of the Kingdom of Kasanje," 355–74; Birmingham, "The Date and Significance of the Imbangala Invasion of Angola," 143–52; Vansina, "More on the Invasions of Kongo and Angola," 421–29; Miller, "The Imbangala and the Chronology of Early Central African History," 549–74.

[2] Miller, *Way of Death*, 140.

ORIGINS

The lists of liberated Africans from Cuba and Brazil and the slave registers of Angola provide evidence that calls for a revision of this view. These two sources were created to protect freed Africans from re-enslavement. In 1819, the British, in association with other powers, established mixed commission courts in Havana, Cuba, and Rio de Janeiro, Brazil, to adjudicate cases involving vessels suspected of violating international treaties restricting the sale of slaves across the Atlantic.[3] The courts confiscated the slave traders' property and freed all Africans found on board. Clerks of the courts then recorded information about all surviving recaptives in bound registers, including names, age, sex, and height, as well as country or nation of origin. The lists of liberated Africans from Cuba and Brazil contain information on approximately 454 Africans shipped from the Congo River, 922 from Loango, 94 from Mayumba, 1,235 from Ambriz, 1,059 from Luanda, and 837 from Benguela. In total, the lists provide information on 4,601 Africans shipped from West Central Africa between 1832 and 1840.[4] Nothing similar to the size, aims, and extent of these lists exists for previous years.

Portuguese colonial officials created the second source, the slave registers of Angola, between 1855 and 1856. These records were part of a process undertaken by the Portuguese colonial administration in Lisbon for the gradual emancipation of slaves and continued freedom of other Africans living under Portuguese rule in Africa.[5] They provide the same kind of information as the lists of liberated Africans from Cuba and Brazil, and indeed they may have been modeled on their Mixed Commission counterparts. Colonial officials registered slaves living under Portuguese rule on the coast as well as in the interior of their territories in Angola. However, since the registers listed the slave

---

[3] Bethell, "The Mixed Commissions," 79–81; Domingues da Silva et al., "The Diaspora," 349–50.

[4] The lists of liberated Africans from Cuba are available on line at Eltis et al., "Voyages"; Eltis and Misevich, "African Origins." The originals are kept in the BNA, FO 313, vols. 58 (*Aguila*), 60 (*Joven Reyna* and *Marte*), and 61 (*Marte, Amália, Diligencia, Empresa*, and *Matilde*). The lists of liberated Africans from Brazil are available in the ANRJ, cod. 184, vol. 4 (*Especulador, Leal*, and *Paquete de Benguela*), cod. 471 (*Duque de Bragança, Rio da Prata, Órion, Brilhante, Feliz*, and *Carolina*), and in the AHI, lata 4, maço 3 (*Brilhante* and a vessel without name).

[5] Visconde d'Athoguia, "Decreto de 14 de Dezembro de 1854." *Diário Do Governo*, 28 December 1854, 305 edition, sec. Ministério dos Negócios da Marinha e Ultramar, Seção do Ultramar.

population that remained in Angola, as opposed to those sold across the Atlantic, not all of them provide information adequate for tracing the origins of slaves shipped to the Americas. Moreover, the continued presence of the Portuguese in the interior of Angola during the mid-nineteenth century further contaminated this source because it incorporated into the registers vast numbers of people previously outside Portuguese influence, such as the Kasanje, whose kingdom the Portuguese invaded in 1850. At a later date, this invasion resulted in the construction of the Portuguese forts of Duque de Bragança and Tala Mungongo, where many Kasanje were listed in the slave registers of Angola.[6] Therefore, only the registers compiled at the coastal settlements are reliable for tracing the origins of slaves sold overseas.

The Angolan registers do, however, include a large number of slaves who were originally intended for sale into the transatlantic trade. The rapid growth of the slave populations of the coastal settlements before and after the abolition of the Brazilian trade confirms this hypothesis. In Luanda, for example, the slave population increased from 2,749 in 1844 to 6,020 in 1850 and to 14,294 in 1856, when Governor José Rodrigues Coelho do Amaral reported the total numbers registered in Angola to the colonial office in Lisbon.[7] In Benguela, the slave population increased from 2,438 in 1844 to 2,634 in 1850 and to 5,566 in 1856.[8] Figures on the earlier slave population of Novo Redondo are not

---

[6] António Rodrigues Neves, *Memoria da Expedição à Cassange Commandada pelo Major Graduado Francisco Salles Ferreira em 1850, Escripta pelo Capitão Móvel d'Ambriz António Rodrigues Neves* (Lisbon: Imprensa Silviana, 1854), passim; Douglas L. Wheeler, "The Portuguese in Angola, 1836–1891: A Study in Expansion and Administration" (Ph.D., Boston University, 1963), 126–80; René Pélissier, *História das Campanhas de Angola: Resistência e Revoltas, 1845–1941* (Lisbon: Editorial Estampa, 1997), vol. 1, 107–44; Jill R. Dias, "Angola." In *Nova História da Expansão Portuguesa: O Império Africano, 1825–1890*, ed. Valentim Alexandre and Jill R. Dias, vol. 10 (Lisbon: Editorial Estampa, 1986), 408–12.

[7] Angola, *Almanak Estatístico da Província d'Angola e suas Dependências para o Anno de 1851* (Luanda: Imprensa do Governo, 1852), 8; Lopes de Lima, *Ensaios*, vol. 3, mapa no. 1; José C. Curto, "The Anatomy of a Demographic Explosion: Luanda, 1844–1850." *International Journal of African Historical Studies* 32, no. 2/3 (1999): 402–03; José C. Curto and Raymond R. Gervais, "The Population History of Luanda during the Late Atlantic Slave Trade, 1781–1844." *African Economic History* 29 (2001): 58–59. See also José Rodrigues Coelho do Amaral to the State Secretary of the Navy and Overseas Affairs, 11 February 1856, AHU, Angola, Papéis de Sá da Bandeira, sala 12, maço 822.

[8] Angola, *Almanak Estatístico*, 9; Lopes de Lima, *Ensaios*, vol. 3, mapa no. 1; Cândido, *Fronteras de Esclavización*, 76. See also José Rodrigues Coelho do Amaral to the State Secretary of the Navy and Overseas Affairs, 11 February 1856, AHU, Angola, Papéis de Sá da Bandeira, sala 12, mç. 822.

available, but they must have followed a similar upward trend, culminating with a population of 1,154 in 1856.[9] Slave registers for Luanda survive for 7,522 Africans, about 53 percent of the total registered at that port.[10] Records of captives registered at Benguela are available for 2,588 Africans, or 46 percent of captives originally registered.[11] Only the slave registers of Novo Redondo appear to be complete.[12] In summary, the slave registers of Luanda, Benguela, and Novo Redondo provide information on 11,264 enslaved Africans, most of whom were originally intended for sale into the transatlantic trade.

When combined, the lists of liberated Africans from Cuba and Brazil and the Angolan records provide information about 15,864 Africans who were enslaved in the interior of West Central Africa during the nineteenth century. However, only about half of these provide information for tracing slave origins. In the nineteenth century, Africans had conflicting concepts of origins and identity. They responded to questions such as "where did you come from?" or "what is your nationality?" in different ways. Hence, most of the 15,864 individuals gave replies that are not useful for the purposes of this study. For example, 814 did not specify a place of origin; 120 referred to places outside West Central Africa, such as Mozambique, São Tomé, and Zanzibar; and 223 individuals mentioned names of places no longer identifiable. Additionally, 456 individuals referred to rivers such as Kwanza or Kwango as their country of origin but, since these rivers crossed the territories of several peoples and the individuals did not provide any additional clues about where they had come from, it is impossible to specify their origins. A further 2,432 Africans did provide a known place of origin, but mostly referred to major slave trading posts situated on the coast or in the interior of Angola, such as Ambaca, Benguela, Boma, Cabinda, or Encoje. Finally, 4,207 individuals indicated a generalized country of origin such as "Angola" or "Congo."

Despite the number of records with no geographic information, 7,612 Africans, close to half of all individuals listed, gave an ethnonym as an answer. Scholars have normally hesitated to use these to trace the origins of slaves carried across the Atlantic. They suspected that these ethnonyms

---

[9] José Rodrigues Coelho do Amaral to the State Secretary of the Navy and Overseas Affairs, 11 February 1856, AHU, Angola, Papéis de Sá da Bandeira, sala 12, mç 822.

[10] AHNA, cod. 2467, 2482, 2524, 2784, 2846, 2862, 3186, 3254, 3260 (Luanda), and box 135 (Luanda).

[11] AHNA, cod. 3160 (Benguela).   [12] AHNA, cod. 2830 (Novo Redondo).

had a European origin. Traders may have imposed ethnonyms on slaves carried across the Atlantic, or slaves themselves may have adopted new ethnonyms as they left Africa and sought to blend into the new milieu in the Americas.[13] Also, enslaved Africans could have been captured and owned by different masters in Africa before they were sold into the Atlantic markets. They may have assimilated the identity or ethnicity of their previous owners before they arrived in the Americas.[14] All these concerns have made historians very cautious about using ethnonyms to trace the origins of captives leaving Africa.

Although these are serious issues, we can have some confidence in the use of ethnonyms in these records. Both sources were created soon after

[13] Robert W. Slenes, "'Malungu, Ngoma Vem!:' África Coberta e Descoberta no Brasil." *Revista USP* 12 (92, 1991): 51–54; Robin Law, "Ethnicity and the Slave Trade: 'Lucumi' and 'Nago' as Ethnonyms in West Africa." *History in Africa* 24 (1997): 205–09; Michael Angelo Gomez, *Exchanging Our Country Marks: The Transformation of African Ties in the Colonial and Antebellum South* (Chapel Hill: University of North Carolina Press, 1998), 2–4 and 144; Mariza de Carvalho Soares, *Devotos da Cor: Identidade Étnica, Religiosidade e Escravidão no Rio de Janeiro, Século XVIII* (Rio de Janeiro: Civilização Brasileira, 2000), 224–30; D. B. Chambers, "Ethnicity in the Diaspora: The Slave Trade and the Creation of African 'Nations' in the Americas." *Slavery and Abolition* 22, no. 3 (2001): 26–27; Beatriz Gallotti Mamigonian, "To Be a Liberated African in Brazil: Labour and Citizenship in the Nineteenth Century" (Ph.D., University of Waterloo, 2002), 46–47; Gwendolyn Midlo Hall, "African Ethnicities and the Meanings of 'Mina.'" In *Trans-Atlantic Dimensions of Ethnicity in the African Diaspora*, ed. Paul E. Lovejoy and David V. Trotman (New York: Continuum, 2003), 64–66; Edward A. Alpers, "'Mozambiques' in Brazil: Another Dimension of the African Diaspora in the Atlantic World." In *Africa and the Americas: Interconnections during the Slave Trade*, ed. José C. Curto and Renée Soulodre-La France (Trenton: Africa World Press, 2005), 43–68; Robin Law, "Ethnicities of Enslaved Africans in the Diaspora: On the Meanings of 'Mina' (Again)." *History in Africa* 32 (2005): 248.

[14] Curtin, *Economic Change*, vol. 1, 34–35; Suzanne Miers and Igor Kopytoff, "African 'Slavery' as an Institution of Marginality." In *Slavery in Africa: Historical and Anthropological Perspectives* (Madison: University of Wisconsin Press, 1977), 10–24; Miller, *Way of Death*, 255; Slenes, "Malungu, Ngoma Vem!," 54–55; Joseph C. Miller, "Central Africa during the Era of the Slave Trade, c.1490s-1850s." In *Central Africans and Cultural Transformations in the American Diaspora*, ed. Linda M. Heywood (New York: Cambridge University Press, 2002), 42–43; Paul E. Lovejoy, "Ethnic Designations of the Slave Trade and the Reconstruction of the History of Trans-Atlantic Slavery." In *Trans-Atlantic Dimensions of Ethnicity in the African Diaspora*, ed. Paul E. Lovejoy and David V. Trotman (New York: Continuum, 2003), 15; Linda M. Heywood and John K. Thornton, *Central Africans, Atlantic Creoles, and the Foundation of the Americas, 1585–1660* (New York: Cambridge University Press, 2007), 169–70; Paul E. Lovejoy, "Transatlantic Transformations: The Origins and Identities of Africans in the Americas." In *Africa, Brazil, and the Construction of Trans-Atlantic Black Identities*, ed. Boubacar Barry, Elisée Soumonni, and Livio Sansone (Trenton: Africa World Press, 2008), 97–98.

Africans landed in the Americas or, in the case of the Angolan registers, while they were still in Africa. Additionally, both sets of documents were created with the assistance of people familiar with the languages and cultures of the individuals recorded. The lists of liberated Africans from Cuba, for instance, include the names of the translators who assisted the court commissioners in registering the recaptives. They were often slaves or freed Africans who had previously come from West Central Africa and become fluent in Spanish and Portuguese. The Brazilian lists are less clear, but they must also have been created with the help of African translators, since the courts there followed the same guidelines as in Cuba. Furthermore, Rio de Janeiro had such a large slave population that many of the languages spoken in West Central Africa were also spoken in the city. As Mary Karasch notes, travelers visiting Rio often remarked on the babble of tongues spoken in the streets.[15]

In Angola, Portuguese colonial officials registered slaves with similar procedures. Given the lengthy presence of the Portuguese on the coast of West Central Africa, they were well acquainted with neighboring populations. Also, they had been compiling censuses of the populations living under Portuguese rule in Angola since the late eighteenth century, and colonial officials had considerable experience with the bureaucratic requirements of such activities.[16] Furthermore, the guidelines for slave registration encouraged slave owners to present all their slaves to colonial officials, since in theory unregistered slaves were automatically freed.[17] They also specified that an inspector should be present at the moment of the registration.[18] There are few reasons to doubt the capacity of local officials and inspectors to engage with Africans. Although Portuguese was the dominant language of the administration, the everyday speech among the local population comprised a range of local African dialects. In fact,

---

[15] Karasch, *Slave Life*, 214–15.

[16] Curto and Gervais, "The Population History of Luanda," 4–26; José C. Curto and Raymond R. Gervais, "A Dinâmica Demográfica de Luanda no Contexto do Tráfico de Escravos do Atlântico Sul, 1781–1844." *Topoi*, no. 4 (2002): 86–97.

[17] Visconde d'Athoguia, "Decreto de 14 de Dezembro de 1854." *Diário do Governo*, 28 December 1854, 305 edition, sec. Ministério dos Negócios da Marinha e Ultramar, Seção do Ultramar, Title 1, Article 2, 1574.

[18] The guidelines specify that the inspection of the slaves should follow the "Regulamento de 25 de Outubro de 1853." See Ibid., Title 1, Article 1, 1574; Visconde d'Athoguia, "Regulamento que Faz Parte do Decreto de 25 de Outubro de 1853, Publicado no Diário do Governo no. 268, de 14 de Novembro de 1853." *Diário do Governo*, 29 November 1853, 281 edition, sec. Ministério dos Negócios da Marinha e Ultramar, Seção do Ultramar, Article 7, 1601.

Kimbundu was the dominant language spoken in Luanda well into the nineteenth century.[19] This fact is all the more important given that at that time Luanda was the largest European community in Africa south of the Sahara, with the possible exception of Cape Town.

Africans had no reason to conceal their ethnicity when questioned by court or Portuguese officials. The lists of liberated Africans from Cuba and Brazil were created to protect Africans from re-enslavement. The slave registers of Angola served a similar purpose. They were created to inhibit the enslavement of free Africans, as well as the re-enslavement of Africans who had gained their freedom after registration. Furthermore, as will be seen below, the ethnonyms available in the lists of liberated Africans and the slave registers align with data from the analysis of other documents used to measure the impact of the slave trade on Africa. The number and proportion of Nsundi or Ndongo slaves leaving West Central Africa in the nineteenth century from the registers, for example, match reports about warfare, predatory trade, and depopulation in the areas where these ethnic groups lived. The form in which some of these ethnonyms appear in the documents also attests to their authenticity. Designations such as "Muxicongo" and "Camundongo" literally mean "I am Kongo" and "I am an inhabitant of Ndongo," in Kikongo and Kimbundu, respectively. Therefore, they are not inventions of slave traders or colonial officials, but authentic expressions of African identity. Finally, although slaves may have been traded several times before they entered the transatlantic traffic, it is doubtful whether the majority of them spent sufficient time enslaved in Africa to adopt the ethnicity of their owners. As will be seen in the next chapter, slaves leaving Angola in the nineteenth century were relatively young, suggesting that they were first generation slaves sold across the ocean soon after their enslavement. All in all, the ethnonyms available in the lists of liberated Africans as well as the slave registers provide reliable information about the origins of slaves leaving West Central Africa in this period.

While ethnonyms often appear with different spellings, they can be organized into modern ethnic and linguistic groups and located on a map of West Central Africa. Research suggests that the ethnolinguistic map of West Africa, another region that served as a major source of slaves for the transatlantic slave trade, shows remarkable continuity throughout the

---

[19] Jan Vansina, "Portuguese vs Kimbundu: Language Use in the Colony of Angola (1575–c.1845)." *Bulletin Des Séances de l'Academie Royale Des Sciences d'Outre Mer* 47 (March 2001): 276–78.

years from the beginning of the slave trade to the present, although political stability is quite another issue.[20] Preliminary analyses of the Bantu languages of Southeast Africa, also a region deeply affected by the slave trade, yield similar results.[21] Furthermore, Portuguese colonial records, in addition to field studies and historical research, provide scholars with a number of maps, lists, and other resources that have enabled them to reconstruct the ethnolinguistic map of West Central Africa for the nineteenth century.[22] The ethnonyms available in the lists of liberated Africans and the slave registers of Angola have been compared with these sources and organized into modern ethnic and linguistic groups. Africans who claimed they came from or were affiliated with the Lunda, Muatianvo, and Muatianbo, for example, were considered as belonging to the Lunda ethnic group – part of the Ruund linguistic group, located east of the Upper Kasai River. After adjusting for the variations in spelling, the records show that slaves shipped from West Central Africa in these years came from 21 linguistic groups, comprising 116 ethnicities spread throughout the region's interior.

[20] P. E. H. Hair, "Ethnolinguistic Continuity on the Guinea Coast." *Journal of African History* 8, no. 2 (1967): 247–49.

[21] P. E. H. Hair, "From Language to Culture: Some Problems in the Systemic Analysis of the Ethnohistorical Records of the Sierra Leone Region." In *The Population Factor in African Studies*, ed. R. P. Moss and R. J. A. R. Rathbone (London: University of London Press, 1975), 74.

[22] These resources include but are not limited to João Carlos Feo Cardoso de Castello Branco e Torres, *Memórias Contendo a Biographia do Vice Almirante Luis da Motta Feo e Torres, a História dos Governadores e Capitaens Generaes de Angola desde 1575 até 1825, e a Descripção Geographica e Politica dos Reinos de Angola e Benguella* (Paris: Fantin, 1825), Map; Lopes de Lima, *Ensaios*, Maps; José de Oliveira Ferreira Diniz, *Populações Indígenas de Angola* (Coimbra: Imprensa da Universidade, 1918), Maps; Mário Milheiros, *Índice Histórico-Corográfico de Angola* (Luanda: Instituto de Investigação Científica de Angola, 1972), Lists; José Redinha, *Distribuição Étnica de Angola* (Luanda: Centro de Informação e Turismo de Angola, 1962), Lisps and Map; Vansina, *Kingdoms of the Savanna*, Maps and Index; Martin, *The External Trade*, Maps and Index; Hilton, *The Kingdom of Kongo*, Maps and Index; Robert W. Harms, *River of Wealth, River of Sorrow: The Central Zaire Basin in the Era of the Slave and Ivory Trade, 1500–1891* (New Haven: Yale University Press, 1981), Maps and Index; Karasch, *Slave Life*, Appendix A; Gladwyn Murray Childs, *Kinship and Character of the Ovimbundu: Being a Description of the Social Structure and Individual Development of the Ovimbundu of Angola, with Observations Concerning the Bearing on the Enterprise of Christian Missions of Certain Phases of the Life and Culture Described* (London: Reprinted for the International African Institute & for the Witwatersrand U.P. by Dawson, 1969), Maps and Index; John K. Thornton, *Africa and Africans in the Making of the Atlantic World, 1400–1800*, 2nd edn. (New York: Cambridge University Press, 1998), Maps and Index; "Ethnologue: Languages of the World," 2009, www.ethnologue.com/.

The records also provide the means to estimate the number of slaves shipped by linguistic and ethnic groups. In 1969, Philip Curtin observed that the number of captives leaving from West Central Africa varied according to ports of embarkation, suggesting that different regions in the interior supplied these ports with slaves. Curtin argued captives embarking at ports north of Luanda usually came from the basin of the Congo River; slaves leaving from ports south of Luanda originated from the central plateau of Angola; and slaves shipped from Luanda itself came not only from its immediate interior but also from the central plateau and the basin of the Congo River.[23] Indeed, Luanda was a case apart, because it was by far the largest single departure point in the history of the transatlantic trade.[24] It is now possible to use estimates of the number of slaves shipped from Luanda and the ports north and south of it to arrive at an approximate distribution of the Africans transported by ethnic and linguistic origins.[25]

Recent studies show that between 1831 and 1855, the period covered by the lists of liberated Africans and the slave registers of Angola, the ports north of Luanda shipped 313,375 slaves. The ports south of it shipped approximately 186,510, while Luanda alone shipped about 267,330.[26]

---

[23] Curtin, *The Atlantic Slave Trade*, 260–62. See also Domingues da Silva, "The Atlantic Slave Trade from Angola," 112–13; Ferreira, "The Suppression," 5.

[24] An up-to-date ranking of the largest ports of slave embarkation is available in David Eltis and David Richardson, eds., *Atlas of the Transatlantic Slave Trade* (New Haven: Yale University Press, 2010), Table 5, 90.

[25] Domingues da Silva, "The Atlantic Slave Trade from Angola," 122; Eltis and Richardson, *Atlas*, 137–53.

[26] Domingues da Silva, "The Atlantic Slave Trade from Angola," 122. Other similar estimates are available in José C. Curto, "The Legal Portuguese Slave Trade from Benguela, Angola, 1730–1828: A Quantitative Re-Appraisal." *África: Revista Do Centro de Estudos Africanos Da Universidade de São Paulo* 16–17, no. 1 (April 1993): 110–15; José C. Curto, "A Quantitative Reassessment of the Legal Portuguese Slave Trade from Luanda, Angola, 1710–1830." *African Economic History*, no. 20 (1992): 15–24; Eltis and Richardson, *Atlas*, 137–53; Eltis, "The Volume and Structure of the Transatlantic Slave Trade," 23–28 and 31–35; Lovejoy, *Transformations in Slavery*, 46–55 and 145–51; Joseph C. Miller, "Legal Portuguese Slaving from Angola: Some Preliminary Indications of Volume and Direction, 1760–1830." *Revue Française d'Histoire d'Outre-Mer* 62, no. 226–27 (1975): 138–56; Miller, "The Slave Trade," 101–02; Joseph C. Miller, "The Numbers, Origins, and Destinations of Slaves in the Eighteenth-Century Angolan Slave Trade," *Social Science History* 13, no. 4 (1989): 393–412; Joseph C. Miller, "The Numbers, Origins, and Destinations of Slaves in the Eighteenth-Century Angolan Slave Trade." In *The Atlantic Slave Trade: Effects on Economics, Societies, and Peoples in Africa, the Americas and Europe*, ed. Joseph E. Inikori and Stanley L. Engerman, 2nd edn. (Durham: Duke University Press, 1998), 89–108.

Since the lists of liberated Africans and the slave registers provide information on the port of departure or, in the case of the slave registers, the places of registration in Angola, the ratio of linguistic and ethnic groups for each of these three regions can be computed and then applied to the estimated numbers shipped from the three port groupings. This operation is important because, without it, the different nature of the sources and the fluctuations in the slave trade can render a distorted picture of the past. As we have seen, most of the records from the lists of liberated Africans from Brazil and Cuba refer to Africans who had embarked from ports north of Luanda, while most of the individuals recorded in the slave registers of Angola were registered in Luanda and ports south of Luanda. Moreover, the number of slaves leaving from each port fluctuated significantly between the 1830s and the 1850s. From the 1830s to the first half of the 1840s, the majority of the slaves departed from Luanda and the ports south of Luanda. From the mid-1840s, however, that picture changed, with the majority leaving from the northern ports. Finally, some ports were simply more involved in the traffic than others and estimates of the proportion of each linguistic and ethnic group forced into the trade must take such differences into consideration. For example, 5 percent of slaves shipped from Luanda who were Kongo is considerably more than 5 percent transported from any of the ports north of Luanda who were Kongo. The sources alone, therefore, cannot account for the size and relative distribution of that migration. They must be adjusted to provide a more accurate picture of the traffic. After completing this operation, the resulting ethnolinguistic subtotals for the three regions can be aggregated and projected on a map of West Central Africa.

Figure 3.1 shows the result of this procedure. It displays the estimated number of slaves leaving West Central Africa between 1831 and 1855 by linguistic groups and the relative position of those groups in the region's interior. The map makes immediately apparent that slaves came from a wide variety of places across West Central Africa. As scholars have already stressed, in the nineteenth century slaves were drawn into the trade from regions situated increasingly farther from the coast.[27] Certainly, Figure 3.1 shows that the enslavement zone at that time covered a vast area of approximately 2.5 million square kilometers; a region larger than the territory of the United States east of the

[27] See, for example, Miller, *Way of Death*, 146–47; Oppen, *Terms of Trade and Terms of Trust*, 59–61; Vansina, "It Never Happened," 403; Thornton, "The Chronology and Causes," 7.

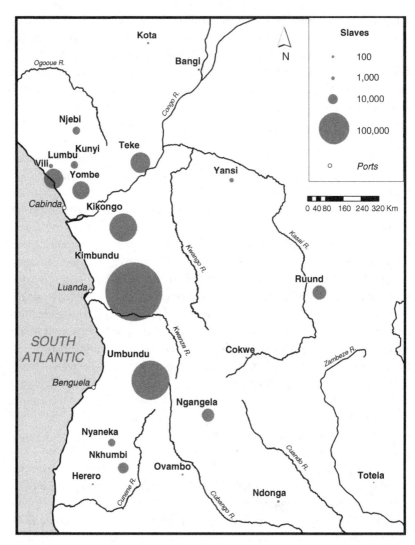

FIGURE 3.1 Estimated number of slaves leaving West Central Africa by linguistic groups, 1831–1855
Source: Appendix B, Table B.24.

Mississippi River. Moreover, captives came from different ecological environments ranging from the Equatorial forest in the north to the arid lands around the Cunene River in the south. In the east, they came from places as distant as the Kasai or Zambeze rivers. Scholars have rightly stressed the extent to which the transatlantic trade expanded throughout the interior of West Central Africa during the nineteenth century.

However, the most important pattern that Figure 3.1 illustrates is that the vast majority of the slaves carried off in this period did not come from these remote regions. It clearly indicates that they belonged to the Kikongo, Kimbundu, and Umbundu linguistic groups, all of whom lived west of the Kwango River. By the nineteenth century, slave traders had long drawn on these groups as sources of captives for the transatlantic trade. Kikongo slaves first appeared in the historical record in the early sixteenth century, when Portuguese traders sailed to Angola to purchase slaves for their sugar plantations at São Tomé, in the Bight of Biafra.[28] Kimbundu slaves are first mentioned shortly thereafter, as Portuguese traders expanded their activities to Luanda, where they founded a colony in 1576.[29] Umbundu slaves began to appear in the records somewhat later, around the late seventeenth century, shortly before the Portuguese built the first military garrisons in the Angolan highlands.[30] By the nineteenth century Kikongo, Kimbundu, and Umbundu speakers were already well-established and historic targets of the transatlantic trade.

Slaves leaving West Central African ports certainly traveled greater distances prior to embarkation than captives leaving from any other broad region of sub-Saharan Africa. However, these distances were shorter than most scholars claim. Patrick Manning, for instance, contends that in the nineteenth century slaves shipped from West Central Africa came from places situated between 600 and 700 kilometers from the coast.[31] Joseph Miller argues that at this time they traveled in caravans departing from Lunda, 500 kilometers distant from Kasanje, which in turn is located about 300 kilometers from the coast.[32] However, Table 3.1 suggests that in the nineteenth century slaves traveled much shorter distances than this. It provides a breakdown of Africans with known ethnonyms by ports of

---

[28] Birmingham, *Trade and Conflict*, 24–25; Hilton, *The Kingdom of Kongo*, 55–59; Vansina, *Kingdoms of the Savanna*, 52–54; Miller, *Way of Death*, 140–46.

[29] Birmingham, *Trade and Conflict*, 32–33 and 46–51; Vansina, *Kingdoms of the Savanna*, 125–30; Miller, *Way of Death*, 140–46.

[30] Birmingham, *Trade and Conflict*, 140–41; Vansina, *Kingdoms of the Savanna*, 197–200; Miller, *Way of Death*, 140–46; Roquinaldo Amaral Ferreira, "Transforming Atlantic Slaving: Trade, Warfare and Territorial Control in Angola, 1650–1800" (Ph.D., University of California, 2003), 71–80; Cândido, *Fronteras de Esclavización*, 28–37.

[31] Manning, *Slavery and African Life*, 70.   [32] Miller, *Way of Death*, 195.

TABLE 3.1 *Percentage of slaves leaving West Central Africa by distance traveled between their origins in the interior and their ports of embarkation (in kilometers), 1831–1855*

Distances (km)	Ports north of Luanda	Luanda	Ports south of Luanda	Total
0–100	10.4	0.2	21.2	11.0
101–200	5.4	15.7	10.5	11.8
201–300	7.8	33.5	21.3	24.1
301–400	20.3	15.1	17.9	17.1
401–500	6.9	2.0	11.8	7.1
501–600	12.8	24.5	13.2	17.8
601–700	34.9	0.6	0.7	6.0
701–800	0.9	1.1	0.3	0.7
801 over	0.7	7.2	3.0	4.3
Total	100.0	100.0	100.0	100.0

Source: Appendix B, Tables B.21, B.22, and B.23.

embarkation and the distances they traveled to reach those ports (or their place of registration). It demonstrates that two out of every three captives traveled distances no greater than 400 kilometers, with the average distance traveled ranging between 200 and 300 kilometers.

But the average is probably subject to some upward bias. The distances that form the basis of Table 3.1 are measured from the heartland of the specified linguistic group, which is often located in places more distant from the coast than the actual population centers. Many Lunda slaves probably originated from areas close to the Kwango River, whereas they were counted in this study as coming from beyond the Kasai River, the traditional heartland of the Ruund-speaking people to which the Lunda belong. This attribution explains the high percentages of Africans coming from regions situated between 500 and 700 kilometers from the coast. Additionally, many Africans who embarked at Luanda but claimed to have come originally from the basin of the Congo River or the Angolan highlands probably did not travel overland from these regions directly to Luanda. They must have traveled first to one of the ports north or south of Luanda and then completed their journey by sea, a much quicker and safer route than crossing dense forests, mountainous regions, and toll roads con-trolled by local rulers. Actual distances travelled were probably shorter than Table 3.1 suggests.

SLAVERY AND SOCIETY

One of the major implications of the above argument is that Africans transported from West Central Africa became slaves as a result of internecine strife rather than as victims of large-scale wars waged throughout the interior. As previously mentioned, scholars claim that in the nineteenth century the majority of slaves sold into the Atlantic were prisoners of wars waged by Ruund speakers from the Lunda Empire. They argue that Lunda rulers were responding to the demand for slaves on the coast of West Central Africa by extending their military activities throughout the interior. This aggression gave them control over the flow of foreign commodities introduced inland via trade with the Americas. Rulers could use these commodities as an important source of revenue and a way of building dependency and loyalty among their subjects.[33]

The supposition that the trade in slaves leaving West Central Africa is connected to the expansion of the Lunda Empire has received further support from research focusing on slavery in Africa. Scholars have long stressed that outsiders were usually the principal targets of enslavement and sale into the trade. Orlando Patterson claims, for example, that natal alienation of slaves was a key component of slave status in any given society.[34] Claude Meillassoux argues that Africans regarded outsiders as the primary candidates eligible for enslavement. He maintains that the slave was above all "the alien *par excellence*, if not the alien in an absolute sense."[35] More recently, Sean Stilwell went even further, arguing that "slaves in Africa were not just outsiders; they were also understood as kinless."[36] In short, the idea that outsiders were perfect candidates for enslavement has shaped much of the current scholarship focusing on the question of who was eligible for enslavement and sale across the Atlantic. These views fit well with the idea that the majority of the slaves leaving West Central Africa in the nineteenth century were prisoners of war.

However, the data presented in this chapter suggest that the majority of the captives in this region had more in common with their captors than

---

[33] Ibid., 78–94 and 146–47; Oppen, *Terms of Trade and Terms of Trust*, 59–61; Vansina, "It Never Happened," 403; Thornton, "The Chronology and Causes," 6–8.

[34] Orlando Patterson, *Slavery and Social Death: A Comparative Study* (Cambridge: Harvard University Press, 1982), 44. For a recent criticism of this view of slavery, see Vincent Brown, "Social Death and Political Life in the Study of Slavery." *American Historical Review* 114, no. 5 (2009).

[35] Claude Meillassoux, *The Anthropology of Slavery: The Womb of Iron and Gold*, trans. Alide Dasnois (Chicago: University of Chicago Press, 1991), 28.

[36] Stilwell, *Slavery and Slaving*, 9.

historians have commonly assumed. A more refined analysis is possible for each of the three principal language groups identified in Figure 3.1. Together the Kikongo, Kimbundu, and Umbundu-speaking peoples accounted for 72 percent of the men, women, and children in our sample. The Lunda Empire subjugated none of these groups. They were more likely to have been enslaved as a result of internal conflicts within their own language communities, perhaps through judicial proceedings, debts, and kidnapping. Figures 3.2, 3.3, and 3.4 take each of these groups in turn and provide a further breakdown of slaves transported by ethnicity.

Figure 3.2 shows that the majority of the Kikongo slaves came from the former Kingdom of Kongo, which in the nineteenth century was largely fragmented as a result of years of civil wars. However, smaller numbers also came from neighboring polities, such as the kingdoms of Ngoyo, Kakongo, and Yaka. All these societies recognized the nominal power and authority of a king, even though this position was sometimes vacant. Kongo had ceased to exist as a centralized kingdom in the seventeenth century, but the king's position still existed and candidates from different royal lineages disputed the throne among themselves.[37] As in other kingdoms, Kikongo society was hierarchical; nobility at the apex, commoners in the middle, and slaves in the lowest tier. Slavery, in fact, predated the transatlantic trade in Kikongo territory, but the incidence of slaves in Kikongo society and the extent to which the trade influenced who, by, and how one could be enslaved likely changed over time. Linda Heywood, among others, argues that the transatlantic trade contributed significantly to changing Kikongo values, laws, and ideas of who could be enslaved.[38] Reflecting on the case of the Kongo in particular, she writes:

In the early seventeenth century, when Kongo stopped expanding and waging wars against its neighbors, elites had the opportunity to manipulate the laws concerning the kinds of crimes for which freeborn Kongos could be enslaved. Civil wars which began in the last quarter of the seventeenth century and which continued into the eighteenth further encouraged this process, and contenders for power enslaved the populations of their rivals. Thus, condemning rebels to slavery

---

[37] Susan Broadhead, "Beyond Decline: The Kingdom of Kongo in the Eighteenth and Nineteenth Centuries." *International Journal of African Historical Studies* 12, no. 4 (1979): 619–20; Jelmer Vos, "The Kingdom of Kongo and Its Borderlands, 1880–1915" (Ph.D., School of Oriental and African Studies, 2005), 33–42; Hilton, *The Kingdom of Kongo*, 218–19; John K. Thornton, *The Kingdom of Kongo: Civil War and Transition, 1641–1718* (Madison: University of Wisconsin Press, 1983), 53.

[38] Heywood, "Slavery," 2–3. See also Vos, "The Kingdom of Kongo," 32–33; Hilton, *The Kingdom of Kongo*, 121–22; Thornton, *The Kingdom of Kongo*, 19–20.

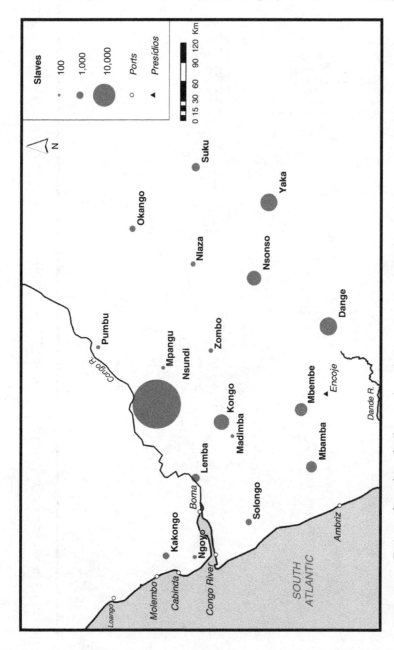

FIGURES 3.2 Estimated number of Kikongo slaves leaving West Central Africa by ethnic groups, 1831–1855
Source: Same as Figure 3.1.

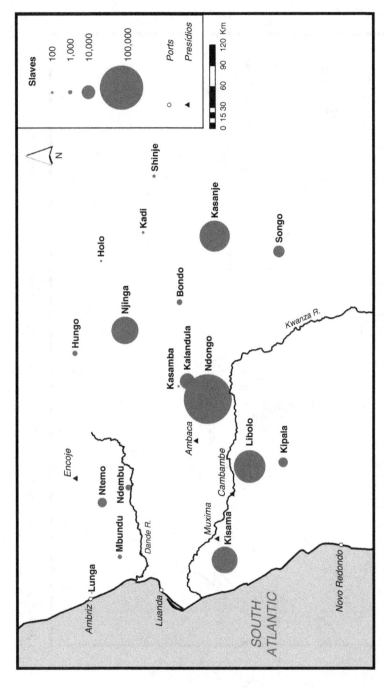

FIGURE 3.3 Estimated number of Kimbundu slaves leaving West Central Africa by ethnic groups, 1831–1855
Source: Same as Figure 3.1.

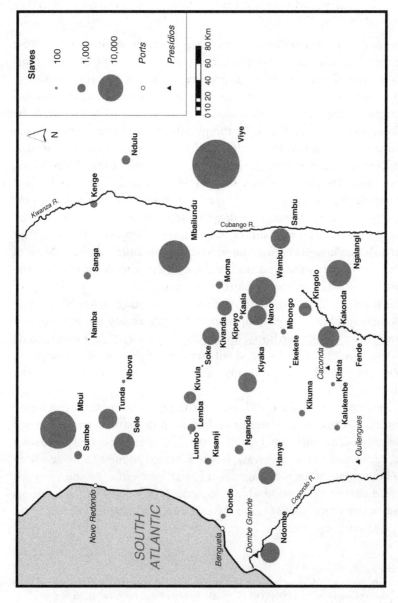

FIGURE 3.4 Estimated number of Umbundu slaves leaving West Central Africa by ethnic groups, 1831–1855
Source: Same as Figure 3.1.

increasingly became the way for freeborn Kongos to lose their freedom. In time, kings and their political rivals openly enslaved free Kongos, selling some to Portuguese and other foreign merchants, sending others as gifts to missionaries and political allies, and keeping the remainder to serve as soldiers, producers or status symbol.[39]

The majority of the Kikongo-speaking captives shipped from West Central Africa in the nineteenth century belonged to the Nsundi ethnic group. The Nsundi inhabited a province of the old Kingdom of Kongo that went by the same name. In the nineteenth century, the Nsundi became victims of a sophisticated trading network dominated by Kikongo speakers at Boma, at the mouth of the Congo River. Norm Schrag points out that Boma elders believed that the Nsundi, as well as the Yombe, another language group situated north of the Congo River, were "enemies against whom they should not make war but [rather] kidnap through deception."[40] These "enemies" were then sold into the Atlantic commerce through the *dingizi* trading system, a commercial network that allowed certain individuals to travel safely through the interior using special insignias belonging to healing cults called *lemba*.[41] Most of these individuals were graduates of the *khimba* schools for youth initiation, organized by chiefs who introduced young free men to knowledge of their spirit world. The graduates used a secret language unknown to other Kikongo speakers and promoted special bonds among the initiates that transcended lineage, territorial domain, and ethnicity.[42] As a result, Boma traders were able to enslave and sell members of the Nsundi ethnic group even though both spoke the same language and shared similar cultural values.

The impact of the slave trade on the Kikongo speakers in the nineteenth century is difficult to determine, but it must have been distributed unevenly across different regions. John Thornton measured the demographic impact of the slave trade on the Kikongo population living within the boundaries of the old Kingdom of Kongo between 1780 and 1789. He argued that in this period about 600,000 people lived in the kingdom from where an average of 6,180 slaves, or approximately 1 percent of the

[39] Heywood, "Slavery," 12.
[40] Norm Schrag, "Mboma and the Lower Zaire: A Socioeconomic Study of a Kongo Trading Community, c.1785–1885" (Ph.D., Indiana University, 1985), 62–63.
[41] John Janzen, *Lemba, 1650–1930: A Drum of Affliction in Africa and the New World* (New York: Garland, 1982), 3–6.
[42] Schrag, "Mboma and the Lower Zaire," 64–65.

total population, were carried annually.[43] This estimate does not include Africans who died during the process of enslavement, transport, and sale on the coast, and is thus a lower bound assessment of the demographic impact of the traffic.

The majority of the slaves shipped came from the kingdom's capital, Mbanza Kongo, which at that time served as the principal stage for the kingdom's civil wars. These slaves were supplemented with other Kikongo speakers captured in different parts of the kingdom, especially Mbrize, Kibangu, and Mbamba Lubota, all three south of Mbanza Kongo.[44] Not all of these slaves were prisoners of war. According to Thornton's estimates, at least 27 percent of all captives shipped from the Kingdom of Kongo were enslaved through raids or judicial proceedings.[45] The impact of the slave trade was particularly destructive in the capital, however. In 1780, the population of Mbanza Kongo numbered about 27,600, but by 1789 it had fallen to 18,950; a decline of 31 percent in just ten years.[46] Nevertheless, the overall impact on the kingdom's population was reduced by the importation of slaves from neighboring regions.[47] In the nineteenth century, the impact of the slave trade on the Kikongo-speaking population likely followed a similar pattern of geographic concentration, but with the majority of the slaves coming from Nsundi rather than Mbanza Kongo.

Similarly, Kimbundu speakers leaving West Central Africa in the nineteenth century were also enslaved as a result of internal conflicts, judicial proceedings, debts, and kidnapping. In fact, their presence in the trade can be established as early as the sixteenth century, when the Portuguese established a colony at Luanda.[48] Figure 3.3 shows the estimated number of Kimbundu slaves entering the traffic between 1831 and 1855 broken down by ethnic group. The majority of them came from decentralized societies organized around clans or lineages headed by one or more powerful individuals who had a voice in decisions affecting the entire society. These societies included the Kisama, Libolo, Ndembu, and Ndongo. However, captives also came from some centralized states such as Holo, Hungu, Kasanje, Njinga, Shinje, and Songo, generally ruled by a chief or king.

---

[43] John K. Thornton, "As Guerras Civis no Congo e o Tráfico de Escravos: A História e a Demografia de 1718 a 1844 Revisitadas." *Estudos Afro-Asiáticos* 32 (1997): 67 and table 1.
[44] Ibid., 67. [45] Ibid., calculated from table 1. [46] Ibid., calculated from table 2.
[47] Ibid., 68.
[48] Birmingham, *Trade and Conflict*, 32–33 and 46–51; Vansina, *Kingdoms of the Savanna*, 125–30; Miller, *Way of Death*, 140–46.

The political impact of the trade on the Kimbundu was particularly destructive. In the sixteenth century, the Ndongo appeared to be on the verge of becoming a centralized society ruled by a king, holder of the title of *ngola*. However, with the increasing demand for slaves on the coast, the Ndongo fell prey to the Portuguese and other Kimbundu societies, notably Kasanje, who raided them for slaves.[49] As a result, the Ndongo fragmented into a number of chiefdoms called *sobados* by the Portuguese. The latter established suzerainty over local peoples by forcing them to sign vassal treaties reducing them to vassal status, and building a number of forts along the Kwanza River, such as Muxima, Cambambe, and Ambaca. These forts, called *presídios*, are identified on Figure 3.3 by dark triangles. The Portuguese then collected tributes from the *sobados* in slaves and other commodities.[50]

In theory, vassals were not allowed to enslave other vassals, but the demand for slaves on the coast was so high that it stimulated rivalry among different *sobas* or chiefs. As a consequence, instead of capturing non-vassals living near their territories, these *sobas* frequently turned against each other to supply the tributes that their suzerains demanded. Vassals enslaved other vassals through raids, kidnappings, and pawning, to an extent that, ironically, alarmed the Portuguese authorities in Luanda. As Roquinaldo Ferreira notes, "by the end of the eighteenth century, enslavement had become so pervasive in regions under nominal Portuguese control that the Luanda administration was forced to intervene on behalf of African vassals."[51] The Portuguese worried about the enslavement of vassals less from humanitarian reasons, but rather because the practice had the potential to undermine their authority in the region. It threatened their ability to recruit laborers to carry out services in the colony and encouraged out migration from regions under Portuguese control.[52] The Portuguese tried to address the problem by creating tribunals and other judicial mechanisms that would ensure all individuals captured were non-vassals, but their efforts produced little results.

[49] Birmingham, *Trade and Conflict*, 17–20 and 91–96; David Birmingham, *Central Africa to 1870: Zambesia, Zaïre and the South Atlantic* (New York: Cambridge University Press, 1981), 75–83.

[50] Birmingham, *Trade and Conflict*, 32–33, 50, and 78–79; Heintze, "Luso-African Feudalism in Angola? The Vassal Treaties of the Sixteenth to the Eighteenth Century," 123; Beatrix Heintze, "Angola nas Garras do Tráfico de Escravos: As Guerras do Ndongo (1611–1630)." *Revista Internacional de Estudos Africanos* 1 (1984): 11–15. Carlos Couto, however, asserts that tributes were paid mostly in goods. See Couto, *Os Capitães-Mores*, 124–33 and 252–56.

[51] Ferreira, *Cross-Cultural Exchange*, 77.   [52] Ibid., 85–86.

The practice of pawning was deeply rooted. The colonial administration simply had neither the resources nor manpower to police the *sobas* and enforce the laws. Ndongo *sobas* also had few options. If they did not enslave vassals, they would have to wage wars against the more powerful kingdoms of eastern Kimbundu land or against the Kisama and Libolo, in the forest south of the Kwanza River, who the Portuguese were unable to subdue. As Ferreira further observes, "the enslavement of African vassals remained central to production of slaves in Angola well into the nineteenth century."[53]

The slave trade had a significant demographic impact on the Ndongo. In 1844, Commander Lopes de Lima traveled to Luanda and consulted the censuses of Portuguese Angola then available in the colonial archives. These censuses began in the late eighteenth century and, because the Ndongo were the largest ethnic group living under Portuguese rule in Angola, they provide valuable evidence about the size of the Ndongo population. According to Lopes de Lima, the censuses indicated that the black population of Portuguese Angola "had grown so little, that it had increased no more than one percent in an interval of twenty years."[54] Modern research supports this assessment, at least for an earlier period. John Thornton has established that the slave trade not only reduced the rate of growth among the black population of Portuguese Angola, but also caused a dramatic imbalance between the number of males and females. He concludes that late eighteenth-century Angola was very much a female world, since females outnumbered males in different age and social categories by as much as 60 percent.[55]

Umbundu speakers, the third major linguistic group represented in the registries, exhibited patterns similar to the Kikongo and Kimbundu populations. The Umbundu lived on the central plateau of Angola intermingled among several different societies. The largest of them, Mbailundu and Viye, were located in the east, at the head of the Kwanza and Cubango rivers. They practiced agriculture but their main economic activity comprised long distance trade. Initially, most of the trade was in salt, copper, iron, wax, ivory, and foodstuffs transported between the coast and the populations living east of the Angolan highlands. However, after the arrival of the Portuguese on the coast of southern Angola in the 1610s,

---

[53] Ibid., 87.   [54] Lopes de Lima, *Ensaios*, vol. 3, 6–7.
[55] John K. Thornton, "The Slave Trade in Eighteenth Century Angola: Effects on Demographic Structures." *Canadian Journal of African Studies* 14, no. 3 (1980): 421–23.

the Umbundu began to exchange a whole new range of goods, including textiles, spirits, and firearms. It is not clear when these societies adopted a centralized form of government, but linguistic evidence and oral traditions show that they were familiar with concepts of kingship as early as the fourteenth century and that many were living under the authority of rulers before the Portuguese reached the highlands in the mid-seventeenth century.[56]

Slavery in Umbundu land also predated the arrival of the Portuguese, and slaves were used in a variety of ways, from concubines, to laborers, and military officers. However, the transatlantic trade from their region began after Portuguese attempts to find copper mines in the interior of Benguela had failed.[57] In the eighteenth century, the trade from the central plateau increased with the opening of Benguela in 1716 to direct trade with Brazil and the establishment of Portuguese forts in the Angolan highlands, especially in Caconda.[58] In the nineteenth century, the trade further expanded, spreading throughout the central plateau. Figure 3.4 presents an estimated ethnic breakdown of the Umbundu-speaking slaves leaving West Central Africa similar to the Kimbundu and Kikongo breakdowns. It shows that the majority of Umbundu captives came from centralized states such as Mbailundu, Viye, Wambu, Kiyaka, Ngalangi, Kivula, Ndulu, Kingolo, Kalukembe, Sambu, Ekekete, Kakonda, and Kitata. These kingdoms collected tribute from other Umbundu kingdoms, such as Kasongi, Ngalangi, Kivanda, Namba, Sanga, Kenge, Kipeyo, Mbongo, and Elende.[59] However, many of the slaves also came from decentralized societies, such as the Mbui, Hanya, and Ndombe.

The Portuguese channeled these slaves through a series of forts that they had constructed along the Coporolo River and on the slopes of the Angolan highland, such as Quilengues, Dombe Grande, and Caconda. To protect their interests in the region, the Portuguese forced the local populations to sign vassal treaties with them, similar to those they signed with the Kimbundu. As Mariana Cândido notes, these treaties offered

[56] Vansina, *How Societies Are Born*, 170–82.
[57] Birmingham, *Trade and Conflict*, 140–41; Maria Emília Madeira Santos, *Viagens de Exploração Terrestre dos Portugueses em África* (Lisbon: Centro de Estudos de Cartografia Antiga, 1978), 138–41; Ferreira, "Transforming Atlantic Slaving," 71–80; Cândido, *Fronteras de Esclavización*, 28–29; Cândido, *An African Slaving Port*, 44–50. Add note on slavery.
[58] Ferreira, "Transforming Atlantic Slaving," 112–21; Cândido, *Fronteras de Esclavización*, 30–32; Cândido, *An African Slaving Port*, 160–64.
[59] Childs, *Kinship and Character*, 168; Merran McCulloch, *The Ovimbundu of Angola* (London: International African Institute, 1952), 2.

Portuguese protection to vassals in exchange for tributes. Some of these tributes could be paid in slaves, but vassals were not allowed to enslave other vassals because "they were considered to have embraced the Christian faith."[60] The Portuguese thus expected their Umbundu vassals to pay tributes by enslaving non-vassals or delivering people who had at least been born into slavery. As with their Kimbundu counterparts, this system did not work. Most of the Umbundu vassals were unable to resist their more powerful, independent neighbors to the east. Some attacked their fellow vassals, fearing they themselves would be enslaved should they fail to pay tributes. Others claimed that they had been attacked by other vassals and maneuvered the Portuguese to launch a punitive expedition against their neighbors. This situation contributed to an atmosphere of violence and insecurity in the plateau. As Cândido writes, "*sobas* who were raided eventually raided others as a way to generate captives who could be exchanged for weapons, alcohol, and other imported goods, indicating the pervasive effects of the transatlantic slave trade."[61]

Although such raids were important, they were not the exclusive source of Umbundu slaves. Debts and judicial proceedings, especially in cases involving accusations of witchcraft, often resulted in significant numbers of slaves. In the mid-nineteenth century, László Magyar, a refugee of the Hungarian revolutions of 1848, moved to the Angolan highlands. He married the daughter of an Umbundu aristocrat and lived in the Kingdom of Viye for almost ten years, from 1849 to 1858, leaving detailed records of his interactions with the several Umbundu kingdoms on the central plateau. He noticed, for example, that among the Umbundu there were two types of slaves: the *fuka* or *hafuka*, in other words, pawns, and the *dongo*, "slaves captured in war or purchased, whose owners had unlimited power over them." "The number of the *dongo*," he continues, "is enormous." He further noticed that "many of them were imported, but there are also many who were enslaved in the land." According to Magyar, the Umbundu had vast numbers of slaves because "among these greedy, jealous, and perpetually in conflict people the least offense ... is considered a *kesila*, a crime, and, since there are no written laws and the customary laws are interpreted and applied in most cases arbitrarily by the powerful in detriment of the vulnerable, we cannot be surprised to find half of the nation enslaved to the other half." Of all crimes, however, witchcraft produced the most slaves. "The dangerous consequences of crimes based on superstitious beliefs," Magyar concludes, "contribute

[60] Cândido, *An African Slaving Port*, 205–06. [61] Ibid., 208.

significantly for the disgrace of the peoples of southern Africa, because at least half of the several millions of slaves exported over the centuries to the Americas, as well as those who stay in Africa, can attribute their sad fate to these imaginary crimes."[62]

Despite the importance of the Umbundu as a source of slaves, Atlantic commerce probably had little impact on the total number of Umbundu speakers living in the central plateau of Angola. Linda Heywood and John Thornton accessed Magyar's accounts and estimated the size of the Umbundu population on the basis of his knowledge of African systems of tax collection. They argue that the total Umbundu population in this period numbered approximately 1,680,150 individuals, living in Kakonda, Kenge, Kisanji, Kiyaka, Mbailundu, Mbui, Ndulu, Ngalangi, Nganda, Sambu, Sele, Sumbe, Viye, and Wambu.[63] The estimates of slaves shipped from the same ethnic groups over the quarter century from 1831 to 1855 is 116,324 individuals, or an average of 4,652 per year. This figure suggests that the proportion of Umbundu slaves sold into the trade each year during the nineteenth century was approximately 0.3 percent of the entire Umbundu population, not a significant proportion. Heywood and Thornton also compared Magyar's figures with other data available for a selected number of Umbundu societies in the late eighteenth century and noted that the Umbundu had grown in the nineteenth century, thanks to the incorporation of slaves from other linguistic groups. The Umbundu kingdoms of the central plateau shared borders with a number of peoples from whom they drew slaves, especially females in the fertile age range. Newcomers included the Nyaneka, Nkhumbi, Ovambo, and notably the Ngangela, a group whose name was originally derived from a derogatory term that Umbundu speakers gave to the people living east of the central plateau.[64] The Umbundu sold some of these slaves to the coast, but they also kept some of them within their

---

[62] László Magyar, *Reisen in Süd-Afrika in den Jahren 1849 bis 1857* (Pest and Leipzig: Lauffer & Stolp, 1859), chap. 7 and 8. I would like to thank Conceição Neto for allowing me to use the forthcoming Portuguese translation by Chá de Caxinde of the German edition of Magyar's work.

[63] These do not include the Massongo, Kubala, Libolo, and Haku, listed in Thornton and Heywood's chart 1, since they were actually Kimbundu speakers. See Linda Heywood and John Thornton, "African Fiscal Systems as Sources for Demographic History: The Case of Central Angola, 1799–1920." *Journal of African History* 29, no. 2 (1988): 213–19.

[64] According to Gladwin Childs, the Ngangela included the Luimbi, Cimbandi, Lucazi, Cyemba, Ngonzelo, Chokwe, and other peoples who lived east of the central plateau. See Childs, *Kinship and Character*, 173, footnote 1.

kingdoms. Consequently, despite the continuation of the slave trade from their area, the Umbundu population actually increased in size between the late eighteenth and the mid-nineteenth centuries.[65]

CONCLUSION

Analysis of the lists of liberated Africans from Cuba and Brazil in addition to the slave registers of Angola challenges current interpretations of the origins of slaves and the ways they entered the transatlantic traffic. Regions adjacent to the coast were the source of most captives, rather than Lunda prisoners from the deep interior. It also draws attention to an important aspect of the history of the transatlantic trade. Africans enslaved and sold one another into the trade for nearly four hundred years, albeit under pressures that emanated from the Atlantic world. However, it should be noted that these individuals did not regard themselves as Africans. In fact, the documentary evidence suggests that they defined themselves on the basis of ties to localized polities, lineages, or ethnic groups. They might speak the same language as their captors, live next to one another, worship the same deities, but they could still be considered "outsiders." This restricted sense of localized identity had disastrous consequences for some communities, such as the Nsundi and the Ndongo. Others were able to minimize the demographic impact of the trade by incorporating slaves from other linguistic groups into their own societies, as did the Umbundu of the central plateau of Angola. It is clear that these localized forms of identity were an essential prerequisite for the continuation of the transatlantic trade in the nineteenth century and probably in earlier centuries too.

---

[65] Heywood and Thornton, "African Fiscal Systems," 223–25; Heywood, *Contested Power in Angola*, 2–3, 10–11, and 17.

4

The Demographic Profile of the Enslaved Population

Any new insights into how captives entered the traffic must take into account their age and sex. The demographic profile of the population forced into the trade provides important clues about master preference for slaves in the Americas. Did they prefer male or female slaves? Adult or children? Did this preference change over time? Why? The sex and age of captives also provide insights into who Africans regarded as eligible for enslavement and sale overseas. Was African preference for slaves any different from that of masters in the Americas? Which was dominant? Could they have been complementary? Only an analysis of African and European conceptions of gender and age, coupled with a careful assessment of the demographic data of slaves forced into the Atlantic, will help clarify these questions.

In the nineteenth century, British efforts to suppress the transatlantic trade increased the demand for slave women in Brazil and Spanish America. Planters in these regions feared that, if Britain succeeded in abolishing the trade, the captive population on their plantations would decline rapidly. They looked to increase the ratio of women to men on their properties in the expectation that the slave population would soon increase by natural means, so negating the need to rely on arrivals from Africa. Indeed, until the abolition of the trade, the growth of the captive population in Brazil and the Caribbean had depended largely on the transatlantic trade. The working conditions on the Brazilian and Cuban plantations were so demanding that planters often preferred to buy able-bodied slaves from Africa rather than raising slave children to adulthood.[1]

---

[1] Carlos Augusto Taunay, *Manual do Agricultor Brasileiro*, ed. Rafael de Bivar Marquese (São Paulo: Companhia das Letras, 2001), 76–80; Maria Graham, *Journal of a Voyage to*

Furthermore, mortality rates among slaves working on plantations, especially sugar plantations, but also rice, coffee, and cotton, were particularly high, restricting the natural growth of slave populations in many parts of the Americas.[2] At the same time, the Industrial Revolution in Europe reduced the cost of merchandise used to obtain slaves, making it possible for planters to buy more able-bodied individuals.[3]

However, planter preferences had little impact on the demographic profile of the slave population leaving West Central Africa after 1800. Although planters tried to increase the number of females on their plantations, males continued to outnumber women in West Central African departures. Moreover, captives sold into the trade during the nineteenth century were on average younger than those sold in previous centuries. All this suggests that planter preferences were but one factor shaping the demographic profile of the traffic from West Central Africa. African enslavers, traders, and owners were also primary agents determining the sex and age patterns of the export trade. This finding has profound implications for the history of the transatlantic trade, because it fundamentally challenges accepted wisdom about who shaped the trade and decided which individuals were eligible for enslavement and sale across the Atlantic.

Scholars in the past have generally claimed that planter preferences were the principal factor shaping the demographic profile of captives embarked from Africa. They have argued that the majority of slaves embarked were men because planters believed that males were more able than females to endure the harsh work conditions on cash crop plantations in the Americas.[4] Additionally, in most European societies, men usually performed most of the heavy labor in agriculture, such as clearing, plowing, and harvesting, while women generally attended to

Brazil and Residence There during Part of the Years 1821, 1822, 1823 (London: Longman, Hurst, Rees, Orme, Brown, and Green, 1824), 289; Alexander Humboldt, *The Island of Cuba*, trans. J. S. Thrasher (New York: Derby and Jackson, 1856), 213–16 and 227–29.

[2] B. W. Higman, *Slave Populations of the British Caribbean, 1807–1834* (Baltimore: Johns Hopkins University Press, 1984), 314–17 and 374–78; Herbert S. Klein and Francisco Vidal Luna, *Slavery in Brazil* (New York: Cambridge University Press, 2010), 167–68; Manuel Moreno Fraginals, *The Sugarmill: The Socioeconomic Complex of Sugar in Cuba, 1760–1860* (New York: Monthly Review Press, 1976), 55, 142–43, and 148.

[3] Eltis, *Economic Growth*, 47–48; Miller, *Way of Death*, 496–502 and 635–36.

[4] Jacob Gorender, *O Escravismo Colonial* (São Paulo: Ática, 1978), 321–24; Fernando Ortiz, *Los Negros Esclavos* (Havana: Editorial de Ciencias Sociales, 1975), 196–99; Eric Williams, *Capitalism and Slavery* (Chapel Hill: University of North Carolina Press, 1994), 38.

household chores, such as making preserves, clothing, and selling home-grown produce in neighboring markets.[5] When Europeans migrated, they took with them their gender perceptions of the division of labor, which they sought to replicate on the cash crop plantations of the Americas. Scholars long accepted that the proportion of approximately two males for every female exported in the overall history of the traffic was the result of planters demanding more slave men than women.

However, in recent decades a number of studies have challenged this interpretation. According to this new view, the majority of slaves sold into the transatlantic trade were men not because planters believed that males could support the labor regime of plantation agriculture better than females but because Africans valued female labor more highly than male labor. Ester Boserup, for example, drew attention to women's participation in African economic development. She observed that women played a central role in both agriculture and trade in Africa.[6] Claire Robertson and Martin Klein then noted the importance of female labor in Africa, stressing that most slaves as well as their owners on the continent were women rather than men.[7] Finally, in a recent publication with Gwyn Campbell and Suzanne Miers, Joseph Miller has also emphasized the importance of women in African economies by showing not only that they outnumbered men in earlier times but also "that they played crucial roles in the politics of the men who brought them into their households, and sometimes also the economies of the women in them."[8]

Such findings have prompted new research into the gender component of the slave trade. For example, after examining the sexual distribution of slaves shipped from Africa by different European carriers, Herbert Klein argued that Africans exercised a direct control over this movement by keeping what for them were more highly valued women off the market. Klein held that the preferences of planters in the Americas and Africans were complementary.[9] David Eltis and Stanley Engerman analyzed sex and age data of slaves sold into the trade between the seventeenth and

---

[5] Carlo M. Cipolla, *Before the Industrial Revolution: European Society and Economy, 1000–1700* (New York: Norton, 1976), 59–60; Louise Tilly and Joan W. Scott, *Women, Work, and Family* (New York: Holt, Rinehart and Winston, 1978), 32–37 and 44–47; Merry E. Wiesner, *Women and Gender in Early Modern Europe*, 2nd edn. (New York: Cambridge University Press, 2000), 108–11.

[6] Ester Boserup, *Woman's Role in Economic Development* (London: Allen & Unwin, 1970), 16–24.

[7] Robertson and Klein, "Women's Importance in African Slave Systems," 3–5.

[8] Miller, "Women as Slaves and Owners of Slaves," 1.

[9] Klein, "African Women," 34–37.

nineteenth centuries and discovered that men made up less than half of all slaves embarked from Africa. They noted the proportion of women dropped markedly from a relatively high level in the seventeenth century, while the number of boys and girls rose strongly into the nineteenth century, with the increase in the ratio of girls being the most dramatic of any of the four categories. They concluded that men were not the dominant sex and age category in the trade and that their relative importance probably declined over time.[10] Finally, Ugo Nwokeji analyzed the trade from the Bight of Biafra and noted that the sex distribution of slaves embarked from this region differed significantly from that of other regions of embarkation in Africa. He observed economic factors alone cannot account for this difference either in Africa or the Americas. Rather, he argues that in this particular region "African conceptions of gender shaped the sex and age structure of the overseas slave trade."[11] All in all, recent studies of the trade have suggested that Africans may have been major, if not the primary, agents shaping the demographic profile of slaves carried across the Atlantic.

MALES AND FEMALES

What was the situation in nineteenth-century West Central Africa? Data on the sex and age of slaves embarked from the region in this period is fragmentary at best. However, they indicate that Africans had a major influence on determining the demography of slave departures. Table 4.1 shows the percentage of males leaving the region between 1781 and 1867 by destination based on 316 voyages available in the "Voyages" database. It confirms the traditional opinion about the sexual distribution of individuals sold into the trade, with males accounting for 68 percent of all captives embarked. The last row of the table shows little variation across regions of disembarkation. The majority of the captives leaving West Central Africa were males regardless of their final destination in the Americas.

However, the proportion of males embarked did increase significantly during the period of the illegal trade. Table 4.1 shows that between 1781 and 1805 about 66 percent of those shipped were males. This proportion decreased to 64 percent between 1806 and 1830, probably the response of Cuban and Brazilian planters to British efforts to abolish the trade. They

[10] Eltis and Engerman, "Was the Slave Trade Dominated by Men?" 241.
[11] Nwokeji, "African Conceptions of Gender," 66.

TABLE 4.1 *Percentage of male slaves leaving West Central Africa by region of disembarkation, 1781–1867*

Years	British and French Caribbean	Cuba	Brazil	Other	Total
1781–1805	65.0 (45.8)	70.4 (7.3)	69.7 (0.8)	64.3 (3.7)	65.7 (57.6)
1806–1830	71.4 (1.5)	61.2 (5.9)	50.0 (0.2)	70.0 (1.2)	64.0 (8.8)
1831–1855	81.5 (1.7)	79.0 (2.8)	67.1 (3.8)	74.3 (16.5)	74.2 (24.8)
1856–1867	91.1 (0.5)	42.6 (0.6)	–	74.1 (8.6)	73.3 (9.7)
Total	66.1 (49.5)	67.3 (16.6)	66.5 (4.8)	72.3 (30.0)	67.9 (100.9)

Note: Numbers in brackets represent thousands of slaves for whom data are available.
Source: David Eltis et al., "Voyages: The Trans-Atlantic Slave Trade Database," Online database, 2008, www.slavevoyages.org.

expected to use the females they had brought to expand the slave population on their plantations in case the British succeeded in their endeavors to cut the traffic completely, but the ratio of males embarked increased sharply to 74 percent between 1831 and 1855 and remained high between 1856 and 1867 despite planter demands for more females.

Planters in general valued males more highly than females but, as we have seen, in the first decades of the nineteenth century there was an increased demand for females. This demand narrowed the price differential between males and females at the main slave markets of the Americas. Manolo Florentino has accessed probate records of slave owners who had lived in rural areas of Rio de Janeiro between 1790 and 1830, then the principal destination for slaves leaving West Central Africa.[12] These records list the value of each individual by age, sex, and origin, that is, whether the slaves were Africans or Creoles. They indicate that planter attitudes toward females were shifting as the British pressed to end the traffic. Among African slaves aged 12 to 55 years old, the price differential between males and females decreased from 25 percent between 1810 and 1812 to 14 percent between 1815 and 1817. In the following years, this figure continued to decline, from 11 percent between 1820 and 1822 to 9 percent between 1825 and 1827. In 1830, the last year of the legal trade to Brazil, and also the final year for which price data are available, the price difference for captives brought from Africa was slightly under 9 percent.[13] Among Creoles in the same age group there was a similar

---

[12] Florentino, *Em Costas Negras*, 59–60.   [13] Ibid., 220.

price pattern between males and females, though less pronounced. The price differential between male and female Creoles decreased sharply from 22 percent between 1815 and 1817 to 11 percent between 1820 and 1822 and then increased again to 14 percent in 1825 to 1827 and to 17 percent in 1830.[14] All in all, the higher relative price for females suggests that planters had changed their attitudes toward the acquisition of females, especially those from Africa.

Pictorial representations of plantation labor in the Americas indicate that planters had no reservations about putting female slaves alongside males in the most demanding tasks. Jerome Handler and Michael Tuite have grouped into a single website images of plantations scenes and agriculture labor published in periodicals, as well as travelers' accounts from the sixteenth to the nineteenth centuries. These images are a rich source for our understanding of the sexual division of labor in the plantations and cities of the Americas.[15] One of the most revealing sets of images, published in 1823, is William Clark's *Ten Views in the Island of Antigua*. It clearly shows women working in every stage of sugar production, including digging, cutting, fetching, and carrying sugar cane.[16] Planters in nineteenth-century Brazil were no different. Henry Koster, who lived in Pernambuco between 1809 and 1815, reported that it was common for slave women to work alongside men in the Brazilian sugar mills. Figure 4.1 is a copy of an image published in Koster's account showing two women working in a sugar mill; one is carrying cane while the other is feeding it to the sugar mill. His interpretation is that "two men and two women are employed in feeding the mill with cane."[17] Maria Graham also noted the use of women in sugar production in Brazil. She travelled throughout the interior of Rio de Janeiro between 1821 and 1823 and saw slave women working in one of the first steam-powered mills then existing in Brazil.[18] Steam-powered milling of sugar cane was a key technological innovation on nineteenth-century plantations.

---

[14] Ibid.

[15] Jerome S. Handler and Michael L. Tuite Jr., "The Atlantic Slave Trade and Slave Life in the Americas: A Visual Record," Online database, (2008), http://hitchcock.itc.virginia.edu/Slavery/.

[16] William Clark, *Ten Views in the Island of Antigua* (London: T. Clay, 1823). Reproduced in Handler and Tuite Jr., "The Atlantic Slave Trade and Slave Life in the Americas," image reference NW0051, NW0052, NW0054, and NW0065.

[17] Henry Koster, *Travels in Brazil* (London: Longman, Hurst, Rees, Orme, and Brown, 1816), 348.

[18] Maria Graham, *Journal of a Voyage to Brazil and Residence There during Part of the Years 1821, 1822, 1823* (London: Longman, Hurst, Rees, Orme, Brown, and Green, 1824), 282–83.

FIGURE 4.1 A sugar mill, Brazil, 1816
Source: Henry Koster, *Travels in Brazil* (London: Longgam, Hurst Rees, Orme, and Brown, 1816), 336. Reproduced from "Internet Archive," 1996-https://archive.org/details/travelsinbrazi00kost.

In 1854, the *Illustrated London News* published an article about the application of this new technology in Brazil, and the image illustrating the article showed three slave women milling sugar cane in one of De Mornay's steam-powered mills on the Caraúna plantation, Pernambuco.[19]

Milling sugar cane may not seem as exacting as toiling in the fields, but it was in fact hard work. Since the sixteenth century, travelers often described the labor routine in Brazilian sugar mills as a hell for blacks.[20] Because the juice had to be extracted from the cane as soon as it was cut, the sugar mill had to operate almost continually from August to the beginning of May of the following year.[21] Moreover, in Brazil the boiling

[19] "Sugar Manufacture in Brazil." *The Illustrated London News* 25 (9 September 1854): 232. A copy of this article's image is available in Handler and Tuite Jr., "The Atlantic Slave Trade and Slave Life in the Americas," image reference pg232.

[20] André João Antonil, *Cultura e Opulência do Brasil* (Belo Horizonte: Itatiaia, 1982), 92–93.

[21] Schwartz, *Sugar Plantations*, 99–106. In Cuba, sugar mills could operate up to 16 hours per day during the peak of the harvest seasons. See Ortiz, *Los Negros Esclavos*, 189.

house was commonly located next to the mill. As a consequence, in addition to the stress of milling cane, workers also had to endure the heat coming from the caldrons of the boiling house.[22]

Work at the sugar mills was particularly dangerous because of the risk of slaves losing a limb while feeding cane between the sugar mill rollers. Henry Koster witnessed such accidents and reported planters' precautions to avoid them. He also noted that some planters began using oxen instead of horses to run their mills, because the screams of the blacks caught in the rollers sometimes caused horses to draw the mill with increased velocity. Oxen, by contrast, moved more slowly and tended to stop rather than speed up when such accidents occurred. Koster describes:

Negros who thrust the cane in between the rollers have sometimes allowed their hands to go too far, and one or both of them having been caught, in some instances, before assistance could be given, the whole limb and even the body has been crushed to pieces. In the mills belonging to owners who pay attention to the safety of their negroes, and whose wish it is to have every thing in proper order, a bar of iron and a hammer are placed close to the rollers upon the table which supports the cane. The bar is intended to be violently inserted between the rollers in case of an accident, so as to open them, and this set at liberty the unfortunate negro. In some instances I have seen lying by the side of the bar and hammer, a well tempered hatchet, for the purpose of severing the limb from the body if judged necessary.[23]

The flames heating the caldrons, intense work routine, and horrendous accidents were enough to evoke the image of hell in the minds of European travelers. Slave women's work, however, was not restricted to planting and milling sugar. Historians have noted that women were employed in a wide variety of activities located in the countryside as well as urban centers. They typically worked as servants, maids, cooks, porters, weavers, sewers, hucksters, washers, midwives, and in many other capacities. Some activities were well-known domains of female slaves, such as wet nursing and prostitution.[24] All the evidence from nineteenth-century Brazil points to female slaves being just as useful to planters as male slaves. Forces shaping the demographic profile of slaves leaving West Central Africa were more likely to have originated in Africa than in the Americas.

Breaking out the regional data into groupings of port of departure provides further evidence of African influence. Table 4.2 shows that over the whole period 69 percent of the slaves embarked were males. However, the proportion of males shipped varied significantly from port to port.

[22] Schwartz, *Sugar Plantations*, 115–18.   [23] Koster, *Travels in Brazil*, 348–49.
[24] Karasch, *Slave Life*, 203–10 and 230–31.

TABLE 4.2 *Percentage of male slaves leaving West Central Africa by port of embarkation, 1781–1867*

Years	Ports north of Luanda	Luanda	Ports south of Luanda	Total
1781–1805	65.7 (26.7)	68.2 (0.6)	74.7 (0.2)	65.9 (27.5)
1806–1830	68.9 (4.4)	53.8 (3.1)	–	62.8 (7.5)
1831–1855	81.0 (13.3)	75.6 (2.9)	62.2 (7.2)	74.5 (23.4)
1856–1867	73.3 (9.8)	–	–	73.3 (9.8)
Total	70.5 (54.2)	63.2 (6.6)	63.3 (7.4)	68.9 (68.2)

Note: Numbers in brackets represent thousands of slaves for whom data are available.
Source: Same as Table 4.1.

In the African-controlled ports located north of Luanda, about 70 percent were males. As we have seen, most came from the Kimbundu, Kikongo, and Vili-speaking peoples, who lived in matrilineal societies where women had a prominent role in decisions about production and reproduction. In contrast, the ratio of males embarked from the Portuguese ports was considerably lower; only 63 percent of those leaving Luanda and the ports south of Luanda were males. The populations inhabiting the hinterlands of these ports were also matrilineal societies; the Kimbundu again, as well as the Umbundu. Since planters in the nineteenth century purchased slaves of both sexes, the variation in the ratio of males shipped from these ports is likely a result of African conceptions of who could be enslaved and who could not. Some societies were simply more open to selling females into the trade than others.

The sexual distribution of slaves embarked from each of these ports also varied considerably over time. In the ports north of Luanda, the proportion of males embarked increased continuously between 1781 and 1855, from 66 to 81 percent, declining thereafter to 73 percent between 1856 and 1867. In contrast, the ratio of males shipped from Luanda declined initially from 68 percent between 1781 and 1805 to 54 percent between 1806 and 1830. However, it increased again to 76 percent between 1831 and 1855. Data for the ports south of Luanda are incomplete, but the evidence available suggests that the proportion of males shipped declined between the eighteenth and nineteenth centuries, from 75 percent between 1781 and 1805 to 62 percent between 1831 and 1855. These data indicate that the populations living in the central plateau were inclined to sell more females into the trade than other populations living in the region's interior.

West Central Africans in general had several reasons for selling more males than females into the trade. Many males were trained soldiers who had been captured in wars waged by different polities within the region. As prisoners of war, they were expensive to maintain and at the same time potentially rebellious. Some of these prisoners came from the central plateau of Angola. They were soldiers of the Nano Wars waged by several Umbundu polities during the first half of the nineteenth century, especially Viye, Mbailundu, and Wambu.[25] African masters, enslavers, and traders in general usually looked to sell these slaves on the coast as soon as they could. This outlet gave them a convenient way of reducing maintenance costs, avoiding potential rebellions, and making a profit from an undesirable "commodity."

A second reason for retaining females was that women were an integral part of the work force throughout the larger region, especially in food production. Europeans frequently commented on women digging, planting, harvesting, and processing food with children strapped on their backs. Father Giovanni Antonio Cavazzi de Montecuccolo travelled throughout the kingdoms of Ndongo, Kongo, and Matamba between 1654 and 1667 and noted that "women performed almost all agricultural work."[26] One of his illustrations depicts a woman with a child strapped on her back preparing the soil for cultivation with a hoe. Over two hundred years later, the Portuguese explorers Hermenegildo Capello and Roberto Ivens, travelling overland from Benguela to Yaka, recorded the same scene near the Kwango River, reproduced here in Figure 4.2.[27] Women's work was essential to the economies of West Central African societies, so much so that African masters, enslavers, and slave traders often considered it more important to hold rather than sell female slaves into the transatlantic trade.

A further reason Africans preferred to retain females lies in the importance of their role in the distribution of wealth and power within West

[25] Bernardino Freire de Figueiredo Abreu e Castro, "Colonia de Mossamedes." *Annaes do Conselho Ultramarino (Parte Não Oficial)* ser. 1 (1855): 152; Joachim John Monteiro, *Angola and the River Congo* (New York: Macmillan and Co., 1876), 289; Pélissier, *História das Campanhas de Angola*, vol. 1, 173–75 and 187–92; Redinha, *Distribuição Étnica de Angola*, 16–17; Catarina Madeira Santos, "Um Governo 'Polido' para Angola: Reconfigurar Dispositivos de Domínio (1750-c.1800)" (Doctorate, Universidade Nova de Lisboa, 2005), 299–308.
[26] João António Cavazzi de Montecucculo, *Descrição Histórica dos Três Reinos de Congo, Matamba e Angola*, trans. Graciano Maria Leguzzano (Lisbon: Junta de Investigações do Ultramar, 1965), vol. 1, 38–39.
[27] Hermenegildo Capello and Roberto Ivens, *De Benguella às Terras de Iácca: Descripção de uma Viagem na Africa Central e Occidental* (Lisbon: Imprensa Nacional, 1881), vol. 1, 53–54 and 177.

AS LAVRAS PERTO DO CU-ANGO

FIGURE 4.2 African Women working the fields near the Kwango River, 1881.
Source: Hermenegildo Capello and Roberto Ivens, *De Benguella às Terras de
Iácca: Descripção de uma Viagem na Africa Central e Occidental* (Lisboa:
Imprensa Nacional, 1881), vol. 1, 177. Reproduced from "Internet Archive,"
1996-, https://archive.org/details/debenguellasterro1cape.

Central African societies. Although power was usually in the hands of
men, most of these societies were matrilineal, which meant that wealth and
power were passed on through maternal lines of succession. This practice
often led men who wanted to protect inherited wealth and power to marry
kinless women so that their inheritance would not be disbursed among
their brothers-in-law or their own children, who were the legal heirs of
their mothers and maternal uncles. Thus, many African men sought to
marry slave women to avoid the dispersal of their wealth and power to the
families of their spouses.[28] Moreover, in most African societies, the

---

[28] Hilton, *The Kingdom of Kongo*, 85–90; Lovejoy, *Transformations in Slavery*, 12–15;
Kristin Mann, *Slavery and the Birth of an African City: Lagos, 1760–1900* (Bloomington:
Indiana University Press, 2007), 76–79; Manning, *Slavery and African Life*, 118–22;

number of dependents a man had commonly served as an important indicator of a man's status.[29] Marrying slave women ensured that any offspring legally belonged to their fathers instead of their mothers and uncles. The African preference for female over male slaves is easy to understand.

YOUNG AND OLD

Culturally specific norms also influenced the age profile of individuals sold into the trade from West Central Africa. Traditionally, planters and slave owners in the Americas purchased more adults than children from Africa because they could put them to work as soon as they arrived. However, in the nineteenth century, slaves leaving the region were younger than in previous centuries, suggesting that, despite the planter preference for adults, the number of children shipped tended to increase over time. Explanations for such a trend are more likely to be found either in Africa or in attempts to suppress the slave trade on the African coast than in Europe.

Comparing age categories of persons sold into the trade is considerably harder than comparing sexual categories. The age an individual enters adulthood differs from culture to culture and is subject to many interpretations. Europeans often recorded the age of slaves purchased in Africa according to their own perceptions of age. In the eighteenth and nineteenth centuries, Europeans believed that individuals entered adulthood when they became eligible for marriage. In southern Europe, females were generally eligible for marriage when they reached puberty at about 12 years old. Males were commonly eligible for marriage about the time they could bear arms and serve in the army. As a result, European females usually reached adulthood before males. The Constitutions of the Archbishopric of Bahia, which guided moral conduct in the Portuguese empire, ruled that females were eligible for marriage when they reached

Joseph C. Miller, "Imbangala Lineage Slavery." In *Slavery in Africa: Historical and Anthropological Perspectives,* ed. Suzanne Miers and Igor Kopytoff (Madison: University of Wisconsin Press, 1977), 211–15; Miller, *Way of Death,* 94–103; Vansina, *Kingdoms of the Savanna,* 219.

[29] Lovejoy, *Transformations in Slavery,* 12–15; Mann, *Slavery and the Birth of an African City,* 79–81; Manning, *Slavery and African Life,* 122–25; Miller, *Way of Death,* 42–53; Alberto da Costa e Silva, *A Manilha e o Libambo: A África e a Escravidão de 1500–1700* (Rio de Janeiro: Nova Fronteira, 2002), 370; Thornton, *Africa and Africans,* 91; Vansina, *Kingdoms of the Savanna,* 194–96.

12 years of age, while males were eligible for marriage only after they turned 14 years old.[30] Thus, by our standards many of the individuals that Europeans recorded as adult slaves were probably teenagers.

Perception of adulthood among West Central Africans during the period of the trade was not very different from that of Europeans previously described. However, in Africa both sexes generally had to undergo rituals of initiation before being considered adults. Because physical signs of adulthood are less clear in males than in females, males had to undergo extensive rituals of initiation that culminated with circumcision. These rituals were frequently carried out in camps outside the home villages, towns, and cities from which the initiates came. Additionally, these rituals introduced young males to techniques of hunting, warfare, and other responsibilities associated with manhood in their societies. In some societies, these rituals could be exceedingly cruel. Galdwyn Childs noted that among the twentieth-century Umbundu speakers of the central plateau of Angola the "hardship and the cruelty of the initiation camps have their parallel in the trading and slave trading expeditions of the past."[31] In any event, Portuguese and West Central Africans probably had similar notions of when individuals reached adulthood.

However, the specifics of carrying slaves across the Atlantic sometimes influenced the way Europeans distinguished children from adults. From the sixteenth to the mid-eighteenth century, for example, Portuguese and Spanish traders identified slave children not by their approximate age but by their height. They counted slaves in terms of *peças da Índia*, or in *piezas de Índia* in Spanish. This term, literally a piece of Asian cloth, referred to one of the most popular commodities used to purchase slaves on the African coast. In the seventeenth century, a *peça* in Spanish contracts for the slave trade equaled the value of a healthy adult, male or female, measuring seven or more quarters of a *vara*.[32] The *vara* was a medieval form of measurement of length that varied over time from region to region. The Seville *vara* was the standard used in the Angolan-Brazilian maritime trade. In the nineteenth century, the length of a Seville *vara* was approximately 83.59 centimeters or 32.9 inches, so the height of a *peça da Índia* in the nineteenth century was about 146 centimeters or 57 inches.[33]

[30] Sebastião Monteiro da Vide, *Constituições Primeiras do Arcebispado da Bahia* (São Paulo: Typographia de António Louzada Antunes, 1853), 109–10, Title 64.

[31] Childs, *Kinship and Character*, 116–17.   [32] Vila Vilar, *Hispanoamerica*, 189–90.

[33] Converted according to the "Real Orden del 9 de Diciembre de 1852." In Cárlos Sanguineti, *Diccionario Jurídico-Administrativo* (Madrid: Imprensa de la Revista de Legislacion y Jurisprudencia, 1858), 643–55.

This was rather short for a healthy adult, male or female. David Eltis showed that in the nineteenth century adult males shipped from any part of the African coast south of the Sahara measured on average between 157 and 166 centimeters, while females measured between 151 and 157 centimeters.[34] In any event, Portuguese slave traders between the sixteenth and the mid-eighteenth century calculated the carrying capacity of their vessels by adding the heights of their slaves in *peças da Índia* and dividing it by a *vara craveira*, which measured about 525 centimeters.[35] In general, three *peças* were allowed for each ton, so that Portuguese and Spanish traders could in fact write contracts for the trade specifying the volume of the cargo to be shipped across the Atlantic.[36] Additionally, this practice allowed customs officials to collect taxes on the basis of able-bodied equivalencies rather than on the actual number of captives. The contract of the Companhia da Guiné, for example, specified that it had to deliver "ten thousand tons of slaves" from Africa to the Spanish Americas between 1699 and 1705.[37] As a consequence, until the eighteenth century, references to children in documents related to the Portuguese and Spanish trades are rare.

In the eighteenth century, the term *peça da Índia* was increasingly replaced by a new term, *cabeça*, indicating a single adult. Because a *cabeça* did not necessarily imply the same labor power as a healthy adult, the Portuguese government began to tax slaves according to different age categories. These categories, however, were also based on the height of the slaves rather than their actual age. The trade contract that the Portuguese government awarded to Manoel Barbosa Torres in 1753 to carry slaves from Angola stated that "the duties for *cabeças* and children who do not fit the established requirements of *peças da Índia* will be paid relative to the *peças da Índia* with the proviso that the children must not be more than four *palmos* tall."[38] *Palmos* was a measurement of length equivalent approximately to 22 centimeters in the nineteenth century.

[34] David Eltis, "Nutritional Trends in Africa and the Americas: Heights of Africans, 1819–1839." *Journal of Interdisciplinary History* 12, no. 3 (1982): 459, Table 1.
[35] J. Lúcio de Azevedo, *Épocas de Portugal Económico*, 4th edn. (Lisbon: Livraria Clássica, 1988), 75–76.
[36] Ibid.
[37] "Assento para a Introdução dos Negros das Índias Espanholas, Feito entre o Conselho Real das Índias e um Sócio da Companhia Real da Guiné, em Madrid a 12 de Julho de 1699." In Carreira, *As Companhias Pombalinas*, 309.
[38] Dom José I, "Carta de Sua Mag. sobre a Remataçam do Contrato dos Direitos Novos que a Rematou Manoel Barbosa Torres dos Direitos dos Escravos q' se Embarcam desta Cid. de Loanda p. os Portos do Brazil." *Arquivos de Angola*, 1, 2, no. 13–15 (1936): 521.

Therefore, slaves considered children could not be taller than 88 centimeters, a very short stature compared to 146 centimeters of a *peça da Índia*.[39]

In the eighteenth century, the Portuguese began to separate children embarked from West Central Africa into two different categories. The first category they called *crias de pé* or children able to stand. The second category they called *crias de peito* or nursing infants. The distinction between *crias de pé* and *crias de peito* resulted from a conflict over how to tax children put on board Portuguese ships on the coast of West Central Africa. Until the eighteenth century, the heights of children were added to those of adults and taxes were then collected in *peças da Índia*. However, as traders and customs officials began to count slaves in *cabeças*, they had to create a new way of taxing children. In 1758 the Portuguese government settled the conflict with a tax reform that levied different taxes on children and adults embarked. *Crias de pé* measuring four *palmos* or less were charged half the taxes paid on adults, while *crias de peito* were tax free and, when shipped together with their mothers, the two counted as only one *cabeça*.[40]

After the Portuguese began to count slaves in *cabeças*, children appeared in the documentation more frequently. Most of them were probably nursing infants and toddlers. Since tax procedures at the Portuguese ports of slave embarkation in West Central Africa stipulated such a short height for children embarked, there were many individuals classified as adults who would be considered children by our own standards and, indeed, may have been by the standards of Europeans and Africans of that time. Nevertheless, tax records of slaves embarked from Luanda provide us with some idea of their age distribution.

In the eighteenth century, children were a significant percentage of the total number of slaves shipped from Luanda. Horácio Gutiérrez analyzed records of taxes collected from vessels carrying slaves from Luanda and estimated the proportion of children shipped for 17 years between 1734 and 1769. These records provide the total number of slaves as well as the number of *crias de pé* and *crias de peito* embarked for the years 1740–1742, 1744, 1747–1749, 1762–1767, and 1769. Gutiérrez also found records showing only totals embarked for the years 1734, 1738, and 1754, but he estimated the proportion of *crias de pé* and *crias de peito*

---

[39] Fortunato José Barreiros, *Memória sobre os Pesos e Medidas de Portugal, Espanha, Inglaterra e França* (Lisbon: Typographia da Academia Real das Sciencias, 1838), 20.

[40] Dom José I, "Ley sobre a Arecadação," 538.

embarked in these years using the average percentage rate of children shipped according to each category in the following four years for which he had data. In total, he calculated that 143,848 slaves were embarked from Luanda in these 17 years. Approximately 9,220 of the total were children; 7,003 *crias de pé* and 2,217 *crias de peito*. According to his estimates, about 6 percent of the slaves embarked from Luanda in those years were children.[41]

Although Gutiérrez recognized the different categories of children embarked, he did not realize that these categories included only individuals measuring up to four *palmos* tall. In fact, the proportion of children shipped could have been much higher according to both European and African perceptions of age during the period of the trade. A more realistic proportion is probably double the percentage Gutiérrez estimated. This is important to emphasize because shipping records with age data available for slaves embarked in West Central Africa during the nineteenth century were not based on Portuguese tax records. Rather, they were created by other institutions in different countries that recorded the age of enslaved individuals according to European and African perceptions of age during the eighteenth and nineteenth centuries. One example of these institutions is the mixed commission courts for the adjudication of vessels accused of illegal trading, which form the basis for much of the age data available in the "Voyages" database.

The database contains 365 records of voyages with age data for slaves shipped from West Central Africa by region of disembarkation between the late eighteenth and the nineteenth centuries. Table 4.3 shows that about 17 percent of all individuals carried were children. Further, the ratio of children embarked varied widely across time. Between 1781 and 1805, about 11 percent of those shipped were children. This percentage increased to 16 between 1806 and 1830. However, during the period of the illegal trade, the percentage of children sold increased sharply to 53 between 1831 and 1855 and to 36 between 1856 and 1867. Traders had never shipped such a large percentage of children before, and the reasons for this increase are difficult to determine. On the one hand, planters in the Americas were not interested in receiving so many children. On the other, Africans were often reluctant to sell children across the Atlantic. Given these positions, it appears that the British efforts to abolish the slave trade created a situation to which both sides had to adjust.

[41] Horácio Gutiérrez, "O Tráfico de Crianças Escravas para o Brasil durante o Século XVIII." *Revista de História, São Paulo* 120 (1989): 60–63.

TABLE 4.3 *Percentage of slave children leaving West Central Africa by region of disembarkation, 1781–1867*

Years	British and French Caribbean	Cuba	Brazil	Other	Total
1781–1805	15.2 (38.8)	21.4 (3.1)	3.2 (58.6)	27.8 (2.4)	10.6 (102.9)
1806–1830	33.4 (1.2)	19.2 (5.2)	4.0 (9.9)	39.7 (1.2)	16.5 (17.5)
1831–1855	55.4 (1.7)	53.1 (2.2)	56.8 (3.8)	49.6 (6.7)	52.9 (14.4)
1856–1867	–	–	–	42.9 (2.3)	42.9 (2.3)
Total	17.5 (41.7)	25.9 (10.5)	8.1 (72.3)	43.2 (12.6)	17.4 (137.1)

Note: Numbers in brackets represent thousands of slaves for whom data are available.
Source: Same as Table 4.1.

Table 4.3 confirms that the percentage of children embarked increased, especially during the period of the illegal trade. In the British and French Caribbean, it increased from 15 percent between 1781 and 1805, to 33 percent between 1806 and 1830, and 55 percent between 1831 and 1855. The percentage of children shipped to Cuba initially decreased from 21 between 1781 and 1805 to 19 between 1806 and 1830. However, from 1831 to 1855 it increased sharply to 53 percent. The percentage of children embarked to Brazil also increased significantly during the nineteenth century, from a range of 3 to 4 between 1781 and 1830 to an impressive 57 between 1831 and 1855. The share of children embarked to other destinations, though always relatively high, also increased during the nineteenth century, from 28 percent between 1781 and 1805 to 40 percent between 1806 and 1830, reaching 50 percent between 1831 and 1855. After this period, the percentage of children shipped to other destinations declined to 43 percent.

The ratio of children shipped varied significantly by port of embarkation. Table 4.4 shows that the ports north and south of Luanda shipped relatively more children than Luanda. In total, children made up about 26 percent of the slaves leaving the northern ports, 47 percent from the southern ports, and only 6 percent from Luanda itself. However, these numbers may be misleading. The "Voyages" database contains too few records of voyages with age data for slaves leaving Luanda between 1831 and 1855, when the proportion of children sold into the slave trade is likely to have increased.

Despite the lack of data, the records available do indicate important variations in the percentage of children exported across time from the various ports of embarkation. Between 1781 and 1805, for example, the

TABLE 4.4 *Percentage of slave children leaving West Central Africa by port of embarkation, 1781–1867*

Years	Ports north of Luanda	Luanda	Ports south of Luanda	Total
1781–1805	16.0 (20.8)	3.2 (57.8)	3.4 (1.5)	8.0 (80.1)
1806–1830	28.3 (3.7)	8.1 (12.9)	–	14.8 (16.6)
1831–1855	50.5 (7.8)	53.4 (2.1)	55.4 (4.1)	52.5 (14.0)
1856–1867	35.7 (2.9)	–	–	35.7 (2.9)
Total	26.4 (35.2)	6.3 (72.8)	46.8 (5.6)	17.1 (113.6)

Note: Numbers in brackets represent thousands of slaves for whom data are available.
Source: Same as Table 4.1.

percentage of children leaving the ports north of Luanda, at 16 percent, was considerably higher than the 3 percent recorded for departure from Luanda and the southern ports together. The societies in the hinterland of these more southerly ports were apparently less open to selling children into the trade than those to the north. However, during the period of the illegal trade, the percentage of children embarked from all ports increased significantly. Between 1831 and 1855, just over half those shipped from all ports in the region were children.

The increase in the proportion of children embarked from West Central Africa is surprising in view of the current understanding of who was eligible for enslavement and sale into the transatlantic trade. Scholars generally stress that African enslavers and traders commonly preferred to sell adults into the external trade and keep children for sale into the domestic market. This interpretation implies that the demand for slave children in Africa was higher than the demand for adult slaves because African slave owners believed that purchasing and owning slave children involved fewer risks and that children adapted more readily to the dominant culture. Adults, on the other hand, were potential escapees, capable of inciting rebellion or murdering their masters, sometimes employing poison and even witchcraft.[42] Scholars of African slavery need to take into account the increasing proportion of children sold from West Central Africa between the late eighteenth and the mid-nineteenth century. Perhaps our current understanding of African slavery in this period

[42] Lovejoy, *Transformations in Slavery*, 16–17; Miers and Kopytoff, "African 'Slavery,'" 53.

needs reassessing, particularly ideas about who was eligible for sale across the Atlantic.

Kikongo speakers living in the interior of the ports north of Luanda were probably more open to selling children into the trade than Kimbundu or Umbundu speakers who lived in the interior of Luanda and the ports south of Luanda. Table 4.4 shows that during the first half-century of our period the proportion of children leaving the northern ports was four to five times higher than at Luanda and possibly at locations to the south, although we have data for only three vessels there. This trend may be related to the methods of enslavement among the Kikongo. As previously noted, kidnapping was one of the primary forms of enslavement among Kikongo speakers, especially at Boma, and children could easily fall victim to such abductions.[43] Kimbundu speakers living in the interior of Luanda were more conservative in determining who could be sold into the trade. Many of them had long suffered the demographic impact of the trade, especially the Ndongo who lived under direct influence of the Portuguese. Perhaps, some Kimbundu societies could not afford to sell women and children into the trade, since the latter were crucial to the very survival of their societies.[44] In the mid-nineteenth century, the ratio of children to adults shipped from Luanda increased, but it should be noted that by then the overall numbers embarked from this port had declined significantly.[45] Finally, the Umbundu also seemed very conservative in their sale of slaves, as the percentage of captives leaving the southern ports was similar to that leaving Luanda. However, the Umbundu populations of the central plateau of Angola were expanding between the late eighteenth and the mid-nineteenth centuries.[46] It may be that they shipped more adults during the legal period of the trade not because they were coping with the demographic impact of the trade, but rather because they could best supply the demand for adult slaves overseas. The proportion of children shipped from the southern ports also increased in the mid-century, but this was more an adjustment to the period of the illegal trade than a shift in Umbundu conceptions of who could be sold across the Atlantic.

Two important factors contributed to the increase in the percentage of children embarked from West Central Africa during the nineteenth

---

[43] Schrag, "Mboma and the Lower Zaire," 62–63.
[44] Thornton, "The Slave Trade in Eighteenth Century Angola," 421–23.
[45] See Chapter 1, Figure 1.2.
[46] Heywood and Thornton, "African Fiscal Systems," 223–25; Heywood, *Contested Power in Angola*, 2–3, 10–11, and 17.

century. Neither had much to do directly with developments on either side of the South Atlantic; rather they were a function of efforts to suppress the trade. First, as British antislave trade activity increased, traders had to find new outlets through which to sell captives across the Atlantic. These outlets assumed the form of clandestine ports of slave embarkation spread along the coast of West Central Africa. British naval cruisers often guarded traditional ports of embarkation, so traders had to move their operations to different places agreed upon in advance with captains of slave vessels. In most of them, captives were maintained not on the coast, but in barracoons located at some distance from the shoreline, in order to disguise their presence from antislave trade cruisers patrolling the coast. These barracoons were built for the sole purpose of housing slaves until the moment of embarkation.[47] Since traders had to constantly change location and run their activities as clandestinely as possible, they could not afford to face resistance from their slaves. In 1847, Portuguese naval officers captured a boat carrying 20 slaves belonging to Manoel José Constantino, who owned a barracoon in Benguela Velha, southern Angola. All of them were male, being eleven under 14 years old, three over 17, and six over 20.[48] In 1851, Captain João Máximo da Silva Rodovalho, commander of the Portuguese naval station in Luanda, reported the destruction of another barracoon, located in Equimina, near Benguela. This barracoon had 354 slaves, of whom 194 were destined for sale into the trade: 50 men, 33 women, 69 boys, 37 girls, and 5 infants.[49] Finally, in 1857, Portuguese naval officers destroyed another barracoon in Porto da Lenha, northern Angola, containing 25 men, 11 boys, and 9 women.[50]

Second, as the demand for slaves in the Americas declined, the number of slaves available for sale in the African domestic market increased. Examining the censuses of Portuguese Angola in the mid-1840s, Lopes de Lima observed that the population had been increasing at the rate of 1 percent in the previous 20 years. "I do not doubt that the causes for such a small increase," he wrote, "lie above all in the slave trade, which forced more than 20,000 souls to leave the ports of Angola and Benguela annually."[51] When discussing the state of slavery in the region, he further noticed that "it is presently in the proportion of *twelve to forty* in relation to the free population; but the number of slaves should increase as the

---

[47] Ferreira, "Dos Sertões ao Atlântico," 38–42; Miller, *Way of Death*, 299–308.
[48] Ferreira, "Dos Sertões ao Atlântico," 38.   [49] Ibid., 147–48.   [50] Ibid., 149–50.
[51] Lopes de Lima, *Ensaios*, vol. 3, 6.

inhabitants of our cities and districts decide to establish plantations rivaling those of Brazil . . . and when the allied sobas in the interior, persuaded that they cannot sell their vassals and prisoners to foreign lands, understand how convenient will be to employ them to grow in their own lands and conduct to the markets these colonial goods that their soil offer and such demand are enjoying in the ports."[52]

Although large numbers of slaves continued to be shipped from West Central Africa until 1850, their real price on the coast began to decline from the beginning of the nineteenth century. Real prices of slaves sold at Luanda, for example, remained constant from the 1800s to the 1810s, varying between 110,395 *réis* to 110,008 *réis*. They declined significantly in the 1820s to approximately 66,901 *réis*, increasing again only on the eve of the abolition of the Brazilian slave trade in the 1830s to 149,123 *réis*.[53] These data indicate that, although large numbers continued to be shipped from West Central Africa until the mid-nineteenth century, the demand for slaves on the coast was losing momentum. Africans who were previously enslaved and sold into the external trade were now being sold into the domestic market. Enslavement in the interior must have declined with time, and the temporary effect of more slaves on the domestic market probably increased the slave population in many societies of West Central Africa, perhaps resulting in many African owners holding a surplus of young captives that they could not afford to raise to adulthood. In no other place that would have been truer than in the central plateau of Angola, where, as László Magyar observed, "the number of *dongo* slaves is very large," with "half of the nation enslaved to the other half," although "slave prices are presently very low, declining to a third since suppression has started."[54]

CONCLUSION

All in all, slaves shipped from West Central Africa included individuals from every sex and age category, but in the nineteenth century they tended to be mostly boys. The demographic profile of slaves transported shows that African conceptions of gender and age helped shape the trade by determining who should be enslaved and sold across the Atlantic. In the nineteenth century, planters in the Americas became more interested in purchasing slave women in response to the British efforts to abolish the

[52] Ibid., vol. 3, 7. [53] See Appendix C, Table C.2.
[54] Magyar, *Reisen in Süd-Afrika*, chap. 7.

trade. Africans, on the other hand, were often reluctant to sell women into the traffic. They also preferred to keep children within the continent rather than selling them overseas. However, given the pressures to suppress the trade, Africans adjusted to the new circumstances and began selling more children into the trade than in previous years. Children were easier to transport and keep at barracoons situated at remote places along the coast of West Central Africa. As the slave trade declined, it is also possible that African traders found themselves with a surplus of captives, including children, that they were disposed to sell across the Atlantic. African conceptions of gender and age combined with the impact of attempts to suppress the trade were important factors determining who could be enslaved and sold into the transatlantic slave trade from West Central Africa.

5

African Patterns of Consumption

Africans exchanged slaves on the coast of West Central Africa for a variety of goods imported from several regions around the world. The majority of slaves were purchased for Asian and European textiles, rum produced in the Americas, and weapons brought largely from Europe. Historians believe that Africans distributed these goods among their loyal followers in order to accumulate power, increase their number of dependents, raise armies to capture more slaves, and expand their influence throughout the region's interior. This interpretation implies that the supply of captives on the coast was in the hands of just a few rulers, who competed for power and access to foreign imports. This process generated a vicious cycle of violence and warfare, which led to the destruction of some societies and the imperial expansion of others, such as the Lunda Empire. Some scholars have seen Africans as politically motivated to participate in the trade, with the economic gains resulting from sales being secondary.[1]

However, prices of slaves leaving Luanda between the late eighteenth and the nineteenth centuries suggest that Africans did respond to economic incentives. Philip Curtin devised a model to examine the participation of Africans in the trade from Senegambia, which measured their political and economic motivations to sell slaves based on variations in the value and number of captives sold across the Atlantic. If the number of individuals shipped varied according to the price for which they were sold,

---

[1] The main supporter of this view is, of course, Miller, *Way of Death*, 51–61. But see also Birmingham, *Trade and Conflict*, 148–49; Dias, "Angola," 335–39; Lovejoy, *Transformations in Slavery*, 149–50; Thornton, "The Chronology and Causes," 6–7; Oppen, *Terms of Trade and Terms of Trust*, 59–61.

it signified that Africans were economically motivated to participate in the trade. In contrast, if the number of individuals shipped did not respond to variations in price, it meant that Africans engaged in the trade for political reasons, such as wars waged in the interest of establishing a state and imperial expansion. These are extreme examples, of course. The actual motivations must have been diverse, but they probably varied within these parameters, making the analysis of the price and number of slaves embarked a useful indicator of the primary reason Africans participated in the trade.[2]

MOTIVATIONS

Because the number of slaves shipped from the Senegambia did not vary according to price, Curtin concluded that in this particular region Africans were more politically than economically motivated to participate in the trade.[3] Since the publication of his study, many historians have begun collecting data on the price and number of captives sold from other African regions and subjecting them to similar analyses but sometimes reaching different conclusions. Philip Le Veen surveyed price data from all regions and argued that Africans were motivated more by economic than political gain. As he explained, the price of captives sold on the coast varied according to the number of slaves shipped. When prices increased, the number of slaves transported increased, and when prices declined, the number of captives shipped also declined. Le Veen claimed that, in general, Africans sold other Africans on the coast not because of their desire to accumulate power, but on account of economic rewards.[4]

The paucity of the price data for slaves embarked from West Central Africa makes similar analyses difficult. However, the custom records of Luanda provide price information about captives shipped from there between 1780 and 1830, which serves as an indicator of the fluctuations in the prices of slaves leaving the larger region. Customs officials reported the prices of slaves embarked from Luanda annually, but they did not record the value for which each captive was sold. Rather, they listed the annual average price of adult slaves embarked. Although the custom records are incomplete, the data available do allow us to calculate the average price by decade and compare it with the number of slaves leaving

[2] Curtin, *Economic Change*, vol. 1, 156–57.   [3] Ibid., vol. 1, 166–68.
[4] Le Veen, "The African Slave Supply Response," 18–21.

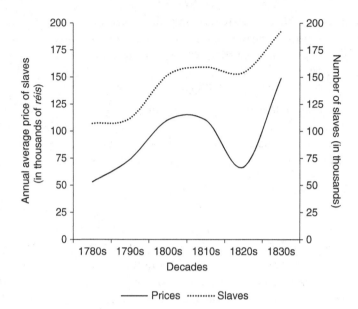

FIGURE 5.1 Comparison between price and number of slaves leaving Luanda by decades, 1780s–1830s
Sources: Prices – Appendix B, Table B.2; Slaves – Daniel B. Domingues da Silva, "The Atlantic Slave Trade from Angola: A Port-by-Port Estimate of Slaves Embarked, 1701–1867." *International Journal of African Historical Studies* 46, no. 1 (2013): 121–22.

Luanda. The prices listed in the records were deflated to reflect real prices and to allow comparison over time. The original data are reproduced together with the deflated prices in Appendix B, Tables B.1 and B.2. The comparison between the price and the number of slaves shipped from Luanda between the 1780s and 1830s is indicated in Figure 5.1.

Figure 5.1 shows that the number of captives embarked varied directly with the prices for which they were sold in Luanda. The trend lines in the number of slaves and the annual average price almost coincide. The only exception is in the 1820s, when the average price of slaves sold declined significantly compared to the number of captives embarked. Otherwise, the lines representing the value and number of slaves transported fluctuated together. When prices increased, the number of captives shipped also increased, when prices declined, the number of slaves embarked declined. This variation shows that traders in the interior were sensitive to changes in demand on the coast. Since Africans dominated the supply of slaves, the variation in the price and number of captives embarked indicates that economic motivations predominated. It also suggests that more than a handful of despotic rulers were willing to participate in this activity.

Slavery had, of course, existed in West Central Africa long before the nineteenth century. Historians still debate whether or not Africans regarded slavery as a system of exchange and economic exploitation before the rise of the transatlantic slave trade. John Thornton argues that Africans viewed slaves as the only form of private, revenue-producing property recognized by law. As such, they were subject to exchange for other slaves as well as for commodities.[5] "When Europeans came to Africa and offered to buy slaves," Thornton notes, "it is hardly surprising that they were almost immediately accepted."[6] Joseph Miller, on the other hand, believes that Africans began to sell slaves as commodities gradually because of the transatlantic trade. According to him, although Africans had long exchanged material goods, such as copper, iron, wax, and salt, among themselves, they regarded the exchange of slaves for goods as something qualitatively different, as gifts among people who had personal obligations to one another. Miller argues that the transatlantic trade changed this form of exchange by adding a new variable, people without previous personal obligations meeting at trading centers with goods to be exchanged exclusively for slaves.[7]

In the nineteenth century, West Central Africans were very familiar with the concept of slavery as a system of exchange and economic exploitation and their desire to obtain consumer goods was the primary reason they enslaved and sold other Africans. The goods they obtained circulated widely throughout the region, and they served as an important medium of exchange, especially for high-value transactions. Historians of Africa often claim that rulers somehow monopolized these goods and used them to raise armies and finance wars.[8] Some of them also argue that

---

[5] Thornton, *Africa and Africans*, 74.   [6] Ibid., 94.   [7] Miller, *Way of Death*, 47–58.

[8] Joseph E. Inikori, "Introduction." In *Forced Migration: The Impact of the Export Slave Trade on African Societies*, ed. Joseph E. Inikori (New York: Africana Publishing Company, 1982), 41–54; Martin A. Klein and Paul E. Lovejoy, "Slavery in West Africa." In *The Uncommon Market: Essays in the Economic History of the Atlantic Slave Trade*, ed. Henry A. Gemery and Jan S. Hogendorn (New York: Academic Press, 1979), 201; Klein, "The Impact of the Atlantic Slave Trade," 235–41; Lovejoy, *Transformations in Slavery*, 110; Claude Meillassoux, "The Role of Slavery in the Economic and Social History of Sahelo-Sudanic Africa." In *Forced Migration: The Impact of the Export Slave Trade on African Societies*, ed. Joseph E. Inikori, trans. R. J. Gavin (New York: Africana Publishing Company, 1982), 80–81; Meillassoux, *The Anthropology of Slavery*, 44–54; Richard L. Roberts, *Warriors, Merchants, and Slaves: The State and the Economy in the Niger Valley, 1700–1914* (Stanford: Stanford University Press, 1987), 18–19; Stilwell, *Slavery and Slaving*, 50–55.

the importation of these goods discouraged African industry and economic development.[9] However, most of the goods imported were destined for personal use, including adornment. Furthermore, they were not substitutes for locally produced items. In fact, they were introduced in such large quantities that the net effect was to reduce their value as luxury items. As a result, the goods brought to West Central Africa generated large numbers of slaves and were dispersed among the wider public, anxious to obtain foreign imports.

African economic interest in the trade is not difficult to explain. Historians of the slave trade have long challenged the assumption that Europeans purchased slaves with gewgaw or trinkets. Scholars have collected lists of trade goods from several regions. They noted that, like peoples in other parts of the Atlantic world, Africans had a sophisticated taste for goods imported from places far away.[10] As previously mentioned, the majority of the slaves shipped were exchanged for textiles, alcohol, and weapons, but these were not the only trade goods used to purchase captives. Since a successful deal depended largely on being able to present the "right" assortment of goods, traders combined them with a wide variety of other items, such as tobacco, beads, and clothing. Commodities used to purchase slaves can therefore provide us with important clues to further understanding why Africans participated in the trade.

CONSUMPTION PATTERNS

As with data on slave prices, lists of imported goods for the period are rare. Only a few records of the merchandise imported at Benguela, for

---

[9] Walter Rodney, *How Europe Underdeveloped Africa* (Washington D.C.: Howard University Press, 1982), 95–103; Inikori, "Introduction," 51–58; Nathan Nunn, "Historical Legacies: A Model Linking Africa's Past to Its Current Underdevelopment." *Journal of Development Economics* 83 (2007): 157–75; Warren Whatley and Rob Gillezeau, "The Fundamental Impact of the Slave Trade on African Economies." In *Economic Evolution and Revolution in Historical Time*, ed. Paul Rhode, Joshua Rosenbloom, and David Weiman (Stanford: Stanford University Press, 2011), 111–34.

[10] See, for example, Richard Bean, "A Note on the Relative Importance of Slaves and Gold in West African Exports." *Journal of African History* 15, no. 3 (1974): 351–56; Metcalf, "A Microcosm of Why Africans Sold Slaves: Akan Consumption Patterns in the 1770s," 377–94; Joseph C. Miller, "Imports at Luanda, Angola: 1785–1823." In *Figuring African Trade: Proceedings of the Symposium on the Quantification and Structure of the Import and Export and Long-Distance Trade of Africa in the Nineteenth Century, c.1800–1913 (St. Augustin, 3–6 January 1983)*, ed. Gerhard Liesegang, Helma Pasch, and Adam Jones (Berlin: Dietrich Reimer Verlag, 1986), 162–244; Richardson, "West African Consumption Patterns," 303–30.

example, have survived. Moreover, Africans who controlled the trade in the ports north of Luanda did not keep written records of the goods imported there, or at least none has ever been located. For this reason, historians have generally used lists of articles at source as they left Europe or the Americas in order to trace African patterns of consumption.[11] After 1807, with the increasing illegality of the slave trade, these lists gradually became scarce. Brazil and Cuba remained the principal markets, with their traders purchasing slaves at the ports north of Luanda, but records of the commodities exported from these countries to those ports are missing.

Customs records from Luanda, by contrast, are more complete and indeed are the best available for sub-Saharan Africa. They allow us to trace the consumption patterns of the populations living in the Luanda hinterland. In the late eighteenth century, customs officials began to report the amount, value, and price of all merchandise legally imported per year, but this information did not reflect the current value of the goods exchanged for slaves. Rather, the figures were estimates that members of the trading board at Luanda calculated by multiplying the amount of goods imported by the annual average price of these goods. By 1823, the records became more accurate, reflecting the value of the merchandise as it entered the port. Joseph Miller has published summaries of these records for the years 1785–1799, 1803–1805, 1809–1810, 1812, 1815–1819, and 1823, but this coverage can now be extended.[12]

New lists of imports at Luanda are now available for the years 1802, 1811, 1813, 1820, 1823–25, 1830–32, 1837, 1857–59, and 1861–1864, and they allow us to extend our analysis to the period of the suppression of the trade. Although the Portuguese prohibited the sale of slaves from their African possessions in 1836, many vessels continued to visit Luanda after that year. As Roquinaldo Ferreira noted, these vessels arrived with goods commonly used to purchase slaves, unloaded them at Luanda, and then departed in ballast to neighboring ports, where they loaded captives clandestinely.[13] This strategy enabled captains to continue using Luanda as a major slaving port, despite the prohibition on selling captives overseas. The customs house at Luanda thus continued to record the bulk of commodities used to purchase slaves through the end of the trade.

---

[11] See, for instance, Richardson, "West African Consumption Patterns," 305–11.
[12] Miller, "Imports at Luanda," 211–41.
[13] Ferreira, "Dos Sertões ao Atlântico," 221–22.

Table 5.1 shows the total value of the merchandise imported at Luanda for the years available between the late eighteenth and the nineteenth centuries in thousands of *réis* distributed across eight different categories. These categories are the same ones that Miller used in his study, and they were adopted here to facilitate a comparison of the eighteenth-century data with those of the legal and illegal period of the slave trade in the nineteenth century. The first category includes alcohol, followed by apparel and notions, Asian textiles, European textiles, foodstuffs, metals and metalware, weapons, and miscellaneous items, such as beads, shells, raw cotton, and tobacco.

The most striking feature about the commodities used by Africans for trading slaves is that the majority of them consisted of articles that did not address the primary needs of the populations living in the interior of West Central Africa. John Thornton noted that Africans had a strong textile manufacturing industry during the period of the slave trade. Although their technology was not comparable to that in Europe, Africans wove excellent cloth from raffia fibers as well as bark and palm trees. Some of these textiles were so fine and delicate that only nobles could afford to wear them. In fact, European visitors frequently compared the cloth produced by Kikongo and Vili weavers to the best produced in Europe.[14] Nevertheless, Asian and European textiles together accounted for approximately 54 percent of Luanda imports by value between the late eighteenth and mid-nineteenth centuries.

Asian textiles accounted for about 24 percent of all goods brought to Luanda. These fabrics were the most important items used to purchase slaves in the interior. Materials most in demand were *cadeás*, *chitas*, *coromandéis*, *lenços*, and *zuartes*. Other textiles imported included *carlangânis*, *casimiras*, *cassas*, *cassadizes*, *damascos*, *dotins*, *dórias*, *elefantes*, *gangas*, *garrazes*, *guingões*, *lapins*, *longuins*, *madapolões*, *mamodins*, *metins*, *musselinas*, *patavares*, and *sanas*. They were dyed white, red, yellow, and blue and came in different patterns such as stripes or checks.[15]

---

[14] John K. Thornton, "Precolonial African Industry and the Atlantic Trade, 1500–1800." *African Economic History*, no. 19 (1990): 10–12.

[15] Luís Frederico Dias Antunes, "Têxteis e Metais Preciosos: Novos Vínculos do Comércio Indo-Brasileiro (1808–1820)." In *O Antigo Regime nos Trópicos: a Dinâmica Imperial Portuguesa (Séculos XVI-XVIII)*, ed. João Fragoso, Maria Fernanda Baptista Bicalho, and Maria de Fátima Silva Gouvêa (Rio de Janeiro: Civilização Brasileira, 2001), 410; Pedro Machado, "Cloths of a New Fashion: Indian Ocean Networks of Exchange and Cloth Zones of Contact in Africa and India in the Eighteenth and Nineteenth Centuries." In *How India Clothed the World: The World of South Asian Textiles, 1500–1850*, ed. Giorgio Riello and Tirthankar Roy (Leiden: Brill, 2009), 68.

TABLE 5.1 *Commodities imported at Luanda (in thousands of réis), selected years, 1785–1864*

Years	Alcohol	Apparel and notions	Asian textiles	European textiles	Foodstuff	Metals and metalware	Miscellany	Weapons	Total
1785–99	1,782,529.8 (23.4)	255,710.2 (3.4)	1,998,810.9 (26.2)	2,089,779.9 (27.4)	487,758.9 (6.4)	77,720.5 (1.0)	647,902.6 (8.5)	287,537.3 (3.8)	7,627,750.1 (100.0)
1802–30	4,184,321.0 (20.7)	622,943.3 (3.1)	5,291,277.7 (26.2)	6,382,707.5 (31.6)	1,025,270.1 (5.1)	522,689.5 (2.6)	800,969.0 (4.0)	1,346,392.4 (6.7)	20,176,570.5 (100.0)
1831–64	2,105,316.1 (18.3)	305,045.9 (2.7)	2,081,601.6 (18.1)	3,318,110.4 (28.9)	1,223,406.3 (10.6)	203,291.8 (1.8)	1,709,171.1 (14.9)	550,247.8 (4.8)	11,496,191.0 (100.0)
Total	8,072,166.9 (20.5)	1,183,699.4 (3.0)	9,371,690.2 (23.8)	11,790,597.8 (30.0)	2,736,435.3 (7.0)	803,701.8 (2.0)	3,158,042.7 (8.0)	2,184,177.4 (5.6)	39,300,511.6 (100.0)

Note: Numbers in brackets represent row percentages.
Sources: Appendix C, Tables C.1 and C.2.

The names associated with some of them give us a hint about their place of origin. Names such as *cambaia*, *jambuseiro*, and *surrate* can be clearly identified with the ports of Cambay, Jambusar, and Surat, on the northwestern coast of India. Others, such as *bengala* and *paliacate*, were clearly Bengal and Pulicat, located on the northeastern coast. Many of the textiles imported through Luanda were simply called *panos da costa*, that is, "fabrics of the coast," which should not be confused with the *panos da costa* from West Africa, which were brought from the Bights of Benin and Biafra for sale in Brazil.[16]

These ports were located near the principal centers of textile production in India, such as Gujarat, Punjab, and Sindh. Some of the fabrics, termed *coromandéis*, came from the Coromandel Coast, on the eastern Indian seaboard, which was also a major production center, along with Bengal, further north in the same region. Local Hindi traders known as *baneanes* transported these cloths overland from the production centers to the coast, where they put them on small vessels to be taken for sale at the principal Portuguese ports in Asia, such as Damão, Diu, and Goa in India, and Macau in China.[17] From there, the textiles were shipped overseas in larger vessels to Portugal and Brazil.

Traditionally, the Portuguese crown held the monopoly over the transportation of goods from its Asian possessions. Since the sixteenth century, all commodities carried from Portuguese Asia had been shipped in a fleet system made up of royal vessels that sailed once or twice per year. These vessels were supposed to deliver the merchandise to Portugal, but they often stopped at Bahia to sell part of their cargo there illegally before crossing the North Atlantic. As a consequence, Bahia became a major center of distribution of Asian textiles in Brazil.[18] The crown tried to suppress this contraband but the practice became so common that in 1672 it made Bahia an official stop in the famous *Carreira da Índia*, or the India Route.[19] From there, Asian textiles were taken to other Brazilian

[16] Antunes, "Têxteis e Metais Peciosos," 410; Machado, "Cloths of a New Fashion," 58–59.

[17] Antunes, "Têxteis e Metais Peciosos," 390–91; Machado, "Cloths of a New Fashion," 58–59. See also Sven Beckert, *Empire of Cotton: A Global History* (New York: Alfred A. Knopf, 2014), 41–52.

[18] José Roberto do Amaral Lapa, *A Bahia e a Carreira da Índia*, Estudos Históricos, 42 (São Paulo: Hucitec, Unicamp, 2000), 1–4.

[19] Roquinaldo Amaral Ferreira, "Dinâmica do Comércio Intracolonial: Geribitas, Panos Asiáticos e Guerra no Tráfico Angolano de Escravos (Século XVIII)." In *O Antigo Regime nos Trópicos: A Dinâmica Imperial Portuguesa (Séculos XVI-XVIII)*, ed. João Fragoso, Maria Fernanda Baptista Bicalho, and Maria de Fátima Silva Gouvêa (Rio de Janeiro: Civilização Brasileira, 2001), 352.

ports, such as Recife and Rio de Janeiro, and traded for slaves in Luanda and Benguela among other places.

In 1765, the crown abolished the fleet system, allowing private traders to purchase textiles in Asia. It tried to restrict the agency of these entrepreneurs by limiting the sale of cloth in certain ports, including Luanda, before it reached Portugal.[20] However, Asian textiles were so crucial for the slave traffic in West Central Africa that Brazilians dominated this branch of the trade even in Portugal. According to Ernestina Carreira, in the final years of the fleet system, about 90 percent of all cloth shipped from Portugal to Brazil was Asian, which traders used to purchase slaves.[21] In the late eighteenth century, Asian textiles accounted for approximately 26 percent of the commodities imported at Luanda by value, and in the nineteenth century, while the trade was still legal, this figure did not change. The huge amount of Asian textiles imported into Luanda no doubt widened consumer choice.

After 1830, during the period of the illegal slave trade, the proportion of Asian textiles brought to Luanda declined significantly to about 18 percent of the total value, as European textiles replaced them as the major import. Europeans always brought cloth produced in their own countries to purchase slaves in the region, but Africans found this cloth inferior to the Asian variety. The principal European fabrics introduced in Luanda included *baés, baetás, bretanhas, brins, calamanhas, chilas, crês, lenços, panos,* and *riscadinhos.* Despite the European technological advancements in textile production at the turn of the nineteenth century, these fabrics were still very rough and had less color variety than the Asian. European textiles were mostly dark and too thick to be worn in the tropics. Since this cloth was more appropriate for temperate climates, the principal consumers of European textiles in West Central Africa were probably the Umbundu, who lived in the central highlands, where the temperature was cooler than any other place in the region.

Most of the European cloth imported through Luanda came originally from England, but the names associated with some fabrics also indicate other regions of provenance. Names like *irlanda, holanda, alemanha,* and *ruão* for example, suggest that Luanda imported cloth from Ireland, the

[20] Ibid., 354.
[21] Ernestina Carreira, "Os Últimos Anos da Carreira da Índia." In *A Carreira da Índia e as Rotas dos Estreitos: Actas do VIII Seminário Internacional de História Indo-Portuguesa,* ed. Artur Teodoro de Matos and Luís Filipe F. Reis Thomaz (Angra do Heroísmo: Barbosa e Xavier, 1998), 826.

Netherlands, Germany, especially Hamburg, and Rouen, in France. These names also imply that such cloths had different styles. Europeans sold their textiles in Lisbon or Porto, from where Portuguese traders loaded them onto transatlantic vessels and resold them to merchants in Brazil. Merchants then exchanged them in Luanda for slaves.

In 1808, with the transfer of the Portuguese court to Rio de Janeiro, European traders were allowed to sell their textiles directly to Brazil. This reduced the costs of using European textiles in the slave trade, as well as shipping and freight costs for the merchandise carried from Portugal to Brazil. British textiles, in particular, benefitted significantly from the opening of the Brazilian ports. Since the British navy had escorted the Portuguese royal family to Brazil, the king granted tax privileges to all British imports.[22] This made British textiles used in the slave trade far cheaper than most other cloth imported from Europe.

Although these incentives helped increase the imports of European goods, during the period of the legal trade in the nineteenth century Africans still preferred Asian materials. Between 1802 and 1830, the percentage of European textiles imported increased to about 32, while the share of Asian textiles remained the same as in the late eighteenth century. However, during the illegal period, this picture changed dramatically. While the value of European fabrics declined to approximately 29 percent, that of Asian fell to 18 percent of the total value of the commodities imported. In the nineteenth century, European technology finally caught up with Asian production techniques.[23] Europeans also had copied the patterns of Asian textiles and were now producing similar fabrics at much lower cost.[24] Textile designs that had typically been produced in India, such as *cadeás, chitas*, and *zuartes*, now began to arrive in Luanda from Europe, especially England.

Brazilian independence in 1822 was another important factor leading to the expansion of European textiles imported through Luanda. Before independence, textiles brought to Brazil from Portuguese possessions in Asia were taxed at the usual domestic import and export rates. However, after independence, trade between Brazil and Portugal was subject to tariffs. This charge inevitably increased costs for Brazilian traders, thus making European textiles the principal cloth brought to Luanda.

Alcohol was the third most imported commodity, constituting about 20 percent of the value of all goods brought to Luanda between 1785 and

[22] Fausto, *História do Brasil*, 122–24.   [23] Beckert, *Empire of Cotton*, 138–46.
[24] Miller, *Way of Death*, 74.

1864. The customs records show that Africans were particularly interested in *aguardente, jeribita*, and wine. *Aguardente*, a distilled by-product of sugar or wine production in Portugal and Brazil, comprised 34 percent of all alcoholic beverages imported at Luanda during that period.[25] *Jeribita* was a sugar-based rum produced in Brazil, which accounted for 22 percent, while wine, which came mostly from the banks of the Douro and Tagus rivers in Portugal, contributed 21 percent.[26] The remaining imported beverages included beer, brandy, cognac, liquor, and a highly aromatic bitter gin called *genebra* or geneva, originally produced in the Netherlands.

African interest in *arguadente* and *jeribita* derived in large part from their high alcoholic content. According to Roquinaldo Ferreira, the alcohol content of the sugar rum that traders used to purchase slaves in the interior could be as high as 60 percent.[27] Joseph Miller believes that it could reach up to 90 percent, though it may have been mixed with water before consumption.[28] The alcoholic content of the wine must have been much lower, between 10 and 13 percent. Although traders also purchased slaves with wine, most of the wine imported at Luanda was probably sold at the numerous taverns that flourished throughout the city as well as at the churches, which used it in the Eucharistic rite. The 1850 census return for Luanda, for example, reported that the port had about 90 taverns, which addressed the needs of both the local population and the community of sailors, soldiers, and visitors from abroad.[29]

The influx of rum and wine through Luanda offered consumers greater variety when compared to the locally produced alcoholic beverages. José Curto claims that Africans living in the hinterland of Luanda produced two types of fermented beverages: *malafu* or *malavu*, a sort of wine made primarily from raphia or extractions from the palm tree, and another, known as *ovallo* or *walo*, a type of beer made of grains such as millet or sorghum.[30] Neither one had a high alcoholic content so, after they were produced, both had to be drunk within a short time period. In contrast, the imported beverages, especially *arguadente* and *jeribita*, could be

[25] Calculated from Appendix C, Table C.3.   [26] Calculated from Appendix C, Table C.3.
[27] Ferreira, "Dinâmica do Comércio Intracolonial," 348.   [28] Miller, *Way of Death*, 465.
[29] "Estatísticas dos Edifícios, Estabelecimentos e Oficinas da Cidade de Luanda Relativa ao Ano de 1850" reproduced in José de Almeida Santos, *Vinte Anos Decisivos de uma Cidade* (Luanda: Câmara Municipal de Luanda, 1970), 167–68.
[30] José C. Curto, *Enslaving Spirits: The Portuguese-Brazilian Alcohol Trade at Luanda and Its Hinterland, c.1550–1830* (Leiden: Brill, 2004), 21–22.

stored for much longer periods, making them more suitable for sale in the long-distance trade than the local variety.[31]

Despite this advantage, Africans continued consuming and producing both *walo* and *malafu*. As late as the 1880s, European travelers commented on the local production and consumption of liquor in the hinterland of Luanda. Hermenegildo Capello and Roberto Ivens, who traveled extensively throughout Angola between 1877 and 1886, observed the production of palm wine. Near the Kwango River, in the Kimbundu-speaking region, they estimated that the production reached "thousands of liters per habitation, judging from the quantity that we have seen consumed in the places we visited."[32] In fact, while the value of imported alcoholic beverages increased during the legal period of the trade, from an annual average of 118 million *réis* to 220 million between 1785–99 and 1802–30, it declined in the illegal period to an average of 210 million *réis*, suggesting that Africans continued to produce and consume large amounts of local alcoholic beverages.

Let us consider the remaining imports by category and their relative importance to the trade. Despite all of the debate about the introduction of firearms to the continent, the customs records of Luanda show that weapons made up less than 6 percent of the value of goods imported. In the seventeenth and eighteenth centuries, the Portuguese tried to avoid exchanging arms for slaves because they feared Africans might use them to attack Portuguese posts in Angola. However, in the face of foreign competition at the ports north of Luanda and pressure from Lisbon's arms dealers, the government relaxed this prohibition.[33] The customs records do not specify the origins of the firearms introduced in West Central Africa. Most of them were probably inexpensive flintlock guns known as "Angola muskets," produced notably in Birmingham, England. Joseph Inikori argues that firearms were a key component in the British slave trade, and the majority of the guns used to purchase slaves were sold in West Central Africa.[34] Until 1807, when the British retreated from the slave trade business, these guns were distributed through the ports north of Luanda but, after that year, they were shipped to Luanda from Brazilian ports opened up to international commerce.

[31] Ferreira, "Dinâmica do Comércio Intracolonial," 346.
[32] Capello and Ivens, *De Benguella às Terras de Iácca*, vol. 2, 143–44.
[33] Birmingham, *Trade and Conflict*, 146–47; Miller, *Way of Death*, 607–08.
[34] Joseph E. Inikori, "The Import of Firearms into West Africa, 1750–1807: A Quantitative Analysis." *Journal of African History* 18, no. 3 (1977): 352.

Portuguese guns were also used to purchase slaves, and they circulated widely in the region's interior. In 1852, David Livingston traveled across the region, from Cape Town to Luanda, and noted that Africans living near the Upper Zambeze River traded Portuguese guns for slave children. He examined one of these guns and saw the inscription *Legítimo de Braga*, meaning "Made in Braga," Portugal. Livingston observed that Makololo chiefs bought these guns from the Mambári, traders of Portuguese and African ancestry who lived near the Kingdom of Viye, in the central plateau of Angola. In exchange for their guns, the Mambári accepted only boys about 14 years old, a pattern discussed in the previous chapter. Livingstone further noted that the children who the Makololo sold to the Mambári were not their own, but "captives of the black races they had conquered."[35]

Africans no doubt used guns in wars and raids, but firearms never replaced traditional weapons in military conflicts in the area. In fact, John Thornton argues that during the period of the slave trade, weapons such as swords, knives, spears, clubs, axes, and shields, as well as bows and arrows figured prominently in most armies across the region. Firearms served only as an additional military resource that Africans used in conjunction with more traditional weapons.[36] Joseph Miller claims that only a small percentage of the guns survived the first few attempts to fire them, and many were unusable from the start.[37] Nevertheless, the potential of these guns to cause death and destruction was intimidating, and African generals could easily harness that potential in raids and military conflicts.

Most of the guns imported through Luanda were probably used for hunting. Guns had a revolutionary impact on Cokwe speakers, for example, who lived near the Upper Kasai River. In the nineteenth century, they broke into the ivory trade from Luanda and Benguela. Historians believe that this activity caused a significant decline in the number of elephants in the region, but it also inaugurated an age of prosperity for the Cokwe, who spread throughout the interior.[38] In the mid-nineteenth century, Cokwe influence in the region became so strong that it rivaled that of their more powerful neighbor, the Lunda Empire.

[35] David Livingstone, *Missionary Travels and Researches in South Africa: Including a Sketch of Sixteen Years' Residence in the Interior of Africa* (New York: Harper & Bros., 1858), 105–06.

[36] John K. Thornton, *Warfare in Atlantic Africa, 1500–1800* (New York: University College London Press, 1999), 107–10.

[37] Miller, *Way of Death*, 88.   [38] Henriques, *Percursos da Modernidade*, 448.

Cokwe art reflects the central importance of firearms in their culture, as is shown by guns decorated with hunter charms, which can be seen in many museums. Further, sculptures of their famous hunter hero, Chibinda Ilunga, depict him holding a gun instead of a bow and arrow.[39]

Although Europeans considered the "Angolan muskets" cheap, Africans had good reason for preferring them to the more sophisticated firearms. The construction of these muskets involved less complicated technology, so blacksmiths could easily repair them using their own tools and knowledge. Isabel Castro Henriques stresses that European travelers in the region often remarked on the ability of local blacksmiths to repair firearms.[40] Similarly, historians have noted that Europeans considered British and French gunpowder superior to Portuguese, because of its higher saltpeter content, which made it more powerful. Africans, on the other hand, favored Portuguese gunpowder because it caused less damage to their weapons, which in turn resulted in fewer deaths to users.[41]

The customs records of Luanda reflected these preferences. While Africans could repair their muskets, they had to be more selective about the gunpowder they used, so the value of gunpowder imported at Luanda was far greater than that of firearms. Gunpowder represented about 70 percent of the value of all of the weaponry imported at Luanda, while firearms made up only 21 percent.[42] The remaining weapons imported included shot lead and blade weapons, such as spears, swords, and knives, especially *facas flamengas* or Flemish knives.

Africans also traded slaves for a number of miscellaneous items, which accounted for approximately 8 percent of the value of all imports. Some of these goods were important for the slave trade, such as tobacco, which accounted for about 11 percent of the miscellaneous items.[43] Most of the tobacco brought to Luanda came from Bahia, Sergipe, Pernambuco, and

---

[39] See the images available in Marie Louise Bastin, *Statuettes Tshokwe du Héros Civilisateur "Tshibinda Ilunga"* (Arnouville-les-Gonesse: Arts d'Afrique Noire, 1978), 63–97; Henriques, *Percursos da Modernidade*, 322.

[40] Henriques, *Percursos da Modernidade*, 320–23.

[41] Martin, *The External Trade*, 111; Miller, *Way of Death*, 91–92. For a similar observation for other African regions see Raymond A. Kea, "Firearms and Warfare on the Gold and Slave Coasts from the Sixteenth to the Nineteenth Centuries." *Journal of African History* 12, no. 2 (1971): 204–05.

[42] Calculated from Appendix C, Table C.10.

[43] Calculated from Appendix C, Table C.9.

Alagoas, in Brazil, which were also major suppliers of tobacco to Europe and West Africa, especially the Bight of Benin, where tobacco was used to purchase slaves. Brazilian tobacco differed from its main competitors because it was covered with molasses, which rendered a sweet and intense flavor well-suited to African taste.[44]

Although Angolans appreciated Brazilian tobacco, it encountered strong competition from local production. Capello and Ivens have observed that tobacco cultivation abounded in the lands of the Bondo, Kikongo speakers who lived near the Kwango River. They once stopped there on the way to Yaka and noted that the Bondo smoked their own tobacco in pipes that passed from hand to hand among a group of smokers. After a short period, this pipe was replaced by another type of pipe made of horn called *mutopa*, with which they smoked *liamba*, a herb Capello and Ivens identified with hemp of the species *Cannabis sativa*. They observed that, though the Bondo appreciated their own tobacco, they viewed the *liamba* as one of their "greatest delights."[45]

Beads, which accounted for about 9 percent of the miscellaneous items imported through Luanda, were also used to buy slaves.[46] It is difficult to tell the exact provenance of these beads. Most of them appear to have originated in Portugal. They were made of glass or porcelain and came in different shapes, sizes, and colors. They appear listed in the records as *missangas, avelórios, contas, contarias, granadas*, and *roncalhas*. Africans used these beads to make necklaces, bracelets, and earrings. They also used them to decorate their hair, clothes, and various utensils, including works of art and religious artifacts.[47]

The customs records include two additional items worth mentioning under the miscellaneous category. The first is shells, listed in the records as *conchas, búzios*, and *zimbo*. In the sixteenth and seventeenth centuries, shells were valued as medium of exchange at Luanda as well as in other African ports, particularly Ouidah, Cape Coast, and Lagos.[48] In Luanda, shells served as currency for small exchanges but with the expansion of the slave trade the value of the shells declined sharply, leading traders

---

[44] Alden, "Late Colonial Brazil," 631–35; Verger, *Fluxo e Refluxo*, 20–26.
[45] Capello and Ivens, *De Benguella às Terras de Iácca*, vol. 2, 26–27.
[46] Calculated from Appendix C, Table C.9.   [47] Miller, *Way of Death*, 86.
[48] Klein and Lovejoy, "Slavery in West Africa," 109–13; Marion Johnson, "The Cowrie Currencies of West Africa. Part II." *Journal of African History* 11, no. 3 (1970): 17–27; Robin Law, *The Slave Coast of West Africa, 1550–1750: The Impact of the Atlantic Slave Trade on an African Society* (Oxford: Clarendon Press, 1991), 48–50, 57–58, and 176–81.

to barter rather than relying on commodity currencies.[49] The customs records show that this trend continued from the late eighteenth to the mid-nineteenth century, when the value of shells declined to insignificance.

The second item worth mentioning is raw cotton, which accounted for approximately 24 percent of all miscellaneous items brought to Luanda, or less than 2 percent of total imports.[50] The reason for such imports is not clear. Perhaps, the cotton was destined for sale to the population living in the Portuguese colonies, but it may have been used to purchase slaves in the interior of West Central Africa. If so, this suggests that Africans were modifying their textile industry to spin and weave cotton cloth for local consumption and trade, a move that could have had important consequences for the relationship between Africans and Europeans. The development of a local cotton cloth industry might have reduced textile importation from Asia and Europe and, as a result, the export of slaves from West Central Africa.

In 1780, Elias Alexandre da Silva Corrêa noted that a species of wild cotton grew widely in Portuguese Angola, especially in Ambaca, Kimbundu land. Africans spun this cotton into yarn, which they used as currency. They also wove it on double-stick looms placed next to the walls of their habitations and made cloth and mats on which many people in Angola, including Portuguese colonizers, slept. According to Corrêa, the fabrics made with this cotton, especially in Kikongo country, "exceeded in perfection and beauty those produced in India."[51] Nevertheless, the use of imported cotton appears to have spread during the nineteenth century. European travelers believed that the region's climate favored the cultivation of imported cotton varieties. David Livingston, travelling across Kimbundu country, saw "cotton growing luxuriantly all around the market places from seeds dropped accidentally. It is seen also about the native huts, and, so far as I could learn, it was the American cotton, so influenced by climate as to be perennial."[52]

The remaining commodities imported were not used exclusively in the slave trade. Foodstuffs, for example, were imported mostly for consumption in the Portuguese colonies. The principal articles were wheat flour, sugar, rice, olive oil, butter, and salt. None of these items, with the

---

[49] Carlos Couto, *O Zimbo na Historiografia Angolana* (Luanda: Instituto de Investigação Científica de Angola, 1973), 37–42; Miller, *Way of Death*, 86.

[50] Calculated from Appendix C, Table C.9.

[51] da Silva Corrêa, *História de Angola*, vol. 1, 155–58.

[52] Livingstone, *Missionary Travels*, 433.

exception of salt, was part of the African diet. Wheat flour and sugar alone made up 42 percent of the value of all food imports, and both were essential to the Portuguese diet.[53] Wheat flour was used in bread, cakes, and other food items, but also in the Eucharistic bread for Catholic mass. Sugar was another central ingredient in the various sweets, desserts, and pastry for which the Portuguese were and remain famous throughout the world. The diet of the African population was based essentially on maize, cassava, and beans, which was an insignificant percentage of the value of food imports.[54] They were probably brought to help traders supplement local food supplies for their slaves, because most of the food consumed in the colonies and exported in slave vessels was produced locally and stored at the public granary.[55] Although food was not used to purchase slaves, it accounted for about 7 percent of all goods imported at Luanda.

Apparel and notions also served a dual purpose: to purchase slaves and for use by Portuguese residents. As clothing denoted social hierarchy among Africans, traders often included it in their bundles of European and Brazilian goods destined for sale in the interior. Traders usually gave these clothes to Africans as gifts to begin negotiations or seal a deal rather than to purchase captives. Africans were particularly interested in caps, hats, and jackets, which they combined with their own outfits, creating a unique sense of fashion and style.[56] Early photographs from the mid-nineteenth century have an abundance of images showing West Central Africans wearing European clothing.[57]

The apparel and notions, however, were not only employed in the slave trade. A large part of them was destined for sale at the Portuguese colonies, especially Luanda and Benguela. These colonies had a significant population of Europeans or people of European ancestry, who wished to maintain contact with their culture and traditions. One way of doing so was to wear clothes from their country of origin and follow the latest trends in European fashion. Apparel and notions for both uses made up only 3 percent of the total value of the commodities imported.

Metals and metalware could also be used to buy slaves, as well as to sell to Portuguese colonists. Iron, in particular, was an important commodity

---

[53] Calculated from Appendix C, Table C.7.

[54] Calculated from Appendix C, Table C.7. See also Venâncio, *A Economia de Luanda*, 57–59.

[55] Miller, *Way of Death*, 86; Venâncio, *A Economia de Luanda*, 63–67.

[56] Miller, *Way of Death*, 79–83.

[57] See, for example, the images available in Heintze, *Pioneiros Africanos*, between pages 96–97, 128–29, 160–61, 192–93, 225–26, and 288–89; Santos, *Nos Caminhos de África*, 272.

used to purchase slaves in other African regions. Indeed, in places like the Upper Guinea coast and the Bight of Benin, the value of a slave was measured in terms of iron bars.[58] However, in West Central Africa, iron as well as other metals played a relatively minor role in the trade. Although Africans had a thriving iron industry, the domestic supply of iron in West Central Africa was sufficient to satisfy the local demand.[59] In fact, the region had such rich deposits of iron ore that the Portuguese tried to build two foundries there during the period of the slave trade; one in Nova Oeiras and another in Trombeta. The ruins of the former remain, but neither one operated for long, because the working conditions the Portuguese imposed were not compatible with those to which African blacksmiths were accustomed.[60]

Portuguese colonists in Luanda and Benguela, by contrast, depended heavily on the imported ironware. Metals like iron, copper, and zinc were crucial for the construction of houses, maintenance of public buildings and, of course, the operation of ports and military facilities. They also needed metals to make tools and a number of other articles essential for everyday life, such as cups, plates, knives, forks, spoons, and hooks. Thus, most of the metals imported at Luanda, no more than 2 percent of the value of all imported goods, were for European use.

CONCLUSION

The customs records of Luanda show that Africans sold other Africans into the trade for consumer goods, especially textiles, alcohol, and weapons imported from Asia, the Americas, and Europe. These goods were not the prime necessities of African life but could and did add to the variety of similar items produced locally. Although Africans had clear preferences for some imported commodities, such as Asian and European textiles, they continued to produce their own goods, like cloths made of raffia and palm trees. Even though they used the opportunity to experiment with new materials, as indicated by the use of imported cotton for textile production, the local industry remained largely independent of foreign

[58] See, for example, Walter Hawthorne, *Planting Rice and Harvesting Slaves: Transformations along the Guinea-Bissau Coast, 1400–1900* (Portsmouth: Heinemann, 2003), 96–98; Law, *The Slave Coast*, 50–51.

[59] Miller, *Way of Death*, 85–86.

[60] Sousa, "Uma Tentativa de Fomento Industrial na Angola Setecentista: A 'Fábrica do Ferro' de Nova Oeiras (1766–1772)," 295–305; Venâncio, *A Economia de Luanda*, 113–23.

imports during the period of the slave trade, raising doubts about the latter's potential to undermine the local economy.

Additionally, the customs records show that most of the goods imported were destined for personal use and adornment. They were not primarily intended to fund raids and wars. Asian and European textiles could indeed have been employed to raise armies. However, they accounted for such a large percentage of the imported goods that their very abundance in the interior casts doubt on their exclusive status, which indicates they would not have power to finance raids and wars. Within Africa, the act of enslavement stemmed from the drive for material gain rather than political power. Foreign goods would only generate large numbers of slaves as long as they were spread among the African population and not concentrated in the hands of rulers. Warfare was far from being the single method of enslavement. The experiences of individual captives, the subject of the following chapter, will point to a wide variety of ways, violent and non-violent, in which Africans found themselves in the hold of a slave ship.

6

Experiences and Methods of Enslavement

Although outsiders were the main target group for capture and sale into the slave trade, insiders were also inadvertently or purposefully taken for the same end. This chapter will examine records and stories of both groups enslaved in the interior of West Central Africa. By the nineteenth century, many societies of the region had long been familiar with the institution of slavery, defined as a system of social, political, and economic exploitation in which people were regarded as valuable properties that could be exchanged for cash or merchandise. Not all captives were sold into the trade; some remained in bondage on the continent. As previously noted, those were mostly women and children, who could be easily integrated in the families of their masters as spouses or dependents. Africans sold into the trade had little to offer in this respect, but they had an exchange value. They were enslaved under specific circumstances, ranging from violent conflicts to judicial proceedings. The experiences of these individuals provide important insights into the question of eligibility for sale in the overseas market.

Contemporaries learned about the experiences of captives by interviewing them. In 1847, Sigismund Wilhelm Koelle disembarked at Freetown, Sierra Leone, as an agent of the Church Missionary Society. He became a linguist at the Fourah Bay Institute, where research into African languages was conducted. In 1854, he published his findings in *Polyglotta Africana*, a well-known book, which is essentially a collection of sample vocabularies of languages spoken by Africans rescued from ships condemned for illegal trading by the Freetown courts.[1] These

---

[1] Koelle, *Polyglotta Africana*; P. E. H. Hair, "Koelle at Freetown: An Historical Introduction." In *Polyglotta Africana*, by Sigismund Wilhelm Koelle, ed. P. E. H. Hair and David Dalby (Graz: Akademische Druck, U. Verlagsanstalt, 1965), 7.

vocabularies cover almost all African regions involved in the trade. The book also provides information about the people Koelle interviewed, such as their names, ages, countries of origin, and the number of their fellow countrymen living in Sierra Leone as well as how they were taken from their original homelands.[2]

Koelle's work is especially valuable for our understanding of the experiences of West Central African captives. In contrast to those from other regions of slave embarkation, captives from this region left little information about their lives and experiences. There are no autobiographies of Africans enslaved in the region's interior.[3] Reconstructed stories about these people in the Americas likewise contain little information on how they were captured and sold in Africa.[4] Apart from Koelle's book, all we have are some fragments reporting the experiences of a few individuals. These fragments, which are available in print as well as in archival documents, together with Koelle's research, provide a valuable record of the experiences of people deprived of their freedom in Africa.[5]

Koelle interviewed 18 liberated Africans from what he termed Congo Angola to build his inventory of words for this region. Although this is a very small number compared to the thousands of individuals dispatched, it includes representatives from almost every major linguistic group forced into the trade. The demographics of Koelle's informants further support

[2] Philip D. Curtin and Jan Vansina, "Sources of the Nineteenth Century Atlantic Slave Trade." *Journal of African History* 5, no. 2 (1964): 186; P. E. H. Hair, "The Enslavement of Koelle's Informants." *Journal of African History* 6, no. 2 (1965): 193.

[3] José C. Curto, "Experiences of Enslavement in West Central Africa." *Social History* 41, no. 82 (2009): 383–88.

[4] Edward Ball, *Slaves in the Family* (New York: Ballantine Books, 1999), 134–37, 147, 174–76, 184, 228, 250–51; Cheryll Ann Cody, "There Was No 'Absalom' on the Ball Plantations: Slave-Naming Practices in the South Carolina Low Country, 1720–1865." *American Historical Review* 92, no. 3 (1987): 563–96; Melinde Lutz Sanborn, "Angola and Elizabeth: An African Family in the Massachusetts Bay Colony." *New England Quarterly* 72, no. 1 (1999): 119–29. Two notable exceptions are John K. Thornton, "The African Experience of the '20. and Odd Negroes' Arriving in Virginia in 1619." *William and Mary Quarterly* 55, no. 3 (1998): 421–34; Heywood and Thornton, *Central Africans, Atlantic Creoles, and the Foundation of the Americas*, 1–9.

[5] Louis Jadin, "Rapport sur les Recherches aux Archives d'Angola du 4 Juillet au 7 Septembre 1952." *Bulletin des Séances de l'Institut Royal Colonial Belge*, no. 24 (1953): 167; Luiz António de Oliveira Mendes, *Memória a Respeito dos Escravos e Tráfico da Escravatura entre a Costa da África e o Brasil*, ed. José Capela (Porto: Escorpião, 1977), 61–62; Felisberto Caldeira Brant Pontes, "Memória de Brant Pontes sôbre a Comunicação das Duas Costas 9/9/1800." In *Apontamentos sobre a Colonização dos Planaltos e Litoral do Sul de Angola*, ed. Alfredo de Albuquerque Felner, vol. 1 (Lisbon: Agência Geral das Colónias, 1940), 248–51.

the use of his data for an assessment of how Africans were enslaved in the region. All interviewees were male, with ages ranging from 14 to 28. Except for three men who remained in Africa for several years, those captured had been immediately sold overseas. Not all of them specified how they were captured. When Koelle interviewed his sample, they were well-established in Sierra Leone, having been there for at least seven years. In fact, one of them, a Kongo man named Mugádu, also known as Thomas Tob, had been living in Freetown for about 40 years when Koelle contacted him. Koelle noted that by the time he interviewed Mugádu, given the man's age, he had held the "office of Kongo head-man," a position found around the Atlantic wherever there was a substantial Kongo population.[6] Koelle's informants provide us with reliable information about the experiences of West Central Africans sent to the Americas after 1807 (see Table 6.1).

The liberated Africans reported two broad methods of enslavement; kidnapping and judicial proceedings. One of the informants said that he was sold by his relatives, but did not give reasons for the transaction.[7] Kidnapping included not only victims of abduction and trickery but also prisoners of wars or raids. Sometimes victims of warfare claimed that they were kidnapped as opposed to being captured, but their background as well as the context in which they were enslaved suggest otherwise. Depending on the circumstance, such as living among former enemies, not everyone felt comfortable enough in admitting to being a prisoner of war. Given the emphasis historians have placed on the role of wars in the slave trade, this method of capture deserves considerable discussion. Scholars generally agree that the majority of slaves sold into the slave trade were prisoners of wars. The question is what kind of wars generated these slaves? Were they large-scale wars that required the mobilization of significant resources and manpower? Or were they local conflicts more accurately described as raids and skirmishes?

WARFARE

The Angolan Wars of the sixteenth and seventeenth centuries have led many historians to believe that large-scale conflicts were the primary

---

[6] Koelle, *Polyglotta Africana*, 13. On the office of Kongo headman, see Marina de Mello e Souza, *Reis Negros no Brasil Escravista: História da Festa de Coroação de Rei Congo* (Belo Horizonte: Editora UFMG, 2002), 159–208.
[7] Koelle, *Polyglotta Africana*, 13–14.

TABLE 6.1 *Koelle's interviewees, c.1847*

Name	Date captured	Ethnolinguistic origin	Age at enslavement	Method of enslavement
Bémbi or William Davis	1832	Umbundu	28	Judicial proceeding/ Witchcraft
Bunsála or Thomas Pratt	1835	Obamba	Unknown	Judicial proceeding/ Adultery
Dsíku or Isaac Manners	1840	Nsundi	23	Kidnapped/ Warfare
Dsíngo or James Job	1829	Teke	Unknown	Judicial proceeding/ Debt
Kadióngo or John Morrison	1837	Kisama	16	Kidnapped/ Abducted
Kindsímbu, Dsindsímbi, or John Baptist	1819	Vili	14	Unspecified
Kúmbu or Thomas Parker	1831	Yombe	Unknown	Judicial proceeding/ Witchcraft
Mugádu or Thomas Tob	1809	Kongo	22	Unspecified
Muséwo or Toki Petro	1794	Songo	15	Kidnapped/ Abducted
Mútomp or William Francis	1835	Kanyok	Unknown	Judicial proceeding/ Misconduct
Nanga or John Smart	1841	Libolo	24	Judicial proceeding/ Debt
Ndsúmu or William Fergusson	1832	Teke	17	Unspecified
Ngónga or John Wilhelm	1834	Kasanje	28	Kidnapped/ Unclear
Nkóngal or James Mafoi	1840	Lunda	23	Kidnapped/ Warfare
Nzinga or Andrew Hobb	1836	Kongo	23	Sold by relatives/ Unspecified
Okiri or Andrew Park	1822	Mbeti	16	Judicial proceeding/ Unspecified

(continued)

TABLE 6.1 *(continued)*

Name	Date captured	Ethnolinguistic origin	Age at enslavement	Method of enslavement
Tut or Charles Wilhelm	1832	Teke	20	Kidnapped/ Unspecified
Unknown	1839	Ngola	22	Unspecified

Source: Sigismund Wilhelm Koelle, *Polyglotta Africana*, ed. P. E. H. Hair and David Dalby (Graz: Akademisch Druck, U. Verlagsanstalt, 1965), 13–15.

method of enslavement in the interior. After the Portuguese founded Luanda in 1575, they formed an alliance with bands of itinerant warriors known as the Jaga. This alliance destabilized a region that was already very politically fragile because of the independence of Ndongo from Kongo. When the Ndongo ruler proved unwilling to accept their trading terms, the Portuguese invaded his realm with the help of the Jaga, replacing him with a ruler more amenable to their interests. This move unleashed a series of military confrontations between claimants to the throne of Ndongo. The faction supported by the Portuguese and the Jaga founded a new polity in the region known as the Imbangala Kingdom of Kasanje.[8] These confrontations resulted in a vast number of prisoners being sent to the Americas during the sixteenth and seventeenth centuries. The Portuguese governors often provoked these conflicts because their income depended largely on the traffic from Luanda.[9] The traffic and political instability contributed to an atmosphere of destruction, violence, and insecurity in the hinterland of Luanda. As a local observer noted, the Angolan Wars led to "carnage on such a large-scale that rivers became polluted with numerous corpses and multitudes of innocent people were captured without cause."[10] Among these multitudes were soldiers and civilians.

In the eighteenth century, Portuguese participation in large-scale African wars began to decline. In 1720, administrative reforms established a salary for high-ranking administrators and prohibited them

---

[8] The traditional account about the Angolan Wars is António de Oliveira de Cadornega, *História Geral das Guerras Angolanas, 1680*, ed. José Matias Delgado (Lisbon: Agência Geral do Ultramar, 1972).

[9] Miller, *Way of Death*, 541–42.

[10] Bishop of Angola to the King, 7 September 1619 in Alfredo de Albuquerque Felner, *Angola: Apontamentos sobre a Ocupação e Início do Estabelecimento dos Portugueses no Congo, Angola e Benguela Extraídos de Documentos Históricos* (Coimbra: Imprensa da Universidade, 1933), 452–56. As quoted and translated by Curto, "Experiences," 390.

from engaging in private commercial activities in the colonies.[11] As a consequence, Portuguese governors based on the coast of Angola were, in theory, no longer able to participate in the trade. Nevertheless, historians continued to view large-scale wars as the primary method of enslavement, but for the eighteenth century they locate these conflicts in the deep interior of West Central Africa at the frontiers of the Lunda Empire. There is some documentary support for this position. During this period, the Portuguese governors in Luanda informed the Colonial Office in Lisbon that the Lunda were conducting military activities deep in the region's interior.[12] Additionally, slave traders operating inland reported on the Lunda campaigns. Manoel Correia Leitão traveled to the valley of the Kwango River between 1755 and 1756 and noted that the Lunda king "is very powerful, and from his realms and domains captains come forth who are sent forth by him to the West, the North, and the South, and other parts with troops of very many people to capture slaves which they sell, according to the place closest to where they take them ... And it is certain that were it not for them, we would not have so many slaves, because, through their ambition and their reputation as conquerors, having become terrestrial Eagles, they raid countries so remote from their Fatherland only to lord it over other peoples."[13]

Lunda military activities along the Kwango River may have been highly destructive, but they did not result in the sale of large numbers on the coast as Leitão argued. Moreover, customs records of slaves shipped from Luanda suggest that large-scale wars inhibited the slave trade rather than stimulated it. David Birmingham, a major proponent of the Lunda origins of slaves embarked from the region, accessed records of slaves shipped from Luanda during the mid-eighteenth century. He noted that, despite the ongoing conflicts along the Kwango River, the number of slaves shipped from Luanda declined in comparison to previous years.[14] As previously mentioned, large-scale wars were not the primary method of enslavement in the interior. This conclusion is not without parallel in other African regions. David Eltis has noted that the number of slaves shipped from the Bight of Benin actually declined in the first half of the eighteenth century as a result of the Dahomean wars, which culminated in

---

[11] Miller, *Way of Death*, 543.   [12] Birmingham, *Trade and Conflict*, 152–54.
[13] Manoel Correia Leitão, "Angola's Eastern Hinterland in the 1750s: A Text Edition and Translation of Manoel Correia Leitão's 'Voyage' (1755–1756)," ed. Eva Sebestyen and Jan Vansina, *History in Africa* 26 (1999): 341–42.
[14] Birmingham, *Trade and Conflict*, 154.

the annexation of Allada and Ouidah, the two principal ports of slave embarkation on the Bight of Benin.[15]

Other military conflict in the interior included frequent and widespread minor wars. In the eighteenth and nineteenth centuries, there were essentially two kinds of military initiatives, one waged by Portuguese colonial officials, the other conducted by different African groups and polities. Although Portuguese governors were no longer allowed to trade slaves, it was part of their mandate to launch punitive expeditions against Africans they considered disruptive or insufficiently loyal to the Crown. Such undertakings included fiscal incentives for slave traders to supply horses for the Luanda Calvary.[16] Portuguese governors could also wage "just wars" against Africans who attacked, or threatened to attack, the Portuguese settlements in Angola.[17] José Curto considers these expeditions large-scale wars, but the number of captives usually reported clearly indicates that they were minor conflicts. There are many examples of these military operations and some of them show the size of these conflicts.

In 1736, the Portuguese launched a military expedition from Benguela against Kakonda in the central plateau of Angola. The records list 77 captives for the royal fifth, a tax equivalent to a fifth part of all goods produced in the Portuguese colonies, paid to the government's treasury. These records show that some 385 individuals were captured overall. In 1744, the Portuguese mounted another expedition against the Ndembu in the interior of Luanda, enslaving 62 females for the royal fifth. The total number of individuals captured must have numbered five times that or approximately 310 captives. In 1761, the Portuguese governor dispatched a small army from Luanda to fight the Hungu who, presumably, invaded Portuguese territory while escaping from a Lunda attack. António de Vasconcelos, Governor of Angola, estimated 15,000 dead or captured among the Hungu. The official figures, however, show that only 803 were allocated to the royal fifth, from a total of 4,015 individuals seized during this campaign. These examples were among the largest expeditions launched by the Portuguese during the eighteenth century but they include only the successful campaigns. Portuguese military expeditions were undermanned, lacked sufficient weapons, and were somewhat sporadic. Clearly, they were not the principal source of the 20,000 or so slaves shipped annually from Luanda and Benguela.

[15] Eltis, "The Volume and Structure of the Transatlantic Slave Trade," 34.
[16] Ferreira, "Transforming Atlantic Slaving," 189–206.
[17] Cândido, *Fronteras de Esclavización*, 162–63.

Nevertheless, based on these examples José Curto concludes, "warfare remained far from a trivial mechanism for the production of slaves."[18]

During the eighteenth and nineteenth centuries, prisoners taken in small-scale conflicts between the different African polities frequently became slaves. Because these conflicts took place in regions outside European influence, we have little information about their causes, how they unfolded, much less the number of prisoners. However, our current knowledge of military logistics in the area suggests these conflicts were seasonal, marked by intense fighting, rapid retreat, and typically involved only a few thousand combatants. John Thornton notes that the savannah was the land of infantry. He argues that horses were unable to survive the climate and, although its main rivers supported considerable boat traffic, the local population never developed a marine culture similar to other African regions, such as the West African coast or along the Niger River.[19] As a consequence, in West Central Africa, military leaders typically employed fleet-footed soldiers to resolve disputes.

Armies usually comprised a combination of conscript and professional warriors. The chain of command varied according to the level of centralization within each society, but a soldier's loyalty to his commander was generally beyond question.[20] Battles occurred mainly during the dry seasons, when men and women were free from farming and armies could move more easily in the interior. The savannah was sparsely populated, making the distribution of food supplies problematic. Mobilized armies had to report with rations. They often took food with them in large baggage trains packed by their wives, who were the principal agricultural workers in most societies of the savannah. These baggage trains were positioned in the middle of marching formations, when armies were on the move, and carefully stationed at a secure place during battles.[21] Given the limited food supplies, and the mobilization of significant productive sectors of the population, these small-scale campaigns usually involved fierce battles in wars that could last up to three years.[22] As previously mentioned, the variations in the climate and agricultural calendar of the region resulted in a seasonal variation in the number of slaves embarked.[23]

---

[18] Curto, "Experiences," 391–92.
[19] John K. Thornton, "The Art of War in Angola, 1575–1680." *Comparative Studies in Society and History* 30, no. 2 (1988): 367–68; Thornton, *Warfare*, 99.
[20] Thornton, "The Art of War," 362–63; Thornton, *Warfare*, 113.
[21] Thornton, "The Art of War," 369–71; Thornton, *Warfare*, 119–20.
[22] Thornton, "The Art of War," 368–69; Thornton, *Warfare*, 120–24.
[23] See Chapter 2.

The number of people captured in individual conflicts was probably small. However, given the frequency of such conflicts and their dispersal in the interior, they generated large numbers of captives for the trade. Prisoners of war were taken to the nearest markets in the interior, where traders from the coast came to purchase them. Sometimes these small-scale conflicts produced so many captives that they flooded inland markets, and African traders needed to take them directly to the ports of embarkation for sale. In 1791, Manoel de Almeida e Vasconcelos, Governor of Angola, noted that Kongo slave traders brought 120 slaves from the interior in one shipment for sale at Ambriz.[24] These unfortunates were probably prisoners of the civil wars at the old Kingdom of Kongo. They were sufficient to fill about half the average carrying capacity of a vessel loading slaves at Ambriz.

Although wars were a common method of enslavement, records of specific individuals enslaved through wars or raids are surprisingly rare. There are in fact only three such records. The earliest refers to the involuntary servitude of Angela who, according to John Thornton and Linda Heywood, was captured during the wars Portugal waged against the Kingdom of Ndongo or in a civil war in the old Kingdom of Kongo. They found that she sailed in the same vessel as the "20 and odd Negroes" who disembarked in Virginia in 1619, from the *São João Batista*. This vessel had left Luanda with some 350 slaves on board. A Dutch privateer, operating in conjunction with an English vessel, intercepted the *São João* off the coast of present-day Venezuela. The Dutch privateer seized slaves from the *São João* and transferred some of them, including Angela, to the English vessel, the *Treasurer*. The Dutch privateer then sailed ahead and delivered the "20 and odd Negroes" to Virginia, while Angela arrived at the same destination four days later in the *Treasurer*. Interestingly, Angela made two more trips in this ship. She went to Bermuda, finally returning to Virginia where she spent the rest of her life working as a servant on the estate of Captain William Pierce at Jamestown.[25]

---

[24] Manoel de Almeida e Vasconcelos to Paulo Martins Pinheiro de Lacerda, 29 January 1791, AHU, CU, Angola, cod. 1627, 79–81.

[25] Heywood and Thornton, *Central Africans, Atlantic Creoles, and the Foundation of the Americas*, 1–9. See also Engel Sluiter, "New Light on the '20. and Odd Negroes' Arriving in Virginia, August 1619." *William and Mary Quarterly*, 3, 54, no. 2 (1997): 397; Thornton, "The African Experience of the '20. and Odd Negroes' Arriving in Virginia in 1619," 421–34.

The second record of particular prisoners of war is in the list of 77 captives representing the royal fifth of the military expedition that the Portuguese launched from Benguela against the Kingdom of Kakonda in 1736. This list includes the names of the individuals allocated to the royal fifth and the estimated value of each person in *réis*.[26] This information was organized into three categories by age and sex; "Negroes," "girls," and "women and children." Of the 77 individuals, 14 were males, including two boys, one of whom was listed separately from his mother; 18 were girls; and 32 were women, including nine with one child each. Finally, a further small group was made up of one young child, two girls, and a male captive of unspecified age. The total value of these slaves at Benguela amounted to 901,000 *réis*.[27] As José Curto noted, excluding the nine children listed with their mothers and the last group, who were dying and consequently deemed worthless, the average value of the remaining 64 was only 14,708 *réis*, less than half the average price of a prime slave sold at Luanda or Benguela.[28] These individuals arrived in Benguela two years after being captured, but their subsequent fate remains unknown.

Koelle's *Polyglotta Africana* provides the third record of individual Africans who forfeited their freedom through wars or raids in West Central Africa. Two of his informants said that neighboring populations kidnapped them in their hometowns. Further, at the time of their enslavement, both were old enough to bear arms and serve in the armies of their countries. Dsíku, for example, also known as Isaac Manners, was a Kikongo speaker from Nsundi, a former province of the Kingdom of Kongo located on the lower Congo River. He said he was born in the town of Kaimatúba, where the Yombe, who lived across the river, kidnapped

---

[26] Isabel Castro Henriques believes that the names available in this document do not belong to the individuals listed but to their African rulers. She claims that the abbreviations "Mle. pelo da terr" and "Ma. pelo da terra" means *moleque* or *moleca proveniente da terra*, that is, boy or girl from the land. However, the preposition "pelo" used in both terms implies that the names belonged to the individuals listed, as in the expression *moleque* or *moleca pelo nome da terra*, that is, how they were called in their lands, because the Portuguese commonly changed the African names of the individuals that they captured for Christian names in Portuguese form. See Isabel Castro Henriques, "A Organização Afro-Portuguesa do Tráfico de Escravos (Séculos XVII-XIX)." In *A Rota dos Escravos: Angola e a Rede do Comércio Negreiro*, ed. João Medina and Isabel Castro Henriques (Lisbon: Cegia, 1996), 164, note 1.

[27] *Avaliação das Cabeças que Chegaram de Benguela em ... Abril de 1738*, enclosed in João Jacques de Magalhães, 29 April 1738, AHU, CU, Angola, box 30 doc. 90. This document is reproduced in Miller, *Way of Death*, xii-xiii; Henriques, "A Organização," 162–64.

[28] Curto, "Experiences," 392–93.

him when he was 23.[29] Dsíku was probably captured in a raid that the Yombe launched from across the Congo River. Nkóngal, or James Mafoi, was a Ruund speaker from the Lunda Empire. According to Koelle, the "Kásas" kidnapped him at his hometown when he was the same age as Dsíku. These "Kásas" were most likely the Kasanje, who lived across the Kwango River and often engaged in military conflicts with the Lunda.[30] Nkóngal may also have been captured in a raid or war, rather than being simply abducted from his hometown by an alien people.

ABDUCTION AND TRICKERY

Although most kidnappings occurred during raids and wars, many Africans were enslaved through abductions, trickery, or simply because of greed. Two of Koelle's informants seem to have been taken from their hometowns. Kadióngo, or John Morrison, a Kimbundu speaker from Kisama, said he had been kidnapped in his hometown when he was 16. He was sold at Luanda and remained there for about five years before being sold into the Atlantic market.[31] Muséwo, or Toki Petro, a Kimbundu speaker from Songo, related that he had been kidnapped when he was 15 and sold in Luanda, where he lived for approximately 21 years working for a Portuguese trader named Henrique Consale or Gonçalves. This slave trader sometimes purchased slaves at Songo. Muséwo was able to maintain contact with his former home by working as a translator. He assimilated much of the Portuguese culture, for his alternate name was a corruption of the Portuguese António Pedro. Although Muséwo claimed he was kidnapped, there is probably more to his story. He may have upset his people in some way, because at his master's death he was freed, yet he did not return home, as one might have expected. Rather, he moved to Brazil, where another Portuguese trader employed him in the trade. Muséwo crossed the Atlantic seven times in six years as a free crewmember on a slaving vessel. On the eighth voyage, an antislave trade cruiser captured his ship and took him to Sierra Leone, where he lived for the next 28 years. Muséwo was about 70 when Koelle interviewed him.[32]

Young men were routinely abducted for sale into the trade. Commander Felisberto Caldeira Brant Pontes, on his voyage from Angola to Bahia on 17 April 1800, met an African sailor who told him a story similar to those of Koelle's informants. According to Brant Pontes, the sailor Domingos was born in a village called Quissuca Quialaceta near the source

[29] Koelle, *Polyglotta Africana*, 15.   [30] Ibid.   [31] Ibid.   [32] Ibid.

of the Zambeze River. Local countrymen kidnapped him when he was about 15. They took him to Massango Nangumbe, from where he traveled to the lands of Quirimbo Quiandua, near the port of Novo Redondo. He was then shipped to Benguela. Domingos reported that his journey in the interior lasted three lunar months and that he was sold to a brother of the captain who commanded the ship in which Brant Pontes was traveling to Bahia. Although the evidence is not clear, Domingos seems to have been working as a sailor on a vessel belonging to this captain's family. On one of his trips to Brazil, he met his former kidnapper working in the port of Rio de Janeiro. This individual claimed that Domingos' father had captured him along with five of his companions after discovering that he was to blame for his son's plight. Domingos' response was that his father's actions were legal, because he had acted with the chief's permission. Two of the five captives remained enslaved in the interior, while Domingos' abductor and three others were taken to Mbailundu, in the central plateau of Angola, where a trafficker from Benguela purchased them and shipped them to Rio de Janeiro.[33] Domingos was about 39 when he told his story to Brant Pontes, and still working as a sailor.

Trickery was often used to enslave the unsuspecting. Nbena, an Umbundu speaker from Ndombe, enjoyed high status in her community as a freeborn owner of both goods and slaves. She was related, moreover, to male leaders within her community and connected through them to males of other Ndombe communities around Benguela.[34] Early one morning in May or June 1817, Nbena and her daughter set out on a journey to Benguela. On the way, they met an old slave woman who worked on the nearby estate of her owner, Lieutenant Colonel António Leal do Sacramento, a black man of means in Benguela. This woman convinced Nbena to interrupt her trip and follow her to Sacramento's house. Once there, she introduced Nbena to Sacramento's wife saying that, as she was too old and tired to work, she had found her master a much younger replacement.[35] Nbena and her daughter were coerced into working without compensation on the estate.

---

[33] Brant Pontes, "Memória." A copy of this document is also available in Felisberto Caldeira Brant Pontes, "Memoria de Brant Pontes sobre a Comunicação da Costa Oriental com a Ocidental de Africa." *Arquivos de Angola* 1, 1, no. 1 (1933): doc. 18. See also Curto, "Experiences," 402; Miller, *Way of Death*, 1–7.

[34] José C. Curto, "The Story of Nbena, 1817–20: Unlawful Enslavement and the Concept of 'Original Freedom' in Angola." In *Trans-Atlantic Dimensions of Ethnicity in the African Diaspora*, ed. Paul E. Lovejoy and David V. Trotman (New York: Continuum, 2003), 44.

[35] Ibid., 49; Curto, "Experiences," 409–10.

However, the two women escaped before their service began, returning to their village where they remained for the next five or six months. In November or December, they again traveled from their village to Benguela. The journey went smoothly but, when they reached their destination, Sacramento's men recognized the "runaways" and promptly recaptured them and took them to him. He branded Nbena and sold her, along with her daughter, for 70,000 *réis* to João de Oliveira Dias, captain of the *Astréa*, a vessel about to depart for Luanda. News of this sale quickly reached Nbena's village, where her relatives mobilized and headed for Benguela. A large crowd surrounded the port's military headquarters, among them five or six Ndombe *sobas*, one of them an uncle of Nbena. These men claimed that Nbena had been illegally enslaved and demanded her back, but she had already left for Luanda.[36]

The situation of Nbena and her daughter raised serious concerns because it overstepped established boundaries as to who could be forced to forfeit their free status and who could not. In a place like Benguela, where the economy depended largely on the slave trade, this apparent disregard for the rights of free individuals caused great unrest. Such cases shook the foundations of many societies in West Central Africa, including the Portuguese colonies, which had a class system based on status – a lower class of slaves, a serving class of commoners, and, at the apex of the social pyramid, the nobility. Alarmed by the crowd, the Governor of Benguela, Manoel de Abreu de Melo e Alvim, decided to try the case in court. He summoned the plaintiffs, including Nbena's family, the Ndombe *sobas*, and a number of other witnesses, who were unanimous in their opinion. Nbena was born free and lived as a free woman until she was enslaved at Sacramento's estate. Sacramento, on the other hand, claimed that Nbena was a slave who had escaped from his estate after being brought there by an old slave woman as her replacement. In response to such a delicate situation, the governor decided in favor of Nbena and ordered Sacramento to return her to Benguela.[37]

Fortunately, Nbena and her daughter were still in Luanda when the governor decided the issue. They were returned to Benguela but not to their village because Sacramento had petitioned for the case to be reopened. The two women were then placed in the custody of a local merchant, Manuel Pereira Gonçalves. Sacramento requested the help of the Governor of Angola at Luanda, Luiz da Mota Feo e Torres, and initiated

[36] Curto, "The Story of Nbena," 49–50; Curto, "Experiences," 410–11.
[37] Curto, "The Story of Nbena," 50; Curto, "Experiences," 411–12.

a judicial challenge against Melo e Alvim that lasted for three years, during which time Nbena and her daughter remained in Benguela. As the authorities could not reach an agreement, Melo e Alvim decided unilaterally to free Nbena and her daughter. Sacramento again pressed the authorities to have the two women returned to him, on the grounds that their successful flight from slavery would set a bad example for the slaves living on his estate. The term of service for both governors then ended and their successors showed little interest in supporting Sacramento, who unwillingly dropped the case.[38] Nbena and her daughter returned home to enjoy freedom surrounded by their family, friends and, ironically, their own slaves.

These two women remained free thanks to their political connections, and local authorities learned a valuable lesson from the incident. Those who lacked insider status or were subject to a quick sale were not so fortunate, such as the case of Catherine Mulgrave Zimmermann. As an eight-year-old, she was captured and put on board the *Heroína*, a slave ship that left for Cuba in 1833 with 303 slaves but was shipwrecked off the Jamaican coast.[39] Catherine survived and grew up as a free woman in Jamaica, and married twice. Johannes Zimmermann, her second husband, says in his letters that Catherine's African name was Gewe and that she was descended from a family of chiefs on her father's side. He claimed that she belonged to a prominent family of mulattos on her mother's side. However, the location of Catherine's hometown remains unclear. Zimmermann mentions that she remembered it as a major seaport where several Europeans lived. Luanda fits this description but since she also referred to snow-covered mountaintops, Cape Town is another possible location. Catherine recalled being on the way to school with her friends when a group of sailors offered them candies, and enticed them onto the *Heroína*, which subsequently set sail across the Atlantic. No political connections were able to intervene but, with the shipwreck of the *Heroína*, Catherine escaped what would otherwise have been a life of harsh work on one of the many sugar plantations of Cuba. She never returned to her hometown, but traveled to Africa with her second husband to work as a teacher and missionary in Ghana.[40]

---

[38] Curto, "The Story of Nbena," 51–59; Curto, "Experiences," 412–13.
[39] Eltis et al., "Voyages," voyage id 41890.
[40] Daniel B. Domingues da Silva, "Catherine Zimmermann-Mulgrave: A Slave Odyssey." In *Voyages: The Transatlantic Slave Trade Database*, ed. David Eltis et al. (Atlanta: Emory University, 2008), www.slavevoyages.org.

Walter Hawthorne, in his recent study on the trade between Brazil and Upper Guinea, argues that Africans enslaved other Africans from necessity. The Balanta, he argues, participated in the trade from Upper Guinea because they needed iron to make tools for use in rice production and weapons. Rice was an important component of the Balanta diet, and Upper Guinea was a region with just as many conflicts as West Central Africa. The Balanta could obtain iron only by participating in the trade. They imported iron bars from Europeans who, until the mid-nineteenth century, were interested in only one commodity from Upper Guinea. These factors clearly support Hawthorne's thesis, which is further bolstered by the social structures of the Balanta.[41]

Hawthorne argues that the Balanta were a decentralized society that valued ideologies of egalitarianism.[42] However, in West Central Africa, as in Upper Guinea, decentralized societies were not the only suppliers of slaves. Moreover, decentralized societies were not immune to greed, which no doubt tempted many Africans. The King of Kongo, Dom Afonso I, was only too aware of the problem as can be seen from his letters. In the sixteenth century, the Kingdom of Kongo was a centralized society but, in spite of his powers, the king was unable to curtail the avarice of some of his subjects, who continued their illegal activities. In 1526, Dom Afonso I wrote to the Portuguese king saying that "every day the [Portuguese] merchants carry away our people, sons of our soil and sons of our nobles and vassals, and our relatives, whom thieves and people of bad conscience kidnap and sell to obtain the coveted things and trade goods of the [Portuguese] Kingdom."[43] A few months later, he wrote again about "thieves and people of bad conscience." The king claimed that they were "*nossos naturaes*," that is, "our people who kidnapped and secreted them [e.g. slaves] away at night for sale to white men."[44]

---

[41] Hawthorne, *From Africa to Brazil*, 64–80.

[42] Walter Hawthorne, "Nourishing a Stateless Society during the Slave Trade: The Rise of Balanta Paddy-Rice Production in Guinea-Bissau." *Journal of African History* 42, no. 1 (2001): 1–3; Hawthorne, *From Africa to Brazil*, 64 and 77–79.

[43] Dom Afonso I to Dom João III, 6 July 1526, in António Brásio, ed., *Monumenta Missionária Africana*, 1 (Lisbon: Agência Geral do Ultramar, 1952), 470–71. As quoted in and translated by Curto, "Experiences," 389.

[44] Dom Afonso I to Dom João III, 18 October 1526, in Brásio, *Monumenta*, 489–90. As quoted in and translated by Curto, "Experiences," 389. See also John K. Thornton, "African Political Ethics and the Slave Trade." In *Abolitionism and Imperialism in Britain, Africa, and the Atlantic*, ed. Derek R. Peterson (Athens: Ohio University Press, 2010), 39–47.

The sixteenth-century Kingdom of Kongo, a centralized society, had laws prohibiting the enslavement and sale of free subjects and vassals. However, by the nineteenth century the kingdom was no longer the same. The new kings had little power over their subjects.[45] In this environment, it was easier to capture and sell fellow Africans. The King of Kongo, Dom Garcia V, annually dispatched an ambassador with three slaves for sale at Luanda to cover the expenses of the education of his son and nephew. They were studying Latin at Luanda's seminary in order to become priests. The sum available to Prince Pedro and his cousin seems to have been sufficient, but in 1812 the prince decided to supplement it by selling his father's ambassador into the slave trade, along with the usual three slaves.[46] Alarmed by this transaction, the Governor of Angola, João de Oliveira Barbosa, sent Prince Pedro and his cousin back to Kongo. Then he set out to search for the ambassador in Brazil. This was a difficult task, since official figures show that, in 1812, 10,704 slaves were shipped from Luanda to five different regions in Brazil; Rio de Janeiro, Bahia, Pernambuco, Maranhão, and Pará.[47] This search was extremely important because the ambassador's sale challenged the accepted norms of eligibility for enslavement. After all, as an envoy from Dom Garcia V, the ambassador was a nobleman who belonged to the Kongo diplomatic corps. Portuguese authorities eventually succeeded in locating the ambassador in Brazil. They made amends by returning him to Luanda from where he travelled back to Kongo. There he could enjoy life again as a free man, ironically in the company of his kidnappers.[48] As in societies throughout the world, greed does not recognize ideology or political organization. It thrived in centralized as well as decentralized societies.

The motives for kidnapping someone and selling him or her into the infamous trade were not always clear. The last two interviewees in Koelle's inventory did not state clearly how they were captured or by whom. They only mentioned that they were kidnapped and sold on the coast. Tut or Charles Wilhelm, a Teke speaker from Tsaye, related that at

---

45 Susan Herlin Broadhead, "Trade and Politics on the Congo Coast, 1770–1870" (Ph.D., Boston University, 1971), 17–18 and 26–31; Broadhead, "Beyond Decline: The Kingdom of Kongo in the Eighteenth and Nineteenth Centuries," 619–20; Vos, "The Kingdom of Kongo," 33–36.
46 Jadin, "Rapport," 167.
47 Curto, "A Quantitative Reassessment," 17 and 24; Joseph C. Miller, "The Political Economy of the Angolan Slave Trade in the Eighteenth Century." *Indian Historical Review* 15 (September 1988): 179; Miller, "The Numbers," 1989, 396–97; Miller, "The Numbers," 1998, 92–93.
48 Curto, "Experiences," 403–04; Jadin, "Rapport," 167.

20 he was kidnapped and hurried to the sea. Tut had lived in Sierra Leone for 17 years by the time Koelle interviewed him. He lived in Lomley, near Freetown, with his wife, who had also come from the same land.[49] Ngónga or John Wilhelm, a Kimbundu speaker from Kasanje, said that he was abducted at 28. He spent two years in the hands of the Portuguese before being sold into the trade, but did not mention who had originally enslaved him. Ngónga was about 43 when Koelle contacted him, and he knew some five other countrymen living in Sierra Leone, but left no further details about his life.[50]

JUDICIAL PROCEEDINGS

Judicial proceedings also generated captives. As previously noted, in many African societies slavery was an integral part of prescribed punishments, even for full members of these societies. It is not surprising to find victims of the slave trade who were originally enslaved as criminals sentenced to banishment or perpetual exile.[51] This fate could occur for several reasons. The available records list misconduct, adultery, debt, and witchcraft as warranting involuntary servitude in the Americas.

Koelle's linguistic inventory provides three examples of individuals sentenced to exile because of misconduct or adultery. Mútomp, or William Francis, a Kanyok speaker from the Katanga plateau, in present-day Democratic Republic of the Congo, said that he grew up at Mámunyikáyint, a day's journey from the Lualaba River, and had one child who could not yet walk when he was "sold on account of bad conduct." He did not elaborate on the nature of his misconduct, but said that he was sold to Mbundu dealers, who took him to Kasanje, where he was resold to Portuguese traders. Mútomp spent two years and a month enslaved in Angola before he was transported to the Americas. He had been in Sierra Leone for 12 years when Koelle interviewed him.[52]

Okiri, or Andrew Park, from Mbeti in present-day Congo Brazzaville, said that he was enslaved at Akuara, when he was about 16, because his mother took him with her after fleeing from his father.[53] It is significant that Okiri suffered the consequences of his mother's flight from the matrimonial home. West Central African societies were generally matrilineal, so inheritance and the distribution of wealth normally followed

---

[49] Koelle, *Polyglotta Africana*, 14.   [50] Ibid.
[51] Ferreira, *Cross-Cultural Exchange*, 66–67.   [52] Koelle, *Polyglotta Africana*, 14.
[53] Ibid.

maternal lines of descent.[54] Moreover, women were the primary agricultural producers in this region.[55] Okiri was neither his father's heir nor an important addition to the household so his father used the justice system to exact revenge. Family dynamics in West Central Africa have changed overtime, but they could clearly have contributed to the enslavement process that fed captives to the plantations and mines of the Americas.

Bunsála, or Thomas Pratt, from Obamba in present-day Gabon, said that he had been married four years when he was enslaved for adultery. The nature of his punishment is significant for our understanding of the role of gender in the process. Although Bunsála did not say whether the person with whom he committed adultery received the same punishment, it is clear that he paid a steep price for violating accepted marital conventions in matrilineal societies. This example is all the more revealing in view of the incidence of polygyny in West Central Africa. Bunsála journeyed five months to the coast, where he was taken to a slave vessel. He had been living in Sierra Leone for 15 years, with some ten other countrymen, when Koelle interviewed him.[56]

In addition to adultery, failure to repay debt could result in slavery and banishment. Dsíngo, or James Job, another of Koelle's interviewees, was sold into the trade for this reason. He was taken from his hometown, Gílibe or Boõõ, near the Congo River when his eldest son was ten.[57] This penalty for debt was so common that even in the Portuguese colonies freeborns could suffer such consequences. According to Portuguese law, enslavement for debt was illegal but there is archival evidence that it in fact happened. José Curto tells the story of a soldier in the Portuguese regiment named José Manuel, who was in danger of losing his freedom because of some merchandise he had borrowed to repay debts he had incurred in the interior. The man who had lent him the items was no other than

---

[54] Anne Hilton, "Family and Kinship among the Kongo South of the Zaire River from the Sixteenth to the Nineteenth Centuries." *Journal of African History* 24, no. 2 (1983): 190; Wyatt MacGaffey, "Lineage Structure, Marriage and the Family amongst the Central Bantu." *Journal of African History* 24, no. 2 (1983): 208; A. Richards, "Some Types of Family Structure amongst the Central Bantu." In *African Systems of Kinship and Marriage*, ed. A. R. Radcliffe-Brown and Cyril Daryll Forde (London: Oxford University Press, 1964), 208. For a different point of view, see Kajsa Ekholm, "External Exchange and the Transformation of Central African Social System." In *The Evolution of Social Systems*, ed. Jonathan Friedman and Michael J. Rowlands (Pittsburgh: University of Pittsburgh Press, 1978), 115–18.

[55] Hilton, "Family and Kinship," 193; MacGaffey, "Lineage," 173–77.

[56] Koelle, *Polyglotta Africana*, 14.   [57] Ibid.

Lieutenant Colonel António Leal do Sacramento, the individual who had tried to sell Nbena and her daughter.

In 1816, José Manuel set out from Benguela to purchase slaves in the central plateau of Angola. Such activity was common among militiamen, who supplemented their income by engaging in the slave trade, the principal export activity of Benguela. However, Manuel's trip did not go well. Somewhere in the interior, he was first robbed of his merchandise and then, for unknown reasons, arrested and subjected to a fine of 46 *panos*, or small pieces of cloth, each valued between 18,000 and 20,000 *réis* in Benguela. Alone and imprisoned in the interior, he had no one to turn to, but a *soba* offered to pay his fine if he agreed to repay him the 46 *panos*. José Manuel promptly accepted the terms of the offer so that he could return home immediately.[58]

Once there, José Manuel tried to repay the *soba* as soon as possible. As someone who depended on the trade to supplement his income, he knew that he had to maintain good relations with African authorities in the interior. He contacted his superior, António Leal do Sacramento, and asked for a loan of 46 *panos* to cover his debts with the *soba*. As Curto noted, Sacramento was a rich man who owned a number of properties in the region as well as a vast retinue of slaves. He at first hesitated to help his subordinate, but reconsidered the request in view of the unusual terms Manuel offered. José Manuel proposed offering Sacramento his personal services for the time it took to repay the debt. According to Curto, Sacramento found this proposal particularly interesting because the value of the debt was not specified. He closed the deal with Manuel, gave him the 46 *panos*, one coat of arms, and one bottle of sugar rum, which Manuel in turn forwarded to the *soba* who released him from his obligation. Free of one debt, Manuel had incurred a worse one. He had become the personal servant and dependent of António Leal do Sacramento.[59]

He continued in this role for almost three years, performing all kinds of chores for his superior. He even carried him in a palanquin, a task usually reserved for slaves. In 1818, José Manuel discovered that Sacramento considered his services fell short of the original value of the goods loaned and consequently was thinking of selling him. Alarmed by this, José

[58] José C. Curto, "Struggling against Enslavement: The Case of José Manuel in Benguela, 1816–20." *Canadian Journal of African Studies* 39, no. 1 (2005): 101–02; Curto, "Experiences," 405–06.

[59] Curto, "Struggling," 102–04; Curto, "Experiences," 406–07.

Manuel mobilized his family and contacted the Governor of Benguela, Melo e Alvim. They argued that José Manuel, in spite of having chosen to become a servant, was a free man and therefore ineligible for slave status with all the inevitable consequences. Curto claims that José Manuel and his family petitioned for the privilege of "original freedom," a right granted to Africans by the Portuguese Crown early on in the trade, which protected those unlawfully enslaved. Melo e Alvim decided to oppose the sale and gave José Manuel and his family more time to arrange the goods necessary to settle his debt.[60]

José Manuel and his family began to assemble the required items to give to Sacramento, who thereupon refused reimbursement of the original debt, demanding instead a *peça da Índia*, a prime adult slave valued at about 90,000 *réis* at that time in Benguela. José Manuel and his family found yet another official in the regiment who, willing to help, gave them a young female slave valued at 64,000 *réis*. Governor Melo e Alvim ordered Sacramento to accept this payment to resolve the issue. Sacramento took the young woman and sold her, but still refused to release Manuel. The governor, unaware the new owner had paid 70,000 *réis* for the woman, ordered her to be returned to Manuel's family, who eventually persuaded Sacramento to take her in exchange for their kinsman.[61] However, Sacramento, not a man to give up easily, petitioned the Governor of Angola, Feo e Torres, to intervene in his favor, initiating a judicial battle between the two governors, as in the case of Nbena. This battle had a similar outcome with one exception. José Manuel remained free but his advocate, Melo e Alvim, was arrested for insubordination and transported to answer for his actions before His Majesty.[62]

The use of human pawns to secure goods against the delivery of slaves provided yet another potential route to transatlantic slave markets. African slave traders usually borrowed merchandise from Europeans to purchase slaves in the interior because of the general scarcity of credit on the coast. In order to secure these loans, they pledged human pawns that they redeemed after exchanging the merchandise advanced for slaves in the interior. These pawns could be slaves, but many were free people with family ties to the debtor. When Africans were unable to redeem their pawns, Europeans kept them for their own trading purposes. Paul

[60] Curto, "Struggling," 104–05; Curto, "Experiences," 407.
[61] Curto, "Struggling," 106–07; Curto, "Experiences," 408–09.
[62] Curto, "Struggling," 107–12; Curto, "Experiences," 409.

Lovejoy and David Richardson argue that pawning was present mostly in West Africa, especially at Old Calabar.[63] However, records of Africans enslaved in the interior of West Central Africa show that the practice was common there too.

In 1793, Luiz António de Oliveira Mendes presented his memoirs of the trade to Brazil to the Scientific Academy of Lisbon. He lived in Bahia while writing the manuscript, which was for the most part based on testimonies collected from people who had lived in Portuguese Angola during the eighteenth century. One of these individuals was Raimundo Jalama, who had worked at Luanda between 1760 and 1770 as an agent of the well-known Companhia Geral de Comércio do Grão Pará e Maranhão and its sister Companhia Geral de Comércio de Pernambuco e Paraíba. Jalama told Mendes several stories about the Angolan trade, one of which concerned two unredeemed pawns who were sold at Luanda, a mother and her daughter, the latter identified by historians as Lucrécia.[64] According to Mendes, Jalama only discovered the women's misfortune after he had bought them. Lucrécia's mother was suffering from what the Portuguese at that time called *banzo*, a psychological condition associated with depression. Jalama initially thought that she missed home and he tried to help by giving her familiar food, but without effect. He then investigated Lucretia's mother's situation further and discovered that her husband had pledged both his wife and daughter for a debt that he had incurred in the interior. When the husband defaulted on the debt, both were forfeited.[65]

The suffering that followed enslavement as a result of debts could be devastating, and the examples in the records attract attention precisely because they are extreme. The case of Nanga, mentioned in the Introduction, is but one example.[66] In transactions involving pawns, the terms were usually implicit in the negotiations between creditors and debtors. The former advanced merchandise needed to buy slaves; the latter used relatives as guarantees. The practice was part of the moral economy based on traditional rights or customs supported by the

---

[63] Lovejoy and Richardson, "Trust," 335–36; Lovejoy and Richardson, "The Business," 67–69.

[64] Curto, "Experiences," 401.   [65] Mendes, *Memória*, 61–62.

[66] Philip Curtin and Jan Vansina believe that Nanga belonged to the Lwena ethnic group, but Koelle's remarks clearly indicate that he was a Libolo, neighbors of the Kisama. The Libolo lived a week's journey from the Kwanza River and two weeks from Luanda. The Lwena lived much farther from Luanda, near the central plateau of Angola. See Curtin and Vansina, "Sources," 204; Koelle, *Polyglotta Africana*, 15.

consensus of the community.[67] As long as both parties abided by the agreement, everyone would benefit but failure to do so could trigger disaster. The revolt of Burra Bene, an African chief who lived at Cape Lopez, in present-day Gabon, provides additional insights into pawning and its potential consequences.

In 1810, Luís Joaquim Lisboa, Governor of the islands of São Tomé and Príncipe, located in the Bight of Biafra, reported to the Portuguese Crown that António José Corrêa, Captain of the brigantine *Boa Sorte* from Pernambuco, had arrived at São Tomé with pawns entrusted to him by Burra Bene. This event caused great concern among the island's traders, because those pledged were free people directly related to the chief of nearby Cape Lopez. Two were women, one of whom was the chief's spouse. According to Lisboa, the captain broke a "very ancient custom" between slave traders from Gabon and São Tomé, because he did not return the pawns after loading his vessel with slaves and leaving the coast of Gabon.[68] The island's traders were very familiar with the institution of pawnship in this region. They frequently visited Gabon to purchase slaves. Customs records from São Tomé and Príncipe indicate that between 1799 and 1811 about 55 percent of the vessels arriving with slaves came from the coast of Gabon.[69] Corrêa was clearly not cognizant of the customs governing the slave trade in this region, but the island traders understood only too well what was at stake as a result of his violation.

António José Corrêa's seizure of Burra Bene's pawns threatened a commercial system based on trust. Because of the scarcity of credit available to purchase slaves, Africans needed to be sure that their pawns would be released when they had met their commitments. Corrêa apparently did not appreciate that important point, so the island's traders petitioned the governor to order him to return Burra Bene's pawns. Corrêa initially resisted the petition but later a judicial order filed with the Crown forced him to comply. Corrêa tried to return the individuals, but it was too late to repair the damage. Governor Lisboa reported that three days after the arrival of the *Boa Sorte*, Burra Bene retaliated for the loss of his pawns by capturing and destroying the vessels of traders from

[67] Edward Palmer Thompson, *Customs in Common* (New York: The New Press, 1991), 187–89.

[68] Daniel B. Domingues da Silva, "O Tráfico de São Tomé e Príncipe, 1799–1811: Para o Estudo de Rotas Negreiras Subsidiárias ao Comércio Transatlântico de Escravos." *Estudos de História, Franca* 9 (2002): 47.

[69] Ibid., 39–41.

São Tomé and Príncipe on the coast of Gabon.[70] Pawning was an important bargaining tool subject to customary laws governing commercial relations, including the norms that determined who could be enslaved and taken to the Americas.

Finally, accusations of witchcraft could also result in enslavement. In contrast to the perceptions of some, Africans across the hinterlands of Luanda, Benguela, and Cabinda deplored witchcraft as alien to their religion. Religion played a central role in African societies in that it was one of the principal means of justifying political power, establishing norms of moral conduct, and making sense of the world in which they lived. African authorities thus usually regarded witchcraft as warranting judicial proceedings, and individuals found guilty of practicing it could be sentenced to death or have their sentence commuted to slavery. Walter Hawthorne notes that many slaves sold on the coast of Upper Guinea in the eighteenth and nineteenth centuries were Africans convicted of practicing witchcraft. He states that the African populations living in that region considered witchcraft one of the most serious of all transgressions.[71] It was no different in West Central Africa. Two of Koelle's informants from this region claimed that they had been enslaved because members of their families were accused of practicing witchcraft. Kúmbu, or Thomas Parker, a Kikongo speaker from the Yombe region, situated north of the Congo River, said that he was enslaved because his sister was accused of practicing witchcraft. He did not give his age at enslavement, but he was already a married man and the father of a five-year-old child.[72] Perhaps because men sold for more than women, it was Kúmbu that was sold into the trade, an indication that his family paid dearly for his sister's offense. The case of Bémbi, or William Davis, provides a further example. Bémbi was an Umbundu speaker from Pangéla, a place Koelle insists is different from Benguela. He grew up in Wodsimbúmba, a day's journey from the sea. According to Koelle, Bémbi was enslaved because his family was accused of using witchcraft to kill the king of his hometown.[73] Apparently, he was not directly involved in the king's murder, but his family may have decided to let him pay for their crimes, since he would fetch a high price on the coast. Bémbi was about 28 when he was enslaved.[74] A charge of witchcraft could endanger entire families.

Judicial procedures also allowed members of a society to enslave their own countrymen. This route to enslavement contrasted widely with that

---

[70] Ibid., 48.   [71] Hawthorne, *From Africa to Brazil*, 81.
[72] Koelle, *Polyglotta Africana*, 14–15.   [73] Ibid., 15.   [74] Ibid.

resulting from wars or raids, because it was aimed at accepted members of society rather than outsiders. Resulting from internal affairs, decisions were made and sanctioned by the community. The demand for slaves on the coast may have increased the range of offenses punishable by enslavement and sale. How this process occurred is still not entirely clear. Linda Heywood offers some clues, pointing out that from the sixteenth century Kongo elites tried to manipulate the kingdom's laws in order to increase the number of criminals sentenced to exile. Elites behaved this way, she argues, because slaves had become the principal exchange currency in the region. Kongo rulers tried to control such abuse by creating offices with specific responsibility for determining the status of slaves sold on the coast.[75] The Portuguese had similar bureaucratic positions at Luanda and Benguela. The Governor of Angola, Miguel António de Melo, reported that such offices still existed in Luanda at the turn of the eighteenth century.[76] As demand for slaves increased, it would not be surprising that African elites felt particularly tempted to manipulate the laws governing the sale of criminals, debtors, and others on the coast of West Central Africa.

CONCLUSION

The experiences of Africans embarked from West Central Africa in the nineteenth century show that, as Robin Law has demonstrated for West Africa, African societies had specific norms governing who was eligible for sale into the trade.[77] Enslaved Africans were usually people situated at the bottom of the social hierarchy of most societies in the region's interior. They included prisoners of war, as well as civilians captured in armed conflicts. Although large-scale wars yielded significant numbers of slaves, most Africans captured in warfare came from small-scale conflicts. Enslaved Africans shipped from the region in the nineteenth century also included victims of abductions, trickery, and greed. These forms of enslavement were primarily aimed at outsiders but, though illegal, they extended to insiders. As we have seen, insiders could be

---

[75] Heywood, "Slavery," 9–12.
[76] António Miguel de Mello, "Angola no Fim do Século XVIII – Documentos." *Boletim da Sociedade de Geografia de Lisboa* 6, no. 5 (1886): 287–88. Roquinaldo Ferreira was able to access some records of such offices and institutions, like the *tribunal de mucanos*. See Ferreira, *Cross-Cultural Exchange*, 99–100.
[77] Law, "Legal and Illegal Enslavement," 514.

legally enslaved through judicial proceedings that ended in their banishment or perpetual exile via the slave trade. These crimes included, but were not limited to, unpaid debts, adultery, and witchcraft. In the nineteenth century, Africans were enslaved through several means; some legal, some not. The fact that both outsiders and, perhaps to a lesser extent, insiders were eligible for enslavement and sale helps explain the longevity of the slave trade.

Conclusion

The origins of slaves leaving West Central Africa in the nineteenth century provide us with an opportunity to understand whom Africans regarded as eligible for enslavement and sale across the Atlantic. The data also highlight the impact of the slave trade on the region. Older claims that the majority of the slaves were prisoners of wars waged by rulers seeking foreign merchandise that cemented alliances, sustained armies, and increased their power are called into question here. This process, the argument goes, had a devastating impact on the region, with rulers seeking captives in places increasingly farther from the coast. As Joseph Miller writes, "the entire series of local transformations, viewed over three centuries of the Angolan slave trade resembled a moving frontier zone of slaving violence."[1] In the nineteenth century, with British efforts to suppress the trade in the North Atlantic, West Central Africa emerged as the principal source of captives for the Americas. The majority were brought to work on the plantations of Cuba and Brazil. Historians believe the number of slaves embarked in this period increased significantly, leading Africans to search for captives in regions more distant from the coast. This book has argued, however, that lists of liberated Africans from Cuba and Brazil, in addition to slave registers made by Portuguese colonial officials in Angola, show that most slaves did not come from lands in the distant interior. It also provides new estimates of the volume of slave departures that show the numbers carried off remained relatively stable from the late eighteenth through to the mid-nineteenth century.

[1] Miller, *Way of Death*, 141.

Despite the British efforts to suppress the traffic, traders continued to purchase slaves in regions situated north of the Equator, such as the Bights of Benin and Biafra. Moreover, though Portuguese, Brazilian, and Spanish traders increased their activities along the coast of West Central Africa, they were able to do so because British, American, and Dutch traders had retreated from the business early in the nineteenth century, allowing the former to buy slaves in ports previously dominated by the latter. Additionally, traders began to search for other sources of slaves in the South Atlantic, such as Mozambique, in Southeast Africa. These other sources of slaves helped ensure that the numbers of those leaving West Central Africa remained stable over time, contradicting the view of historians who believe that the expansion of Portuguese, Brazilian, and Spanish activity increased the volume of the trade and perhaps the incidence of warfare in the region's interior.

Slaves were transported to the Americas through a complex network of merchants, brokers, and traders. These individuals might specialize in a specific function or segment of the trade, but they frequently took on several roles. Brokers could become merchants and finance their own slaving expeditions after they accumulated sufficient resources. This triage was flexible, but operated within environmental conditions that helped shape the trade. The gyres of the South Atlantic, for instance, contributed significantly to the development of a bilateral slaving system, with voyages beginning in the Americas as opposed to Europe. The rainy seasons in West Central Africa also influenced the trade by helping Africans determine the best seasons of the year to plant, harvest, conduct long distance trade, and wage wars.

Although these environmental conditions helped shape the trade, merchants, brokers, and traders had plenty of opportunities for individual agency. Until 1830, during the period of the legal trade, they carried slaves from traditional ports of embarkation and relied on official facilities and administration available on both sides of the Atlantic. However, after 1830, during the illegal period, they had to develop ways to bypass antislave trade cruisers in order to continue shipping slaves. Traders went to great lengths to counterfeit papers and use flags from different countries, including the United States, in order to avoid inspection or capture. They also had to find new ports to load slaves, some of which were located in remote places, where captives were maintained in barracoons. Despite these difficulties, the network of merchants, brokers, and traders continued to function into the second half of the nineteenth century.

Slaves came from approximately 21 linguistic groups and 116 ethnicities spread throughout the interior of West Central Africa. The majority came from regions relatively close to the coast, especially from the Kikongo, Kimbundu, and Umbundu linguistic groups. None of these were invaded much less conquered by the Lunda Empire in this period and the origins of those embarked give little indication of a slaving frontier moving deeper into the interior. Rather, slaves came mostly from within their own linguistic groups and were a mix of criminals condemned to banishment, kidnap victims, and prisoners of wars between neighboring societies. These forms of enslavement did not depend on the will of rulers or their thirst for power, and they probably involved far less violence than large-scale wars between different linguistic groups.

The origins of slaves also show that the demographic impact of the trade on the populations living in the interior was unevenly distributed and that Africans coped with it in different ways. As we have seen, the trade had a profound effect on the Ndongo, Kimbundu speakers who lived in the hinterland of Luanda. By the mid-nineteenth century, the Ndongo population had declined substantially as a result of years of slave trading, and had far fewer males than females. In contrast, Umbundu speakers, who lived in the central plateau of Angola, had a very different experience. Although they served as a major source of slaves, the trade's impact on the Umbundu populations was less severe, since just a small percentage of the total Umbundu population was forced into the Atlantic.

Africans were not only victims of the slave trade but also perpetrators of it. In fact, the transatlantic trade depended largely on African traders and enslavers, who captured the majority of the slaves in the interior and sold them on the coast. However, the use of the term "African" in this context is something of a misnomer given that Africans did not regard each other as Africans. They identified more with their ethnicity, polity, ruler, or religion than with the fact that they lived in the same continent. As Nathan Huggins posited many years ago, Africans who participated actively in the trade "saw themselves as selling people other than their own."[2]

Africans participated in the trade based on criteria as to who could be enslaved and who could not. Gender and age played an important role in this determination. Africans were often reluctant to sell adult women into the trade. Even when prices of female slaves in the Americas

[2] Huggins, *Black Odyssey*, 20.

increased, such as on the eve of the Brazilian abolition in 1830, Africans continued selling more males than females. They considered women too important in their own societies to sell them on the coast in the same numbers as men. In addition to their reproductive function, women were regarded as the primary food producers in many West Central African societies. Further, most societies in the region were matrilineal and practiced polygyny, so free men often married slave women in order to avoid bequeathing their inheritance to the lineage of their wives. This stress on the importance of women in society shaped the demographic profile of the slaves leaving West Central Africa.

Africans enslaved one another more for economic than political gains. Some historians believe that the number of slaves shipped from Africa bore no relationship to fluctuations in price, since most captives shipped were prisoners of wars taken in political conflicts between African rulers. However, prices of slaves sold from Luanda, the principal port of embarkation in the region, show that Africans responded positively to the demand for captives in the Americas. The more prices increased in Luanda, the greater the number of slaves embarked. This relationship between prices and slaves dispatched clearly indicates that the trade did not depend exclusively on the thirst for power of African rulers. Many Africans participated in the trade in order to obtain foreign commodities imported from Europe, Asia, and the Americas.

The principal commodities used to purchase slaves were textiles, alcohol, and weapons; none of which supplied the primary needs of the populations living in the interior. They were mostly consumer goods, which added variety to what was produced locally but did not displace local products. Africans continued making their own cloth and alcohol as well as fighting with their traditional weapons until late in the nineteenth century. Foreign imports brought to West Central Africa during the slave trade era were not among the principal causes of the later underdevelopment of the region. Additionally, these goods were introduced in such large quantities that they lost their luxury status.

Stories of those who were sold into the trade confirm that it was not just warfare that generated slaves. Although raids and wars generated large numbers of captives, Africans had many other ways of enslaving other Africans, such as legal proceedings, pawning, trickery, or simply kidnapping. It was not only outsiders who became victims. Africans also enslaved and sold people from their own linguistic and ethnic groups into the trade, a fact frequently overlooked in the history of Atlantic slavery. This practice indicates that Africans were familiar with the concept of slavery as an institution for political, social, and economic exploitation and that this institution did not exclude insiders from being enslaved and sold across the Atlantic.

Finally, the origins of slaves leaving West Central Africa cannot be traced on a map as a frontier of violence moving continuously eastward. The range of interests, peoples, and forms of enslavement involved in the trade were so diverse that it is impossible to represent the origins as a single wave moving from the coast to the interior. Causes of enslavement and sources of slaves were clearly multiple and must have overlapped but, more important, they depended ultimately on the values, customs, and beliefs of the populations engaged in the trade. Thus, a close study of the origins of the slaves leaving West Central Africa in the nineteenth century offers new insights into whom Africans regarded as eligible for enslavement and sale across the Atlantic as well as the impact of the transatlantic trade on this vast region.

Appendix A – Slave Origins Data

The origins of slaves leaving Angola in the nineteenth century were traced using two sets of documents. The first were the lists of liberated Africans compiled by the mixed commission courts of Havana and Rio de Janeiro; the second, the slave registers of Luanda, Benguela, and Novo Redondo. The original data for the lists of liberated Africans from Cuba are available in the "African Origins" portal.[1] The data for those disembarked in Brazil as well as for the slaves registered in Angola are available in the dissertation that preceded this book, which also contains additional notes on both sets of documents.[2] Table A.1 summarizes the estimates described in Chapter 3. Readers who wish to generate their own estimates, or who would like to provide a different interpretation about the ethnonyms selected, are advised to use the raw data available in the materials mentioned above.

TABLE A.1 *Estimated number of slaves leaving West Central Africa by linguistic and ethnic groups, 1831–1855*

Linguistic groups	Ethnic groups	Estimated number of slaves
Bangi	Kanga	262
Bangi	Ngele	262
Cokwe	Cokwe	397

(continued)

[1] Eltis and Misevich, "African Origins."
[2] Daniel B. Domingues da Silva, "Crossroads: Slave Frontiers of Angola, c.1780–1867" (Ph. D., Emory University, 2011).

TABLE A.1 *(continued)*

Linguistic groups	Ethnic groups	Estimated number of slaves
Herero	Himba	392
Kimbundu	Bondo	1,818
Kimbundu	Holo	349
Kimbundu	Hungo	1,609
Kimbundu	Kadi	492
Kimbundu	Kalandula	12,660
Kimbundu	Kasamba	262
Kimbundu	Kasanje	49,156
Kimbundu	Kipala	4,807
Kimbundu	Kisama	37,070
Kimbundu	Libolo	54,059
Kimbundu	Lunga	87
Kimbundu	Mbundu	1,062
Kimbundu	Ndembu	1,726
Kimbundu	Ndongo	126,213
Kimbundu	Njinga	38,759
Kimbundu	Ntemo	4,848
Kimbundu	Pende	262
Kimbundu	Shinje	606
Kimbundu	Songo	6,890
Kikongo	Dange	6,288
Kikongo	Kakongo	948
Kikongo	Kongo	4,709
Kikongo	Lemba	1,312
Kikongo	Madimba	262
Kikongo	Mbamba	2,290
Kikongo	Mbembe	3,102
Kikongo	Mpangu	262
Kikongo	Ngoyo	318
Kikongo	Nlaza	525
Kikongo	Nsonso	4,222
Kikongo	Nsundi	46,103
Kikongo	Okango	787
Kikongo	Pumbu	318
Kikongo	Solongo	787
Kikongo	Suku	1,399
Kikongo	Yaka	6,037
Kikongo	Zombo	436
Kota	Okota	611
Kunyi	Kunyi	5,774
Lumbu	Lumbu	2,010

(continued)

TABLE A.I *(continued)*

Linguistic groups	Ethnic groups	Estimated number of slaves
Ndonga	Ndundo	56
Ndonga	Nkusu	517
Ndonga	Nyengo	260
Ngangela	Kangala	56
Ngangela	Luio	336
Ngangela	Luvale	2,862
Ngangela	Mbande	112
Ngangela	Mbunda	168
Ngangela	Mbwela	560
Ngangela	Ndungo	168
Ngangela	Ngangela	12,200
Ngangela	Nyemba	280
Njebi	Nzabi	6,299
Nkhumbi	Nkhumbi	11,880
Nyaneka	Kilenge	4,878
Nyaneka	Kipungu	224
Nyaneka	Kwankua	56
Nyaneka	Lenda	56
Nyaneka	Ngambo	336
Nyaneka	Wila	168
Ovambo	Dombondola	56
Ovambo	Kwanyama	224
Ovambo	Ovambo	56
Ruund	Lunda	19,501
Ruund	Ndemba	56
Teke	Mbe	433
Teke	Monjolo	16,195
Teke	Teke	56
Teke	Tio	25,157
Teke	Tsintsege	525
Totela	Totela	262
Umbundu	Donde	341
Umbundu	Ekekete	56
Umbundu	Fende	56
Umbundu	Hanya	4,257
Umbundu	Kaala	224
Umbundu	Kakonda	6,653
Umbundu	Kalukembe	504
Umbundu	Kenge	743
Umbundu	Kikuma	543
Umbundu	Kingolo	2,408

(continued)

TABLE A.1 *(continued)*

Linguistic groups	Ethnic groups	Estimated number of slaves
Umbundu	Kipeyo	2,912
Umbundu	Kisanji	672
Umbundu	Kitata	280
Umbundu	Kivanda	4,145
Umbundu	Kivula	2,184
Umbundu	Kiyaka	5,183
Umbundu	Lemba	962
Umbundu	Lumbo	56
Umbundu	Mbailundu	14,522
Umbundu	Mbongo	448
Umbundu	Mbui	19,379
Umbundu	Moma	784
Umbundu	Namba	56
Umbundu	Nano	5,153
Umbundu	Nbova	173
Umbundu	Ndombe	5,573
Umbundu	Ndulu	1,161
Umbundu	Ngalangi	9,552
Umbundu	Nganda	1,176
Umbundu	Ovimbundu	784
Umbundu	Sambu	5,688
Umbundu	Sanga	713
Umbundu	Sele	6,696
Umbundu	Soke	56
Umbundu	Sumbe	896
Umbundu	Tunda	5,545
Umbundu	Viye	33,050
Umbundu	Wambu	10,952
Vili	Loango	41,262
Yansi	Muyanji	2,100
Yombe	Yombe	32,769
Total		767,215

Source: See text.

Appendix B – Slave Prices Data

Information on prices of slaves leaving West Central Africa in the nineteenth century is extremely rare. The prices used here were originally collected from reports of commodities imported and exported from Luanda, the principal port of slave embarkation on the coast of West Central Africa. Colonial officials began to issue these reports in the late eighteenth century, following administrative reform in the Portuguese Empire.[1] They dispatched these reports annually to Lisbon and, during the French occupation of Portugal, to Rio de Janeiro. Unfortunately, only a few of these reports survive to the present-day.[2] They give the quantity, price, and total value of all merchandise, including slaves, imported and exported from Luanda.

Colonial officials reported the price of slaves in terms of annual averages calculated on the number of adult slaves embarked. Although they were generally purchased with imported commodities, colonial officials communicated the cost of slaves embarked in *réis* (sing. *real*), the Portuguese currency in Angola. Table B.1 shows the prices of slaves leaving Luanda as they appear in the reports available between the eighteenth and nineteenth centuries. Because the value of the *real* changed significantly with inflation, these prices were deflated using an index built with prices of 35 domestic and foreign articles traded in

[1] Curto and Gervais, "The Population History of Luanda," 4–12; Curto and Gervais, "A Dinâmica Demográfica de Luanda," 86–90.
[2] Florentino, *Em Costas Negras*, 160; Joseph C. Miller, "Slave Prices in the Portuguese Southern Atlantic, 1600–1830." In *Africans in Bondage: Studies in Slavery and the Slave Trade*, ed. Paul E. Lovejoy (Madison: University of Wisconsin, 1986), 67. References to surviving reports are listed in the sources of Table C.1.

TABLE B.1 *Prices of slaves leaving Luanda as reported by colonial officials, 1780–1830*

Years	Prices in *réis*	Years	Prices in *réis*
1780	53,000	1813	75,000
1790	59,000	1815	70,000
1802	67,940	1816	68,000
1803	69,550	1817	75,000
1804	72,500	1818	75,000
1805	75,000	1819	75,000
1808	67,000	1820	75,000
1809	72,000	1823	60,000
1810	70,000	1824	65,000
1811	70,000	1825	70,000
1812	69,000	1830	150,000

Sources: 1808, 1811 and 1820: Manolo Florentino, *Em Costas Negras*, 160. 1780, 1790, and 1830: Joseph C. Miller, "Slave Prices in the Portuguese Southern Atlantic," 67. 1802–1805, 1809–1810, 1812–1819, 1823–1825: AHU, CU, Angola, box 106 doc. 5; box 109 doc. 54, box 112 doc. 47; box 115 doc. 14; box 121 doc. 6; box 121A doc. 35; box 127 doc. 1; box 128 doc. 26; box 131 doc. 11; box 132 doc. 26; box 133 doc. 3; box 134 doc. 24; box 138 doc. 56; box 144 doc. 92; and box 159 doc. 13.

TABLE B.2 *Prices of slaves leaving Luanda deflated by decades, 1780–1830*

Years	Nominal prices in *réis*	Silbering indices	Reindex to 1780s	Real prices in *réis*
1780s	53,000	102.6	100.0	53,000
1790s	59,000	128.4	125.1	73,836
1800s	70,570	160.5	156.4	110,395
1810s	72,444	155.8	151.9	110,008
1820s	65,000	105.6	102.9	66,901
1830s	150,000	102.0	99.4	149,123

Sources: Table B.1 and Norman J. Silbering, "British Prices and Busyness Cycles," 232–33.

pounds in Britain between 1779 and 1850.[3] Table B.2 shows these prices deflated by decade between 1780 and 1830.

[3] Norman J. Silbering, "British Prices and Business Cycles, 1779–1850." *Review of Economics and Statistics* 5 (1923): 232–33.

Appendix C – Exchange Commodities Data

The following tables were built with data originally compiled from the customs records of Luanda. They show the value of the commodities imported through that port in thousands of *réis*. It should be noted that customs officials did not record the current value of the merchandise brought there. Rather, the numbers available are estimates that members of the trading board calculated multiplying the amount of goods imported by their annual average price. As a consequence, they should not be regarded as accurate numbers but only as approximations. Nevertheless, they provide an important indication of the principal commodities used to purchase slaves in the interior of West Central Africa.

Tables C.1 and C.2 show the total value and percentage of the commodities imported by categories: alcohol, apparel and notions, Asian textiles, European textiles, foodstuff, metals and metalware, miscellany articles, and weapons. Tables C.3 to C.10 provide the value of the principal articles imported within each of these categories. All values are in thousands of *réis*. Figures for the periods 1785–94 and 1823–25 are provided in the sources in aggregates only as opposed to individual years. The records for 1830–31 provide just a summary of the main commodities imported. Arithmetic mistakes in the sources have been corrected. Missing totals were calculated multiplying the amount of the merchandise imported by the price for which it was sold. Missing prices were estimated with basis on the average price of the same good for the years immediately before and after with data available.

TABLE C.1 *Commodities imported at Luanda by categories (in thousands of réis), 1785–1864*

Years	Alcohol	Apparel and notions	Asian textiles	European textiles	Foodstuff	Metals and metalware	Miscellany	Weapons	Total
1785–94	1,055,507.1	157,265.7	1,358,806.9	1,306,617.5	348,361.2	57,299.2	382,504.6	202,870.8	4,869,232.9
1795	175,387.9	11,346.2	128,359.0	106,328.6	31,907.4	2,436.3	76,594.6	32,705.5	565,065.5
1796	177,919.0	17,923.2	62,682.2	72,176.3	26,910.1	1,103.8	44,687.6	14,330.5	417,732.6
1797	213,989.7	30,346.2	205,632.4	258,751.6	30,745.9	1,880.3	78,739.6	15,710.6	835,796.3
1798	73,268.9	16,644.3	97,777.9	116,912.2	18,182.0	7,663.6	23,194.1	2,019.5	355,662.6
1799	86,457.2	22,184.6	145,552.5	228,993.8	31,652.3	7,337.4	42,182.2	19,900.4	584,260.3
1802	192,831.6	63,943.2	248,630.9	311,232.9	85,015.8	18,326.6	54,503.9	25,827.9	1,000,312.7
1803	175,245.4	41,150.8	233,334.8	300,692.0	70,598.2	34,652.0	63,056.8	76,928.2	995,658.3
1804	206,170.8	59,875.6	179,411.1	277,714.9	96,144.3	32,331.0	67,410.1	62,309.9	981,367.6
1805	255,923.0	20,965.0	201,954.9	529,813.5	—	—	5,242.4	49,514.0	1,063,412.8
1809	165,992.0	11,070.8	121,745.5	207,033.6	33,654.7	24,494.7	18,499.0	6,500.9	588,991.3
1810	155,576.6	22,175.5	274,180.1	320,368.8	38,407.0	13,215.1	44,061.7	12,994.5	880,979.3
1811	130,909.8	38,731.6	215,276.2	332,129.5	38,981.4	17,601.1	39,983.4	58,130.4	871,743.4
1812	167,173.0	24,273.2	264,471.9	286,677.2	47,230.4	38,206.5	32,355.6	33,386.8	893,774.5
1813	195,513.2	10,654.7	329,560.8	300,801.4	33,412.6	11,727.1	26,998.6	691.4	909,359.8
1815	203,278.1	24,035.8	282,046.3	310,429.7	55,293.8	39,109.2	41,126.8	50,573.2	1,005,892.8
1816	172,374.0	33,164.0	244,383.0	465,285.7	55,872.4	52,622.7	41,114.7	66,369.4	1,131,185.9
1817	309,129.1	46,027.1	333,067.4	496,741.8	55,741.6	49,331.5	64,946.2	152,936.4	1,507,921.0
1818	294,498.7	45,046.9	481,934.7	360,776.8	58,539.3	28,357.7	48,937.9	232,717.6	1,550,809.6

1819	221,443.4	54,935.6	687,882.9	534,125.3	60,590.3	24,419.5	60,481.8	119,924.4	1,763,803.1
1820	221,722.4	53,408.9	604,457.5	636,879.8	61,003.3	23,906.4	61,428.7	75,979.4	1,738,786.1
1823–25	962,301.7	73,484.7	588,939.8	627,094.7	190,473.3	114,388.5	116,579.9	312,088.0	2,985,350.7
1830	154,238.2	-	-	84,910.0	44,311.7	-	14,241.8	9,520.0	307,221.8
1831	259,330.0	-	-	105,430.0	49,162.1	-	20,709.0	30,625.0	465,256.1
1832	136,159.6	-	-	132,010.0	36,390.0	-	10,667.7	34,545.0	349,772.3
1837	150,628.6	76,155.2	117,854.1	811,564.8	55,741.3	23,297.0	90,380.6	181,603.4	1,507,225.2
1857	309,428.3	45,078.1	411,774.0	619,968.7	203,620.1	24,335.7	376,624.5	63,268.4	2,054,097.7
1858	190,472.0	38,880.9	354,665.0	460,611.1	248,406.4	25,576.6	268,709.3	64,362.7	1,651,683.9
1859	348,396.3	46,663.8	316,514.6	390,909.1	197,262.9	32,393.9	245,138.0	79,510.9	1,656,789.5
1861	241,168.8	47,320.7	430,995.5	325,304.1	160,169.8	28,471.7	291,139.2	60,937.3	1,585,507.1
1862	206,877.8	20,125.7	219,217.7	184,033.1	98,276.6	22,364.4	182,237.2	8,279.1	941,411.6
1863	158,209.4	16,741.6	114,430.8	160,843.6	93,393.6	29,631.3	113,059.8	11,614.7	697,924.8
1864	104,645.3	14,080.0	116,149.9	127,435.9	80,983.4	17,221.2	110,505.9	15,501.3	586,522.8
All years	8,072,166.9	1,183,699.4	9,371,690.2	11,790,597.8	2,736,435.3	803,701.8	3,158,042.7	2,184,177.4	39,300,511.6

Sources:

1785–94	IHGB DL 794,28
1795–97	BNRJ, Seção de Manuscritos 15-3-33.
1798	AHU, CU, Angola, box 89 doc. 79
1799	AHU, CU, Angola, box 93A, doc. 48
1802	AHU, CU, Angola, box 106 doc. 5
1803	AHU, CU, Angola, box 109 doc. 54
1804	AHU, CU, Angola, box 112 doc. 47
1805	AHU, CU, Angola, box 115 doc. 14
1808	ANRJ, JC, box 448 bundle 1
1809	AHU, CU, Angola, box 121 doc. 6

1809	ANRJ, JC, box 448 bundle 1
1809	ANRJ, JC, box 449 bundle 1
1810	AHU, CU, Angola, box 121A doc. 35
1812	AHU, CU, Angola, box 127 doc. 1
1812	ANRJ, JC, box 449 bundle 1
1813	AHU, CU, Angola, box 128 doc. 26
1813	ANRJ, JC, box 449 bundle 1
1815	AHU, CU, Angola, box 131 doc. 11
1815	ANRJ, JC, box 449 bundle 1
1816	AHU, CU, Angola, box 132 doc. 26
1816	ANRJ, JC, box 449 bundle 1
1817	AHU, CU, Angola, box 133 doc. 3
1818	AHU, CU, Angola, box 134 doc. 24
1818	ANRJ, JC, box 449 bundle 1
1819	AHU, CU, Angola, box 138 doc. 56
1819	ANRJ, JC, box 449 bundle 1
1820	ANRJ, JC, box 449 bundle 1
1823–25	AHU, CU, Angola, box 159 doc. 13
1830–32	AHU, CU, Angola, box 176 doc. 11
1837	AHU, SEMU, Angola, box 593 folder 4
1857–59	*Boletim Oficial do Governo Geral da Província de Angola*, nos. 646, 706, and 762.
1861–64	AHU, SEMU, Angola, box 629, folder 28 and box 638 folder 37.

TABLE C.2 *Commodities imported at Luanda by categories (in row percentages), 1785–1864*

Years	Alcohol	Apparel and notions	Asian textiles	European textiles	Foodstuff	Metals and metalware	Miscellany	Weapons	Total
1785–94	21.7	3.2	27.9	26.8	7.2	1.2	7.9	4.2	100.0
1795	31.0	2.0	22.7	18.8	5.6	0.4	13.6	5.8	100.0
1796	42.6	4.3	15.0	17.3	6.4	0.3	10.7	3.4	100.0
1797	25.6	3.6	24.6	31.0	3.7	0.2	9.4	1.9	100.0
1798	20.6	4.7	27.5	32.9	5.1	2.2	6.5	0.6	100.0
1799	14.8	3.8	24.9	39.2	5.4	1.3	7.2	3.4	100.0
1802	19.3	6.4	24.9	31.1	8.5	1.8	5.4	2.6	100.0
1803	17.6	4.1	23.4	30.2	7.1	3.5	6.3	7.7	100.0
1804	21.0	6.1	18.3	28.3	9.8	3.3	6.9	6.3	100.0
1805	24.1	2.0	19.0	49.8	–	–	0.5	4.7	100.0
1809	28.2	1.9	20.7	35.2	5.7	4.2	3.1	1.1	100.0
1810	17.7	2.5	31.1	36.4	4.4	1.5	5.0	1.5	100.0
1811	15.0	4.4	24.7	38.1	4.5	2.0	4.6	6.7	100.0
1812	18.7	2.7	29.6	32.1	5.3	4.3	3.6	3.7	100.0
1813	21.5	1.2	36.2	33.1	3.7	1.3	3.0	0.1	100.0
1815	20.2	2.4	28.0	30.9	5.5	3.9	4.1	5.0	100.0
1816	15.2	2.9	21.6	41.1	4.9	4.7	3.6	5.9	100.0

1817	20.5	3.1	22.1	32.9	3.7	3.3	4.3	10.1	100.0
1818	19.0	2.9	31.1	23.3	3.8	1.8	3.2	15.0	100.0
1819	12.6	3.1	39.0	30.3	3.4	1.4	3.4	6.8	100.0
1820	12.8	3.1	34.8	36.6	3.5	1.4	3.5	4.4	100.0
1823–25	32.2	2.5	19.7	21.0	6.4	3.8	3.9	10.5	100.0
1830	50.2	–	–	27.6	14.4	–	4.6	3.1	100.0
1831	55.7	–	–	22.7	10.6	–	4.5	6.6	100.0
1832	38.9	–	–	37.7	10.4	–	3.0	9.9	100.0
1837	10.0	5.1	7.8	53.8	3.7	1.5	6.0	12.0	100.0
1857	15.1	2.2	20.0	30.2	9.9	1.2	18.3	3.1	100.0
1858	11.5	2.4	21.5	27.9	15.0	1.5	16.3	3.9	100.0
1859	21.0	2.8	19.1	23.6	11.9	2.0	14.8	4.8	100.0
1861	15.2	3.0	27.2	20.5	10.1	1.8	18.4	3.8	100.0
1862	22.0	2.1	23.3	19.5	10.4	2.4	19.4	0.9	100.0
1863	22.7	2.4	16.4	23.0	13.4	4.2	16.2	1.7	100.0
1864	17.8	2.4	19.8	21.7	13.8	2.9	18.8	2.6	100.0
All years	20.5	3.0	23.8	30.0	7.0	2.0	8.0	5.6	100.0

Sources: Same as Table C.1.

TABLE C.3 *Alcohol imported at Luanda (in thousands of réis), 1785–1864*

Years	Aguardente	Jeribita	Liquors	Wine	Other	Total
1785–94	70,949.5	683,621.0	10,605.0	289,746.0	585.6	1,055,507.1
1795	7,157.0	141,078.5	–	27,120.0	32.4	175,387.9
1796	5,425.8	131,012.0	324.0	41,060.0	97.2	177,919.0
1797	7,314.2	143,700.5	144.0	62,750.0	81.0	213,989.7
1798	901.4	56,311.5	541.9	15,490.2	24.0	73,268.9
1799	881.4	60,672.0	510.0	24,083.0	310.7	86,457.2
1802	77,580.0	50,150.0	1,536.8	63,452.6	112.2	192,831.6
1803	5,883.0	112,125.0	760.5	56,328.1	148.8	175,245.4
1804	8,906.8	134,880.0	784.8	60,999.2	600.0	206,170.8
1805	179,177.0	–	586.0	76,160.0	–	255,923.0
1809	155,737.2	–	465.6	9,769.2	20.0	165,992.0
1810	1,000.0	102,520.0	829.2	51,045.0	182.4	155,576.6
1811	1,995.0	82,875.0	906.2	44,445.2	688.4	130,909.8
1812	–	123,440.0	1,348.4	41,819.4	565.2	167,173.0
1813	–	154,594.0	952.0	39,838.2	129.0	195,513.2
1815	200.0	168,073.6	850.0	33,614.5	540.0	203,278.1
1816	1,310.0	115,240.0	1,134.0	54,280.0	410.0	172,374.0
1817	1,235.0	171,562.5	546.0	135,660.0	125.6	309,129.1

1818	600.0	199,083.5	200.0	94,352.0	263.2	294,498.7
1819	1,072.1	184,090.0	4,724.5	30,834.0	722.8	221,443.4
1820	1,072.1	184,090.0	4,903.5	30,834.0	822.8	221,722.4
1823–25	604,045.0	–	7,257.8	350,570.4	428.5	962,301.7
1830	135,697.2	–	–	18,541.0	–	154,238.2
1831	203,623.5	–	–	55,706.5	–	259,330.0
1832	120,792.3	–	–	15,367.3	–	136,159.6
1837	85,788.6	–	2,158.5	57,295.1	5,386.4	150,628.6
1857	226,507.3	–	5,058.5	75,089.5	2,773.0	309,428.3
1858	126,625.0	–	8,910.0	53,276.0	1,661.0	190,472.0
1859	235,419.2	–	6,168.5	102,146.6	4,662.0	348,396.3
1861	140,624.3	–	4,193.5	93,396.0	2,955.0	241,168.8
1862	156,911.5	–	5,979.4	40,028.7	3,958.2	206,877.8
1863	108,141.1	–	5,243.6	37,760.5	7,064.1	158,209.4
1864	60,150.8	–	3,105.8	36,917.7	4,471.0	104,645.3
All years	2,732,723.2	2,999,119.1	80,728.0	2,219,776.1	39,820.6	8,072,166.9

Sources: Same as Table C.1.

TABLE C.4 *Apparel and notions imported at Luanda (in thousands of réis), 1785–1864*

Years	Barrets	Clothing	Corals	Hats	Other	Total
1785–94	17,178.0	46,646.8	7,518.0	29,391.3	56,531.6	157,265.7
1795	1,272.0	1,101.8	5,247.0	2,769.0	956.4	11,346.2
1796	30.0	7,727.1	3,519.0	4,288.8	2,358.3	17,923.2
1797	903.0	11,252.8	2,664.0	7,023.6	8,502.8	30,346.2
1798	264.8	3,558.3	294.6	4,957.2	7,569.3	16,644.3
1799	113.7	4,557.4	1,637.0	5,268.8	10,607.8	22,184.6
1802	857.7	8,841.1	39,158.0	7,137.3	7,949.1	63,943.2
1803	1,049.1	16,354.2	8,640.0	7,182.0	7,925.6	41,150.8
1804	7,976.4	15,447.0	6,448.0	9,869.4	20,134.8	59,875.6
1805	1,186.5	7,877.5	–	11,533.4	367.6	20,965.0
1809	85.0	6,924.3	–	1,346.0	2,715.6	11,070.8
1810	750.4	6,388.5	1,782.0	4,535.2	8,719.4	22,175.5
1811	2,215.4	9,297.1	12,280.0	6,279.4	8,659.7	38,731.6
1812	1,305.6	6,313.4	736.0	6,842.6	9,075.6	24,273.2
1813	708.6	2,684.8	1,656.0	2,022.6	3,582.7	10,654.7
1815	1,824.0	5,232.8	1,152.0	6,207.0	9,620.0	24,035.8
1816	2,976.0	6,033.6	3,200.0	7,495.0	13,459.4	33,164.0
1817	5,520.0	4,932.0	3,968.0	6,494.0	25,113.1	46,027.1

1818	1,464.0	7,237.8	9,600.0	5,729.5	21,015.6	45,046.9
1819	1,563.9	17,950.7	8,178.0	19,196.0	8,047.0	54,935.6
1820	1,563.9	18,133.5	8,178.0	17,628.0	7,905.5	53,408.9
1823–25	8,688.0	35,521.4	12,082.0	8,737.0	8,456.4	73,484.7
1830	-	-	-	-	-	-
1831	-	-	-	-	-	-
1832	-	-	-	-	-	-
1837	5,604.0	22,582.2	5,499.2	37,242.5	5,227.3	76,155.2
1857	4,892.0	13,993.5	14,274.6	11,108.0	810.0	45,078.1
1858	2,862.0	11,631.9	13,038.0	11,349.0	-	38,880.9
1859	610.0	10,453.2	21,005.0	14,595.6	-	46,663.8
1861	3,716.6	19,942.6	12,100.0	10,885.0	676.5	47,320.7
1862	2,899.1	10,175.8	80.0	3,428.6	3,542.2	20,125.7
1863	678.7	10,191.3	22.5	996.0	4,853.1	16,741.6
1864	1,366.7	8,364.3	560.5	294.1	3,494.5	14,080.0
All years	82,125.0	357,348.6	204,517.4	271,831.8	267,876.5	1,183,699.4

Sources: Same as Table C.1.

TABLE C.5 *Asian textiles imported at Luanda (in thousands of réis), 1785–1864*

Years	Cadeás	Chitas	Coromandéis	Lenços	Zuartes	Other	Total
1785–94	274,915.6	151,602.4	223,429.5	130,560.6	357,997.0	220,301.8	1,358,806.9
1795	11,406.2	12,352.7	52,878.0	5,054.4	39,079.6	7,588.1	128,359.0
1796	5,545.6	14,845.7	10,808.0	2,962.4	18,821.6	9,698.9	62,682.2
1797	20,478.7	47,409.0	38,304.0	2,669.6	69,375.8	27,395.3	205,632.4
1798	12,475.5	12,490.7	17,165.0	5,610.0	29,999.0	20,037.7	97,777.9
1799	16,685.1	12,731.1	28,220.4	2,641.4	61,959.6	23,314.8	145,552.5
1802	39,874.3	22,415.4	39,721.0	28,276.4	65,165.7	53,178.2	248,630.9
1803	49,742.4	36,834.7	56,975.5	17,057.1	29,017.4	43,707.7	233,334.8
1804	36,990.0	27,440.8	27,200.0	12,968.0	33,992.0	40,820.3	179,411.1
1805	-	43,190.1	67,325.0	29,041.0	-	62,398.8	201,954.9
1809	-	12,245.4	26,585.0	13,478.4	40,665.0	28,771.7	121,745.5
1810	28,009.0	12,101.9	35,524.0	32,399.9	115,099.3	51,046.0	274,180.1
1811	31,705.0	8,250.3	35,524.5	3,158.1	103,071.9	33,566.5	215,276.2
1812	30,400.1	5,617.5	53,486.4	14,707.7	113,449.0	46,811.2	264,471.9
1813	39,186.6	6,557.3	116,883.0	11,871.8	93,902.0	61,160.1	329,560.8
1815	36,852.0	6,425.5	51,772.5	18,274.6	114,402.0	54,319.7	282,046.3
1816	47,115.0	9,317.0	76,500.0	24,400.0	28,135.0	58,916.0	244,383.0
1817	142,720.0	6,224.0	79,740.0	2,712.0	54,565.0	47,106.4	333,067.4

Year							
1818	177,084.8	2,724.0	228,904.0	5,804.0	20,850.0	46,567.9	481,934.7
1819	79,343.0	95,370.3	105,088.0	119,771.8	157,894.0	130,415.8	687,882.9
1820	79,343.0	95,370.3	105,088.0	344.4	193,626.0	130,685.8	604,457.5
1823–25	18,466.0	111,472.2	103,472.0	45,951.0	205,248.0	104,330.6	588,939.8
1830	-	-	-	-	-	-	-
1831	-	-	-	-	-	-	-
1832	-	-	-	-	-	-	-
1837		36,422.5			62,313.1	19,118.5	117,854.1
1857		254,892.0			95,826.0	61,056.0	411,774.0
1858		171,908.0			129,985.0	52,772.0	354,665.0
1859		184,478.0			76,761.6	55,275.0	316,514.6
1861		267,349.7			92,855.9	70,789.9	430,995.5
1862		149,318.1			35,231.5	34,668.1	219,217.7
1863		82,807.7			14,382.7	17,240.5	114,430.8
1864		74,770.5		361.0	17,641.5	23,376.9	116,149.9
All years	1,178,337.9	1,974,934.8	1,580,593.8	530,075.5	2,471,312.2	1,636,436.1	9,371,690.2

Sources: Same as Table C.1.

TABLE C.6 *European textiles imported at Luanda (in thousands of réis), 1785–1864*

Years	Baetás	Chilas	Fazendas	Lenços	Panos	Other	Total
1785–94	170,070.5	63,432.0	–	–	285,023.2	788,091.8	1,306,617.5
1795	–	9,072.0	–	9,879.0	32,073.2	55,304.4	106,328.6
1796	–	4,963.0	–	4,022.0	22,105.0	41,086.3	72,176.3
1797	–	16,114.0	–	100,393.0	34,224.0	108,020.6	258,751.6
1798	26,714.4	8,267.4	–	4,545.4	11,356.8	66,028.2	116,912.2
1799	26,283.7	14,110.2	–	4,868.6	58,376.5	125,354.8	228,993.8
1802	39,947.3	27,621.0	–	4,643.6	86,967.1	152,053.9	311,232.9
1803	37,039.0	28,944.0	–	7,074.4	53,050.1	174,584.6	300,692.0
1804	58,860.0	15,000.0	–	6,748.6	38,731.3	158,375.0	277,714.9
1805	38,768.1	50,340.0	–	1,965.0	63,077.2	375,663.2	529,813.5
1809	30,127.2	20,545.0	–	1,153.2	37,457.2	117,751.0	207,033.6
1810	33,574.5	43,844.0	–	14,571.5	62,719.1	165,659.7	320,368.8
1811	54,050.8	51,700.0	–	21,677.2	60,580.5	144,121.0	332,129.5
1812	28,895.7	69,672.0	–	12,596.8	78,743.3	96,769.4	286,677.2
1813	39,023.0	59,109.8	–	19,554.6	98,497.1	84,617.0	300,801.4
1815	33,605.3	68,812.5	–	12,700.0	107,981.8	87,330.1	310,429.7
1816	73,151.8	72,810.0	–	13,067.0	125,111.0	181,145.9	465,285.7
1817	14,294.4	74,610.0	–	27,368.8	228,094.0	152,374.6	496,741.8

1818	13,104.2	-	-	26,495.2	153,782.6	167,394.9	360,776.8
1819	65,507.1	154,400.0	-	19,497.5	131,845.1	162,875.7	534,125.3
1820	65,507.1	154,400.0	-	138,928.9	131,845.1	146,198.7	636,879.8
1823–25	32,149.0	99,828.0	21,405.6	46,658.0	48,411.4	378,642.7	627,094.7
1830	-	-	84,910.0	-	-	-	84,910.0
1831	-	-	105,430.0	-	-	-	105,430.0
1832	-	-	132,010.0	-	-	-	132,010.0
1837	31,408.4	-	575,641.1	67,380.8	73,068.0	64,066.5	811,564.8
1857	11,390.0	-	457,447.2	105,742.0	7,824.0	37,565.5	619,968.7
1858	36,741.0	-	333,340.8	61,905.8	10,185.0	18,438.5	460,611.1
1859	19,870.0	-	274,629.6	77,081.5	10,065.0	9,263.0	390,909.1
1861	14,100.0	-	213,765.6	85,963.1	3,560.0	7,915.4	325,304.1
1862	4,766.8	-	104,415.5	57,330.3	1,297.0	16,223.6	184,033.1
1863	3,707.4	-	112,165.1	33,680.0	2,294.0	8,997.1	160,843.6
1864	4,476.3	-	54,149.6	54,081.2	410.0	14,318.8	127,435.9
All years	1,007,132.7	1,107,594.9	2,469,310.1	1,041,573.0	2,058,755.3	4,106,231.8	11,790,597.8

Sources: Same as Table C.1.

TABLE C.7 Foodstuff imported at Luanda (in thousands of réis), 1785–1864

Years	Olive oil	Rice	Sugar	Vinegar	Wheat flour	Other	Total
1785–94	42,649.6	42,517.5	17,630.0	39,200.0	66,830.4	139,533.7	348,361.2
1795	8,416.0	3,435.0	7,891.2	1,520.0	4,200.0	6,445.2	31,907.4
1796	1,792.0	2,302.5	2,904.0	4,350.0	10,584.0	4,977.6	26,910.1
1797	5,600.0	3,487.5	4,488.0	3,880.0	10,180.8	3,109.6	30,745.9
1798	754.8	1,468.8	5,036.2	1,295.2	4,129.1	5,498.0	18,182.0
1799	5,112.0	4,557.6	5,357.8	1,218.0	3,407.0	11,999.9	31,652.3
1802	7,210.0	5,556.0	6,188.4	3,429.0	45,294.0	17,338.4	85,015.8
1803	6,265.0	4,624.0	8,773.5	2,108.5	24,572.4	24,254.8	70,598.2
1804	5,400.0	9,366.0	19,172.5	7,152.0	27,891.6	27,162.2	96,144.3
1805	–	–	–	–	–	–	–
1809	3,450.0	1,755.0	2,234.0	254.0	8,335.7	17,626.1	33,654.7
1810	2,420.0	3,318.0	5,859.7	470.0	7,902.0	18,437.3	38,407.0
1811	4,650.0	3,920.0	6,062.4	971.0	5,272.5	18,105.5	38,981.4
1812	2,750.0	5,400.0	7,906.2	114.0	10,587.5	20,472.7	47,230.4
1813	1,250.0	3,180.0	5,838.9	1,040.0	11,089.8	11,013.9	33,412.6
1815	3,200.0	4,320.0	13,991.6	264.0	13,875.0	19,643.2	55,293.8
1816	4,500.0	6,000.0	15,402.0	216.0	8,250.0	21,504.4	55,872.4
1817	1,150.0	7,440.0	20,344.0	1,830.0	1,750.0	23,227.6	55,741.6
1818	1,900.0	7,200.0	31,840.4	1,380.0	1,680.0	14,538.9	58,539.3
1819	4,588.5	3,060.0	10,639.2	3,400.0	12,754.0	26,148.7	60,590.3

1820	4,588.5	2,952.0	10,685.2	3,400.0	12,754.0	26,623.7	61,003.3
1823–25	17,337.0	15,344.0	20,237.0	2,040.0	45,800.0	89,715.3	190,473.3
1830	2,600.0	888.8	11,634.0	2,700.0	24,170.4	2,318.6	44,311.7
1831	5,500.0	530.6	15,624.0	7,950.0	16,394.4	3,163.1	49,162.1
1832	1,000.0	1,530.8	8,106.0	7,575.0	15,465.6	2,712.6	36,390.0
1837	3,079.6	3,389.3	10,889.9	8,213.6	6,498.0	23,671.0	55,741.3
1857	9,084.0	20,965.3	58,095.0	7,599.0	53,538.8	54,338.1	203,620.1
1858	8,540.0	30,772.0	65,570.3	21,127.0	48,561.5	73,835.6	248,406.4
1859	10,746.8	9,523.0	47,698.6	8,798.0	41,392.0	79,104.6	197,262.9
1861	4,416.3	7,463.9	24,031.0	10,001.7	27,843.3	86,413.5	160,169.8
1862	3,991.5	5,376.4	24,361.8	3,076.7	22,967.4	38,502.8	98,276.6
1863	3,978.2	5,286.1	16,072.1	2,447.2	18,424.3	47,185.8	93,393.6
1864	3,014.4	4,169.2	7,738.2	3,905.1	21,999.6	40,157.0	80,983.4
All years	190,934.1	231,099.2	518,302.8	162,925.1	634,395.0	998,779.2	2,736,435.3

Sources: Same as Table C.1.

TABLE C.8 *Metals and metalware imported at Luanda (in thousands of réis), 1785–1864*

Years	Cutlery	Ironware	Lead	Nails	Wire	Other	Total
1785–94	324.0	7,690.0	2,645.8	12,000.0	-	34,639.4	57,299.2
1795	97.9	2,080.0	112.0	-	-	146.4	2,436.3
1796	-	800.0	44.0	-	19.8	240.0	1,103.8
1797	276.5	1,200.0	46.0	-	0.0	357.8	1,880.3
1798	3,694.2	1,206.6	80.0	-	92.3	2,590.4	7,663.6
1799	657.3	247.9	302.0	354.0	1,201.3	4,574.9	7,337.4
1802	1,947.7	1,375.0	975.6	4,233.8	142.8	9,651.7	18,326.6
1803	1,066.4	2,795.0	505.5	15,789.4	105.8	14,389.9	34,652.0
1804	2,004.8	3,258.0	3,480.6	5,985.3	975.0	16,627.4	32,331.0
1805	-	-	-	-	-	-	-
1809	1,371.3	-	48.0	22,234.2	44.4	796.8	24,494.7
1810	2,324.0	220.0	267.0	1,977.3	314.5	8,112.2	13,215.1
1811	5,854.9	100.0	496.8	1,146.0	456.0	9,547.4	17,601.1
1812	5,431.5	129.0	399.3	27,548.0	34.0	4,664.8	38,206.5
1813	3,587.8	217.6	264.0	2,239.5	80.4	5,337.8	11,727.1
1815	8,728.4	236.0	455.0	25,524.0	70.0	4,095.8	39,109.2
1816	5,812.0	299.0	547.5	41,648.0	120.0	4,196.2	52,622.7
1817	9,830.2	176.0	1,164.0	30,360.0	300.0	7,501.3	49,331.5

1818	8,264.8	132.0	1,932.0	10,806.0	600.0	6,622.9	28,357.7
1819	6,775.4	–	514.8	1,520.0	7,315.8	8,293.5	24,419.5
1820	4,138.3	–	514.8	2,112.0	7,315.8	9,825.5	23,906.4
1823–25	17,146.2	–	22,562.4	42,803.7	28,434.0	3,442.2	114,388.5
1830	–	–	–	–	–	–	–
1831	–	–	–	–	–	–	–
1832	–	–	–	–	–	–	–
1837	100.0	8,954.5	667.8	–	12,212.5	1,362.2	23,297.0
1857	6,115.0	10,831.8	1,320.0	–	–	6,068.9	24,335.7
1858	13,410.0	8,080.6	352.0	–	–	3,734.0	25,576.6
1859	5,551.0	17,389.0	1,342.5	–	–	8,111.4	32,393.9
1861	3,513.5	9,910.0	2,566.1	140.1	35.2	12,306.8	28,471.7
1862	4,617.0	11,430.1	447.4	–	218.6	5,651.3	22,364.4
1863	3,760.9	11,683.2	746.4	2,097.0	639.6	10,704.2	29,631.3
1864	2,212.5	8,780.9	111.5	423.0	734.4	4,958.9	17,221.2
All years	128,613.6	109,222.1	44,910.7	250,941.3	61,462.1	208,551.9	803,701.8

Sources: Same as Table C.1.

TABLE C.9 *Miscellany articles imported at Luanda (in thousands of réis), 1785–1864*

Years	Beads	Chinaware	Cotton	Drugs	Furniture	Soap	Tobacco	Other	Total
1785–94	53,762.7	12,604.0	-	31,900.0	4,000.0	-	31,252.4	248,985.5	382,504.6
1795	2,800.0	2,580.0	-	393.6	21,960.0	48.0	4,775.6	44,037.4	76,594.6
1796	2,600.0	660.0	-	931.2	22,068.0	144.0	4,639.2	13,645.2	44,687.6
1797	18,100.0	615.0	-	1,978.8	24,660.0	144.0	6,696.8	26,545.0	78,739.6
1798	4,389.4	668.8	-	805.2	820.0	255.0	3,909.9	12,345.9	23,194.1
1799	6,131.4	1,476.0	-	2,104.5	787.8	383.8	6,563.5	24,735.1	42,182.2
1802	14,644.4	1,827.0	-	4,695.9	4,910.5	78.6	6,636.0	21,711.5	54,503.9
1803	25,465.2	3,660.0	-	3,625.3	2,476.0	251.9	11,735.2	15,843.2	63,056.8
1804	14,298.0	4,358.6	-	6,404.0	2,998.0	415.5	17,093.6	21,842.3	67,410.1
1805	180.0	-	-	-	-	-	3,734.0	1,508.4	5,242.4
1809	180.0	1,486.0	130.0	1,312.4	25.6	674.2	8,489.3	6,201.5	18,499.0
1810	12,989.2	2,732.5	865.4	2,580.3	276.8	8,578.8	5,383.6	10,655.1	44,061.7
1811	2,522.0	11,046.0	2,722.2	2,174.0	1,989.6	1,036.8	4,010.4	14,482.4	39,983.4
1812	2,466.0	2,522.8	1,474.0	2,543.0	576.8	3,246.0	6,285.9	13,241.1	32,355.6
1813	3.0	2,765.0	1,504.5	4,635.0	210.0	956.6	8,189.7	8,734.8	26,998.6
1815	1,782.0	2,566.0	125.0	1,686.4	3,405.5	2,328.0	14,661.4	14,572.5	41,126.8
1816	2,460.0	2,780.0	150.0	2,147.8	6,674.8	1,236.0	8,869.9	16,796.2	41,114.7
1817	3,306.0	4,411.0	250.0	2,648.1	9,625.4	2,432.0	14,010.4	28,263.3	64,946.2

1818	2,115.0	5,096.6	381.3	2,874.8	4,366.8	2,885.8	1,213.4	30,004.3	48,937.9
1819	18,661.0	5,610.0	72.2	11,162.0	297.6	2,834.5	961.8	20,882.7	60,481.8
1820	18,661.0	5,610.0	72.2	10,662.0	297.6	2,834.5	1,111.1	22,180.3	61,428.7
1823–25	2,323.2	4,410.0	2,106.0	4,530.9	624.4	3,239.6	31,211.0	68,134.8	116,579.9
1830	–	2,766.8	–	–	–	3,504.0	7,738.5	232.5	14,241.8
1831	–	3,115.8	–	–	–	6,096.0	11,023.5	473.7	20,709.0
1832	–	2,741.9	–	–	–	2,964.0	4,667.5	294.3	10,667.7
1837	6,358.3	12,689.4	7,070.0	4,566.2	2,263.5	1,322.6	9,341.4	46,769.2	90,380.6
1857	8,232.5	19,488.0	188,163.0	7,138.0	2,531.0	38,912.6	30,333.0	81,826.4	376,624.5
1858	25,506.8	21,302.0	153,868.0	13,872.0	2,859.0	3,011.7	17,498.5	30,791.3	268,709.3
1859	16,903.0	15,599.5	105,281.0	10,345.0	9,029.5	4,073.9	26,136.3	57,769.8	245,138.0
1861	7,687.0	10,248.3	152,982.8	8,555.5	9,347.0	33,411.5	9,418.9	59,488.1	291,139.2
1862	9,071.7	7,172.1	76,276.6	4,693.7	3,001.2	3,082.9	21,240.8	57,698.3	182,237.2
1863	8,347.4	9,022.2	30,118.6	2,065.2	1,867.8	4,958.3	12,256.9	44,423.5	113,059.8
1864	8,948.6	5,358.2	29,727.7	1,152.4	1,648.0	9,292.2	11,729.3	42,649.5	110,505.9
All years	300,714.6	188,989.4	753,340.4	154,183.2	145,598.2	144,633.1	362,818.8	1,107,765.0	3,158,042.7

Sources: Same as Table C.1.

TABLE C.10 Weapons imported at Luanda (in thousands of réis), 1785–1864

Years	Ammunition	Blade weapons	Firearms	Gunpowder	Total
1785–94	403.2	41,315.4	110,230.2	50,922.0	202,870.8
1795	-	16,848.0	5,952.5	9,905.0	32,705.5
1796	-	3,568.0	857.5	9,905.0	14,330.5
1797	19.2	1,112.4	4,639.0	9,940.0	15,710.6
1798	0.4	720.4	848.7	450.0	2,019.5
1799	7.5	10,106.6	9,538.8	247.5	19,900.4
1802	159.2	14,218.5	4,429.4	7,020.8	25,827.9
1803	8,576.0	8,657.2	31,391.0	28,304.0	76,928.2
1804	6,000.0	6,009.9	27,800.0	22,500.0	62,309.9
1805	-	-	7,464.0	42,050.0	49,514.0
1809	-	50.9	200.0	6,250.0	6,500.9
1810	129.9	834.0	274.0	11,756.6	12,994.5
1811	268.0	1,762.8	8,539.0	47,560.6	58,130.4
1812	27.0	1,320.8	639.0	31,400.0	33,386.8
1813	64.0	552.4	75.0	-	691.4
1815	60.0	1,607.2	606.0	48,300.0	50,573.2
1816	45.0	656.4	668.0	65,000.0	66,369.4
1817	18.0	878.4	1,540.0	150,500.0	152,936.4
1818	12.0	699.6	3,206.0	228,800.0	232,717.6
1819	156.0	6,833.6	11,374.8	101,560.0	119,924.4

Year					
1820	500.0	9,534.6	11,714.8	54,230.0	75,979.4
1823–25	34,180.0	3,452.0	30,096.0	244,360.0	312,088.0
1830	-	-	-	9,520.0	9,520.0
1831	-	-	-	30,625.0	30,625.0
1832	-	-	-	34,545.0	34,545.0
1837	230.6	16,039.5	86,941.0	78,392.4	181,603.4
1857	-	-	27,820.0	35,448.4	63,268.4
1858	-	2,600.0	21,295.0	40,467.7	64,362.7
1859	-	100.0	20,178.0	59,232.9	79,510.9
1861	-	1,490.0	30,902.7	28,544.6	60,937.3
1862	19.0	-	8,248.1	12.0	8,279.1
1863	8.0	-	3,212.6	8,394.1	11,614.7
1864	-	-	2,210.0	13,291.3	15,501.3
All years	50,883.0	150,968.6	472,891.0	1,509,434.8	2,184,177.4

Sources: Same as Table C.1.

Bibliography

A) ARCHIVAL SOURCES

A.1) Arquivo Histórico do Itamaraty, Rio de Janeiro, Brazil

Coleções Especiais, *Brilhante*, lata 4, maço 3, pasta 1.

A.2) Arquivo Histórico Nacional de Angola, Luanda, Angola

Registro de Escravos da Cidade de Luanda, cod. 2862.
Registro de Escravos de Benguela, cod. 3160.
Registro de Escravos de Luanda, box 135.
Registro de Escravos de Luanda, cod. 2845.
Registro de Escravos de Luanda, cod.3254.
Registro de Escravos de Luanda, cod. 3260.
Registro de Escravos de Novo Redondo, cod. 2830.
Registro de Escravos do Distrito de Luanda, cod. 2467.
Registro de Escravos do Distrito de Luanda, cod. 2482.
Registro de Escravos do Distrito de Luanda, cod. 2524.
Registro de Escravos do Distrito de Luanda, cod. 3186.

A.3) Arquivo Histórico Ultramarino, Lisbon, Portugal

Conselho Ultramarino, Angola
Box 30 doc. 90
Box 65 doc. 64
Box 66 doc. 68, 69, 70, 74
Box 68 doc. 29, 54
Box 69 doc. 34
Box 76 doc. 18, 102

Box 77 doc. 31
Box 78 doc. 57
Box 83 doc. 66
Box 85 doc. 28
Box 89 doc. 79
Box 93A doc. 48
Box 106 doc. 5
Box 109 doc. 54
Box 110 doc. 33
Box 112 doc. 47
Box 115 doc. 14, 45
Box 121 doc. 6, 32
Box 121A doc. 31, 32, 35, 36
Box 125 doc. 46
Box 127 doc. 1
Box 128 doc. 26
Box 129 doc. 63
Box 131 doc. 11, 45
Box 132 doc. 26
Box 133 doc. 3
Box 134 doc. 24
Box 138 doc. 56
Box 144 doc. 94
Box 147 doc. 34
Box 159 doc. 13
Box 176 doc. 11
Cod. 1627
Cod. 1634
Papéis de Sá da Bandeira, sala 12, maço 822
Secretaria de Estado da Marinha e Ultramar, Angola
Box 593 folder 4
Box 629 folder 28
Box 638 folder 37

A.4) Arquivo Nacional, Rio de Janeiro, Brazil

Junta do Comércio, box 448 bundle 1.
Junta do Comércio, box 449, bundle 1.
Registro das Cartas de Alforria, *Carolina*, cod. 184, vol. 3, ff. 90–96 v.
Registro das Cartas de Alforria, *Duquesa de Bragança*, cod. 471, ff. 1–9.
Registro das Cartas de Alforria, *Escuna Feliz*, cod. 184, vol. 3, ff. 72–81.
Registro das Cartas de Alforria, *Especulador*, cod. 184, vol. 4, ff. 1–5.
Registro das Cartas de Alforria, *Leal*, cod. 184, vol. 4, ff. 14–19.
Registro das Cartas de Alforria, *Órion*, cod. 184, vol. 3, ff. 43 v-51 v.
Registro das Cartas de Alforria, *Paquete de Benguela*, cod. 184, vol. 4, ff. 19 v-23 v.

Registro das Cartas de Alforria, *Rio da Prata*, cod. 471, ff. 9 v-16 v.

A.5) Arquivo Nacional Torre do Tombo, Lisbon, Portugal

Registo Geral de Mercês, Dona Maria I, Book 16.
Registo Geral de Mercês, Dona Maria I, Book 29.

A.6) Biblioteca Nacional, Rio de Janeiro, Brazil

Seção de Manuscritos 15–3-33.

A.7) British National Archives, Kew, England

Foreign Office Series 313, *Amalia*, vol. 61, ff. 71–91.
Foreign Office Series 313, *Aguila*, vol. 58, ff. 43–102.
Foreign Office Series 313, *Diligencia*, vol. 61, ff. 92–141.
Foreign Office Series 313, *Empresa*, vol. 61, ff. 190–230.
Foreign Office Series 313, *Joven Reyna*, vol. 60, ff. 84–110.
Foreign Office Series 313, *Marte*, vol. 60, ff. 134–137.
Foreign Office Series 313, *Matilde*, vol. 61, ff. 231–257.

A.8) Instituto Histórico e Geográfico Brasileiro, Rio de Janeiro, Brazil

"Relação das Fazendas, Gêneros, e mais Objectos de Importação que Entraram nesta Cidade de São Paulo da Assunção, desde o Ano de 1785, em que Teve Princípio o Estabelecimento da Alfândega até o Ano de 1794 ... " Luanda, 20 November 1797, João Álvares de Melo, DL 794,28.

A.9) Manuscripts, Archives and Rare Books Library, Emory University, U.S.A.

Logbook of the Yacht Wanderer, Wanderer (Ship) Records, Mss. 172.

B) PUBLISHED PRIMARY SOURCES

Abreu e Castro, Bernardino Freire de Figueiredo. "Colonia de Mossamedes." *Annaes do Conselho Ultramarino (Parte Não Oficial)* ser. 1 (1855): 151–55.
Angola. *Almanak Estatístico da Província d'Angola e suas Dependências para o Anno de 1851*. Luanda: Imprensa do Governo, 1852.
Antonil, André João. *Cultura e Opulência do Brasil*. Belo Horizonte: Itatiaia, 1982.

Athouguia, Visconde d' "Decreto de 14 de Dezembro de 1854." *Diário do Governo*. 28 December 1854, 305 edition, sec. Ministério dos Negócios da Marinha e Ultramar, Seção do Ultramar.

"Regulamento que Faz Parte do Decreto de 25 de Outubro de 1853, Publicado no Diário do Governo no. 268, de 14 de Novembro de 1853." *Diário do Governo*. 29 November 1853, 281 edition, sec. Ministério dos Negócios da Marinha e Ultramar, Seção do Ultramar.

Barreiros, Fortunato José. *Memória sobre os Pesos e Medidas de Portugal, Espanha, Inglaterra e França*. Lisbon: Typographia da Academia Real das Sciencias, 1838.

Bonavides, Paulo, and Roberto Amaral. *Textos Políticos da História do Brasil*. 3rd edn., 10 vols. Brasília: Senado Federal, 2002.

Brant Pontes, Felisberto Caldeira. "Memoria de Brant Pontes sobre a Comunicação da Costa Oriental com a Ocidental de Africa." *Arquivos de Angola*, 1, 1, no. 1 (1933): doc. 18.

"Memória de Brant Pontes sôbre a Comunicação das Duas Costas 9/9/1800." In *Apontamentos sobre a Colonização dos Planaltos e Litoral do Sul de Angola*, edited by Alfredo de Albuquerque Felner, 1:248–51. Lisbon: Agência Geral das Colónias, 1940.

Brásio, António, ed. *Monumenta Missionária Africana*. 15 vols. 1. Lisbon: Agência Geral do Ultramar, 1952.

Brazil. *Collecção das Leis do Império do Brazil de 1831: Actos do Poder Legislativo*. Rio de Janeiro: Typographia Nacional, 1875.

Cadornega, António de Oliveira de. *História Geral das Guerras Angolanas, 1680*, edited by José Matias Delgado. Lisbon: Agência Geral do Ultramar, 1972.

Capello, Hermenegildo, and Roberto Ivens. *De Benguella às Terras de Iácca: Descripção de uma Viagem na Africa Central e Occidental*. Lisbon: Imprensa Nacional, 1881.

"Catálogo dos Governadores do Reino de Angola." *Arquivos de Angola*, 1, 3, no. 34–36 (1937): 459–549.

Cavazzi de Montecucculo, João António. *Descrição Histórica dos Três Reinos de Congo, Matamba e Angola*. Translated by Graciano Maria Leguzzano. 2 vols. Lisbon: Junta de Investigações do Ultramar, 1965.

Clark, William. *Ten Views in the Island of Antigua*. London: T. Clay, 1823.

Coimbra, Carlos Dias, ed. *Livro de Patentes do Tempo do Sr. Salvador Correia de Sá e Benevides*. 2 vols. Luanda: Instituto de Investigação Científica de Angola, 1958.

Dom José I. "Carta de Sua Mag. sobre a Remataçam do Contrato dos Direitos Novos que a Rematou Manoel Barbosa Torres dos Direitos dos Escravos q' se Embarcam desta Cid. de Loanda p. os Portos do Brazil." *Arquivos de Angola*, 1, 2, no. 13–15 (1936): 515–28.

"Ley para Ser Livre, e Franco o Commercio de Angola, e dos Portos, e Sertões Adjacentes." *Arquivos de Angola*, 1, 2, no. 13–15 (1936): 531–35.

"Ley sobre a Arecadação dos Direitos dos Escravos, e Marfim, que Sahirem do Reino de Angola, e Pórtos da sua Dependencia." *Arquivos de Angola*, 1, 2, no. 13–15 (1936): 537–40.

Dom Pedro II. "Ley sobre as Arqueações dos Navios que Carregarem Escravos, 28 de Março de 1684." *Arquivos de Angola*, 1, 2, no. 11–12 (1936): 313–20.

Ellison, Thomas. *The Cotton Trade of Great Britain*. London: Effingham Wilson, 1886.

Felner, Alfredo de Albuquerque. *Angola: Apontamentos sobre a Ocupação e Início do Estabelecimento dos Portugueses no Congo, Angola e Benguela Extraídos de Documentos Históricos*. Coimbra: Imprensa da Universidade, 1933.

Ferreira Diniz, José de Oliveira. *Populações Indígenas de Angola*. Coimbra: Imprensa da Universidade, 1918.

Graham, Maria. *Journal of a Voyage to Brazil and Residence There during Part of the Years 1821, 1822, 1823*. London: Longman, Hurst, Rees, Orme, Brown, and Green, 1824.

Great Britain. *Irish University Press Series of British Parliamentary Papers: Slave Trade*. 95 vols. Shannon: Irish University Press, 1968.

Humboldt, Alexander. *The Island of Cuba*. Translated by J. S. Thrasher. New York: Derby and Jackson, 1856.

Johnson, William Henry. *Cotton and Its Production*. London: Macmillan, 1926.

Koelle, Sigismund Wilhelm. *Polyglotta Africana*, edited by P. E. H. Hair and David Dalby. Graz: Akademische Druck, U. Verlagsanstalt, 1965.

Koster, Henry. *Travels in Brazil*. London: Longman, Hurst, Rees, Orme, and Brown, 1816.

Laet, Joannes de. *Iaerlijck Verhael van de Verrichtingen der Geoctroyeerde West-Indische Compagnie in derthien Boecken. Tweede Deel: Boek IV–VII (1627–1630)*, edited by S. P. L'Honoré Naber. 's-Gravenhage: Martinus Nijhoff, 1932.

Leitão, Manoel Correia. "Angola's Eastern Hinterland in the 1750s: A Text Edition and Translation of Manoel Correia Leitão's 'Voyage' (1755–1756)." Edited by Eva Sebestyen and Jan Vansina. *History in Africa* 26 (1999): 299–364.

Livingstone, David. *Missionary Travels and Researches in South Africa: Including a Sketch of Sixteen Years' Residence in the Interior of Africa*. New York: Harper & Bros., 1858.

Lopes de Lima, José Joaquim. *Ensaios sobre a Statistica das Possessões Portuguezas*. 5 vols. Lisbon: Imprensa Nacional, 1844.

Magyar, László. *Reisen in Süd-Afrika in den Jahren 1849 bis 1857*. Pest and Leipzig: Lauffer & Stolp, 1859.

Mello, António Miguel de. "Angola no Fim do Século XVIII – Documentos." *Boletim da Sociedade de Geografia de Lisboa* 6, no. 5 (1886): 284–304.

"Regimento da Alfandega da Cidade de Saõ Paulo d'Assumpçaõ Capital do Reino de Angola, 21 de Outubro de 1799." *Arquivos de Angola*, 1, 2, no. 11–12 (1936): 359–447.

Mendes, Luiz António de Oliveira. *Memória a Respeito dos Escravos e Tráfico da Escravatura entre a Costa da África e o Brasil*, edited by José Capela. Porto: Escorpião, 1977.

Monteiro, Joachim John. *Angola and the River Congo*. New York: Macmillan and Co., 1876.

Neves, António Rodrigues. *Memoria da Expedição à Cassange Commandada pelo Major Graduado Francisco Salles Ferreira em 1850, Escripta pelo*

Capitão Móvel d'Ambriz António Rodrigues Neves. Lisbon: Imprensa
  Silviana, 1854.
Sanguineti, Cárlos. *Diccionario Jurídico-Administrativo*. Madrid: Imprensa de la
  Revista de Legislacion y Jurisprudencia, 1858.
Silva Corrêa, Elias Alexandre da. *História de Angola*, edited by Manuel Múrias.
  2 vols. Lisbon: Editorial Ática, 1937.
Smith, Adam. *An Inquiry into the Nature and Causes of the Wealth of Nations*. 2
  vols. London: W. Strahan and T. Cadell, 1776.
"Sugar Manufacture in Brazil." *The Illustrated London News* 25, September 9,
  1854: 232.
Tams, Georg. *Visit to the Portuguese Possessions in South-Western Africa*.
  London: T. C. Newby, 1845.
Taunay, Carlos Augusto. *Manual do Agricultor Brasileiro*, edited by Rafael de
  Bivar Marquese. São Paulo: Companhia das Letras, 2001.
Torres, João Carlos Feo Cardoso de Castello Branco e. *Memórias Contendo
  a Biographia do Vice Almirante Luis da Motta Feo e Torres, a História dos
  Governadores e Capitaens Generaes de Angola desde 1575 até 1825, e a
  Descripção Geographica e Politica dos Reinos de Angola e Benguella*. Paris:
  Fantin, 1825.
Vide, Sebastião Monteiro da. *Constituições Primeiras do Arcebispado da Bahia*.
  São Paulo: Typographia de António Louzada Antunes, 1853.

c) NEWSPAPER SOURCES

Boletim Oficial do Governo Geral da Província de Angola, Luanda, Angola, nos.
  646, 706, and 762.

d) SECONDARY SOURCES

Adelman, Jerry. *Sovereignty and Revolution in the Iberian Atlantic*. Princeton:
  Princeton University Press, 2006.
Alden, Dauril. "Late Colonial Brazil, 1750–1808." In *The Cambridge History of
  Latin America*, edited by Leslie Bethell, 2: 601–60. New York: Cambridge
  University Press, 1984.
Alden, Dauril, and Joseph C. Miller. "Out of Africa: The Slave Trade and the
  Transmission of Smallpox to Brazil, 1560–1831." *Journal of
  Interdisciplinary History* 18, no. 2 (1987): 195–224.
Alencastro, Luiz Felipe de. *O Trato dos Viventes: Formação do Brasil no Atlântico
  Sul*. São Paulo: Companhia das Letras, 2000.
Alpers, Edward A. "'Mozambiques' in Brazil: Another Dimension of the African
  Diaspora in the Atlantic World." In *Africa and the Americas:
  Interconnections during the Slave Trade*, edited by José C. Curto and
  Renée Soulodre-La France, 43–68. Trenton: Africa World Press, 2005.
Anstey, Roger. *The Atlantic Slave Trade and British Abolition, 1760–1810*.
  Atlantic Highlands: Humanities Press, 1975.

Antunes, Luís Frederico Dias. "Têxteis e Metais Preciosos: Novos Vínculos do Comércio Indo-Brasileiro (1808–1820)." In *O Antigo Regime nos Trópicos: a Dinâmica Imperial Portuguesa (Séculos XVI–XVIII)*, edited by João Fragoso, Maria Fernanda Baptista Bicalho, and Maria de Fátima Silva Gouvêa, 379–420. Rio de Janeiro: Civilização Brasileira, 2001.

Arruda, José Jobson de A. *O Brasil no Comércio Colonial*. São Paulo: Editora Ática, 1980.

Azevedo, J. Lúcio de. *Épocas de Portugal Económico*. 4th edn. Lisbon: Livraria Clássica, 1988.

Bal, Willy. "Portugais Pombeiro, Commerçant Ambulant du 'Sertão.'" *Annali dell'Istituto Universitario Orientalis, Naples* 7 (1965): 123–61.

Ball, Edward. *Slaves in the Family*. New York: Ballantine Books, 1999.

Bastin, Marie Louise. *Statuettes Tshokwe du Héros Civilisateur "Tshibinda Ilunga."* Arnouville-les-Gonesse: Arts d'Afrique Noire, 1978.

Bean, Richard. "A Note on the Relative Importance of Slaves and Gold in West African Exports." *Journal of African History* 15, no. 3 (1974): 351–56.

Beckert, Sven. *Empire of Cotton: A Global History*. New York: Alfred A. Knopf, 2014.

Behrendt, Stephen D. "Ecology, Seasonality, and the Transatlantic Slave Trade." In *Soundings in Atlantic History: Latent Structures and Intellectual Currents, 1500–1830*, edited by Bernard Bailyn and Patricia L. Denault, 44–85. Cambridge: Harvard University Press, 2009.

Bellagamba, Alice, Sandra E. Greene, and Martin A. Klein. "Finding the African Voice." In *African Voices on Slavery and the Slave Trade*, edited by Alice Bellagamba, Sandra E. Greene, and Martin A. Klein, 11–14. New York: Cambridge University Press, 2013.

Bethell, Leslie. *The Abolition of the Brazilian Slave Trade: Britain, Brazil and the Slave Trade Question, 1807–1869*. Cambridge: Cambridge University Press, 1970.

"The Mixed Commissions for the Suppression of the Transatlantic Slave Trade in the Nineteenth Century." *Journal of African History* 7, no. 1 (1966): 79–93.

Birmingham, David. *Central Africa to 1870: Zambesia, Zaïre and the South Atlantic*. New York: Cambridge University Press, 1981.

"The Date and Significance of the Imbangala Invasion of Angola." *Journal of African History* 6, no. 2 (1965): 143–52.

Trade and Conflict in Angola: The Mbundu and Their Neighbours under the Influence of the Portuguese, 1483–1790. Oxford: Clarendon Press, 1966.

Boahen, A. A. "New Trends and Processes in Africa in the Nineteenth Century." In *General History of Africa*, edited by J. F. A. Ajayi, vol. 6. London: Heinemann, 1989.

Boserup, Ester. *Woman's Role in Economic Development*. London: Allen & Unwin, 1970.

Boxer, C. R. "Salvador Correia de Sá E Benevides and the Reconquest of Angola in 1648." *Hispanic American Historical Review* 28, no. 4 (1948): 483–513.

Salvador de Sá and the Struggle for Brazil and Angola, 1602–1686. London: University of London Press, 1952.

The Golden Age of Brazil, 1695–1750: Growing Pains of a Colonial Society.
Berkeley: University of California, 1962.
Broadhead, Susan Herlin. "Beyond Decline: The Kingdom of Kongo in the
Eighteenth and Nineteenth Centuries." *International Journal of African
Historical Studies* 12, no. 4 (1979): 615–50.
"Trade and Politics on the Congo Coast, 1770–1870." Ph.D., Boston
University, 1971.
Brown, Vincent. "Social Death and Political Life in the Study of Slavery."
American Historical Review 114, no. 5 (2009).
Caldeira, Arlindo Manuel. "Angola and the Seventeenth-Century South Atlantic
Slave Trade." In *Networks and Trans-Cultural Exchange: Slave Trading in
the South Atlantic, 1590–1867*, edited by David Richardson and Filipa
Ribeiro da Silva, 101–42. Leiden: Brill, 2014.
Calonius, Erik. *The Wanderer: The Last American Slave Ship and the
Conspiracy That Set Its Sails.* New York: St. Martin's Press, 2006.
Cândido, Mariana P. *An African Slaving Port and the Atlantic World: Benguela
and Its Hinterland.* New York: Cambridge University Press, 2013.
*Fronteras de Esclavización: Esclavitud, Comercio e Identidad en Benguela,
1780–1850.* Translated by María Capetillo Lozano. Mexico: El Colegio
de México, 2011.
"Merchants and the Business of the Slave Trade in Benguela C. 1750–1850."
African Economic History 35 (2007): 1–30.
"South Atlantic Exchanges: The Role of Brazilian-Born Agents in Benguela,
1650–1850." *Luso-Brazilian Review* 50, no. 1 (2013): 53–82.
"Trans-Atlantic Links: The Benguela-Bahia Connections, 1700–1850."
In *Paths of the Atlantic Slave Trade: Interactions, Identities, and Images*,
edited by Ana Lúcia Araújo, 239–72. Amherst: Cambria Press, 2011.
Cardoso, Carlos Alberto Lopes. "Dona Ana Joaquina dos Santos Silva: Industrial
Angolana da Segunda Metade do Século XIX." *Boletim Cultural da Câmara
Municipal de Luanda* 37 (1972): 5–14.
Carreira, António. *As Companhias Pombalinas de Navegação, Comércio
e Tráfico de Escravos entre a Costa Africana e o Nordeste Brasileiro.*
Bissau: Centro de Estudos da Guiné Portuguesa, 1969.
Carreira, Ernestina. "Os Últimos Anos da Carreira da Índia." In *A Carreira da
Índia e as Rotas dos Estreitos: Actas do VIII Seminário Internacional de
História Indo-Portuguesa*, edited by Artur Teodoro de Matos and Luís Filipe
F. Reis Thomaz, 809–34. Angra do Heroísmo: Barbosa e Xavier, 1998.
Carvalho, Marcus J. M. de. *Liberdade: Rotinas e Rupturas do Escravismo no
Recife, 1822–1850.* Recife: Universidade Federal de Pernambuco, 2002.
Chambers, D. B. "Ethnicity in the Diaspora: The Slave Trade and the Creation of
African 'Nations' in the Americas." *Slavery and Abolition* 22, no. 3 (2001):
25–39.
Childs, Gladwyn Murray. *Kinship and Character of the Ovimbundu: Being
a Description of the Social Structure and Individual Development of the
Ovimbundu of Angola, with Observations Concerning the Bearing on the
Enterprise of Christian Missions of Certain Phases of the Life and Culture*

Described. London: Reprinted for the International African Institute & for the Witwatersrand U.P. by Dawson, 1969.

Cipolla, Carlo M. *Before the Industrial Revolution: European Society and Economy, 1000–1700*. New York: Norton, 1976.

Clarence-Smith, William Gervase. "The Portuguese Contribution to the Cuban Slave and Coolie Trades in the Nineteenth Century." *Slavery and Abolition* 5, no. 1 (1984): 25–33.

Cody, Cheryll Ann. "There Was No 'Absalom' on the Ball Plantations: Slave-Naming Practices in the South Carolina Low Country, 1720–1865." *American Historical Review* 92, no. 3 (1987): 563–96.

Coghe, Samuël. "The Problem of Freedom in a Mid-Nineteenth Century Atlantic Slave Society: The Liberated Africans of the Anglo-Portuguese Mixed Commission in Luanda (1844–1870)." *Slavery and Abolition* 33, no. 3 (2012): 479–500.

Costa e Silva, Alberto da. *A Manilha e o Libambo: A África e a Escravidão de 1500–1700*. Rio de Janeiro: Nova Fronteira, 2002.

Couto, Carlos. *Os Capitães-Mores em Angola no Século XVIII: Subsídios para o Estudo da sua Actuação*. Luanda: Instituto de Investigação Científica de Angola, 1972.

O Zimbo na Historiografia Angolana. Luanda: Instituto de Investigação Científica de Angola, 1973.

Crosby, Alfred W. *Ecological Imperialism: The Biological Expansion of Europe*. New York: Cambridge University Press, 1986.

Curtin, Philip D. *Economic Change in Precolonial Africa: Senegambia in the Era of the Slave Trade*. 2 vols. Madison: University of Wisconsin Press, 1975.

The Atlantic Slave Trade: A Census. Madison: University of Wisconsin Press, 1969.

Curtin, Philip D., and Jan Vansina. "Sources of the Nineteenth Century Atlantic Slave Trade." *Journal of African History* 5, no. 2 (1964): 185–208.

Curto, José C. "A Quantitative Reassessment of the Legal Portuguese Slave Trade from Luanda, Angola, 1710–1830." *African Economic History*, no. 20 (1992): 1–25.

Enslaving Spirits: The Portuguese-Brazilian Alcohol Trade at Luanda and Its Hinterland, c.1550–1830. Leiden: Brill, 2004.

"Experiences of Enslavement in West Central Africa." *Social History* 41, no. 82 (2009): 381–415.

"Struggling against Enslavement: The Case of José Manuel in Benguela, 1816–20." *Canadian Journal of African Studies* 39, no. 1 (2005): 96–122.

"The Anatomy of a Demographic Explosion: Luanda, 1844–1850." *International Journal of African Historical Studies* 32, no. 2/3 (1999): 381–405.

"The Legal Portuguese Slave Trade from Benguela, Angola, 1730–1828: A Quantitative Re-Appraisal." *África: Revista do Centro de Estudos Africanos da Universidade de São Paulo* 16–17, no. 1 (April 1993): 101–16.

"The Origin of Slaves in Angola: The Case of Runaways, 1850–1876." Presented at the Seventh European Social Science and History Conference, Lisbon, 2008.

"The Story of Nbena, 1817–20: Unlawful Enslavement and the Concept of 'Original Freedom' in Angola." In *Trans-Atlantic Dimensions of Ethnicity in the African Diaspora*, edited by Paul E. Lovejoy and David V. Trotman, 43–64. New York: Continuum, 2003.

Curto, José C., and Raymond R. Gervais. "A Dinâmica Demográfica de Luanda no Contexto do Tráfico de Escravos do Atlântico Sul, 1781–1844." *Topoi*, no. 4 (2002): 85–138.

"The Population History of Luanda during the Late Atlantic Slave Trade, 1781–1844." *African Economic History* 29 (2001): 1–59.

Davis, David Brion. *Inhuman Bondage: The Rise and Fall of Slavery in the New World*. New York: Oxford University Press, 2006.

Davis, Natalie Zemon. *The Return of Martin Guerre*. Cambridge: Harvard University Press, 1983.

Delgado, Ralph. *História de Angola*. 4 vols. Lisbon: Banco de Angola, 1970.

Dias, Jill R. "Angola." In *Nova História da Expansão Portuguesa: O Império Africano, 1825–1890*, edited by Valentim Alexandre and Jill R. Dias, 10: 317–556. Lisbon: Editorial Estampa, 1986.

"Famine and Disease in the History of Angola, c.1830–1930." *Journal of African History* 22, no. 3 (1981): 349–78.

Dias, Manuel Nunes. *Fomento e Mercantilismo: A Companhia Geral do Grão Pará e Maranhão (1755–1778)*. 2 vols. Belém: Universidade Federal do Pará, 1970.

Domingues da Silva, Daniel B. "Catherine Zimmermann-Mulgrave: A Slave Odyssey." In *Voyages: The Transatlantic Slave Trade Database*, edited by David Eltis, David Richardson, Stephen Behrendt, and Manolo Florentino. Atlanta: Emory University, 2008. www.slavevoyages.org.

"Crossroads: Slave Frontiers of Angola, c.1780–1867." Ph.D., Emory University, 2011.

"O Tráfico de São Tomé e Príncipe, 1799–1811: Para o Estudo de Rotas Negreiras Subsidiárias ao Comércio Transatlântico de Escravos." *Estudos de História, Franca* 9 (2002): 35–51.

"The Atlantic Slave Trade from Angola: A Port-by-Port Estimate of Slaves Embarked, 1701–1867." *International Journal of African Historical Studies* 46, no. 1 (2013): 107–22.

"The Atlantic Slave Trade to Maranhão, 1680–1846: Volume, Routes and Organisation." *Slavery and Abolition* 29, no. 4 (2008): 461–501.

"The Supply of Slaves from Luanda, 1768–1806: Records of Anselmo da Fonseca Coutinho." *African Economic History* 38 (2010): 53–76.

Domingues da Silva, Daniel B., David Eltis, Philip Misevich, and Olatunji Ojo. "The Diaspora of Africans Liberated from Slave Ships in the Nineteenth Century." *Journal of African History* 55, no. 3 (2014): 347–69.

Drescher, Seymour. *Abolition: A History of Slavery and Antislavery*. New York: Cambridge University Press, 2009.

The Mighty Experiment: Free Labor versus Slavery in British Emancipation. New York: Oxford University Press, 2002.

Dubois, Laurent. *Avengers of the New World: The Story of the Haitian Revolution*. Cambridge: Belknalp Press of Harvard University Press, 2004.

Ekholm, Kajsa. "External Exchange and the Transformation of Central African Social System." In *The Evolution of Social Systems*, edited by Jonathan Friedman and Michael J. Rowlands, 115–36. Pittsburgh: University of Pittsburgh Press, 1978.

Eltis, David. *Economic Growth and the Ending of the Transatlantic Slave Trade.* New York: Oxford University Press, 1987.

"Nutritional Trends in Africa and the Americas: Heights of Africans, 1819–1839." *Journal of Interdisciplinary History* 12, no. 3 (1982): 453–75.

"Slave Departures from Africa, 1811–1867: An Annual Time Series." *African Economic History*, no. 15 (1986): 143–71.

"The British Contribution to the Nineteenth Century Trans-Atlantic Slave Trade." *Economic History Review* 32, no. 2 (1979): 211–27.

"The British Trans-Atlantic Slave Trade after 1807." *Maritime History* 4, no. 1 (1974): 1–11.

"The Nineteenth Century Transatlantic Slave Trade: An Annual Time Series of Imports into the Americas Broken Down by Region." *Hispanic American Historical Review* 67, no. 1 (1987): 109–38.

The Rise of African Slavery in the Americas. New York: Cambridge University Press, 2000.

"The Volume and Structure of the Transatlantic Slave Trade: A Reassessment." *William and Mary Quarterly* 58, no. 1 (2001): 17–46.

Eltis, David, and Stanley L. Engerman. "Was the Slave Trade Dominated by Men?" *Journal of Interdisciplinary History* 23, no. 2 (1992): 237–57.

Eltis, David, Frank D. Lewis, and Kimberly McIntyre. "Accounting for the Traffic in Africans: Transport Costs on Slaving Voyages." *Journal of Economic History* 70, no. 4 (2010): 940–63.

Eltis, David, and David Richardson, eds. *Atlas of the Transatlantic Slave Trade.* New Haven: Yale University Press, 2010.

Engerman, Stanley L., Herbert S. Klein, Robin Haines, and Ralph Shlomowitz. "Transoceanic Mortality: The Slave Trade in Comparative Perspective." *William and Mary Quarterly* 58, no. 1 (2001): 93–118.

Fage, J. D. "Slavery and the Slave Trade in the Context of West African History." *Journal of African History* 10, no. 3 (1969): 393–404.

Falola, Toyin, and Paul E. Lovejoy. "Pawnship in Historical Perspective." In *Pawnship in Africa: Debt Bondage in Historical Perspective*, edited by Toyin Falola and Paul E. Lovejoy. Boulder: Westview Press, 1994.

Fausto, Boris. *História do Brasil.* 8th edn. São Paulo: Editora da Universidade de São Paulo, 2000.

Ferreira, Roquinaldo. *Cross-Cultural Exchange in the Atlantic World: Angola and Brazil during the Era of the Slave Trade.* New York: Cambridge University Press, 2012.

"Dinâmica do Comércio Intracolonial: Geribitas, Panos Asiáticos e Guerra no Tráfico Angolano de Escravos (Século XVIII)." In *O Antigo Regime nos Trópicos: a Dinâmica Imperial Portuguesa (Séculos XVI-XVIII)*, edited by João Fragoso, Maria Fernanda Baptista Bicalho, and Maria de Fátima Silva Gouvêa, 339–78. Rio de Janeiro: Civilização Brasileira, 2001.

"Dos Sertões ao Atlântico: Tráfico Ilegal de Escravos e Comércio Lícito em Angola, 1830–1860." M.A., Universidade Federal do Rio de Janeiro, 1996.

"Slaving and Resistance to Slaving in West Central Africa." In *The Cambridge World History of Slavery*, edited by David Eltis and Stanley L. Engerman, 3: 111–31. New York: Cambridge University Press, 2011.

"The Suppression of the Slave Trade and Slave Departures from Angola, 1830s-1860s." *História Unisinos* 15, no. 1 (2011): 3–13.

"Transforming Atlantic Slaving: Trade, Warfare and Territorial Control in Angola, 1650–1800." Ph.D., University of California, 2003.

Fick, Carolyn. *The Making of Haiti: The Saint-Domingue Revolution from Below*. Knoxville: University of Tennessee Press, 1990.

Finkelman, Paul. "Regulating the African Slave Trade." *Civil War History* 54, no. 4 (2008): 379–405.

Florentino, Manolo. *Em Costas Negras: Uma História do Tráfico Atlântico de Escravos entre a África e o Rio de Janeiro, Séculos XVIII e XIX*. São Paulo: Companhia das Letras, 1997.

"The Slave Trade, Colonial Markets, and Slave Families in Rio de Janeiro, Brazil, ca.1790-ca.1830." In *Extending the Frontiers: Essays on the New Transatlantic Slave Trade Database*, edited by David Eltis and David Richardson, 275–312. New Haven: Yale University Press, 2008.

Flory, Rae Jean. "Bahian Society in the Mid-Colonial Period: The Sugar Planters, Tobacco Growers, Merchants and Artisans of Salvador and the Recôncavo, 1680–1725." Ph.D., University of Texas, 1978.

Fogel, Robert William, and Stanley L. Engerman. *Time on the Cross: The Economics of American Negro Slavery*. Boston: Little Brown, 1974.

Fragoso, João Luís Ribeiro. "A Nobreza da República: Notas sobre a Formação da Primeira Elite Senhorial do Rio de Janeiro (Séculos XVI e XVII)." *Topoi*, no. 1 (2000): 43–122.

Freudenthal, Aida. *Arimos e Fazendas: A Transição Agrária em Angola, 1850–1880*. Luanda: Chá de Caxinde, 2005.

Geggus, David. "The French and Haitian Revolutions, and Resistance to Slavery: An Overview." *Revue Française d'Histoire d'Outre-Mer* 76, no. 282–83 (1989): 107–24.

Genovese, Eugene D. *From Rebellion to Revolution: Afro-American Slave Revolts in the Making of the Modern World*. Baton Rouge: Louisiana State University Press, 1979.

Ginzburg, Carlo. *The Cheese and the Worms: The Cosmos of a Sixteenth-Century Miller*. Translated by Anne Tedeschi and John Tedeschi. Baltimore: Johns Hopkins University Press, 1980.

Ginzburg, Carlo, and Carlo Poni. "The Name and the Game: Unequal Exchange and the Historiographic Marketplace." In *Microhistory and the Lost Peoples of Europe*, edited by Edward Muir and Guido Ruggiero, translated by Eren Branch, 1–10. Baltimore: Johns Hopkins University Press, 1991.

Gomez, Michael Angelo. *Exchanging Our Country Marks: The Transformation of African Ties in the Colonial and Antebellum South*. Chapel Hill: University of North Carolina Press, 1998.

Gorender, Jacob. *O Escravismo Colonial*. São Paulo: Ática, 1978.

Green, Toby. *The Rise of the Trans-Atlantic Slave Trade in Western Africa,
    1300–1589.* New York: Cambridge University Press, 2012.
Gross, Cary P., and Kent A. Sepkowitz. "The Myth of the Medical Breakthrough:
    Smallpox, Vaccination, and Jenner Reconsidered." *International Journal of
    Infectious Diseases* 3, no. 1 (July 1, 1998): 54–60.
Guedes, Roberto, and João Luís Fragoso. "Alegrias e Artimanhas de uma Fonte
    Seriada: Os Códices 390, 421, 424 e 425: Despachos de Escravos
    e Passaportes da Intendência de Polícia da Corte, 1819 – 1833." In *Tráfico
    Interno de Escravos e Relações Comerciais no Centro-Sul do Brasil, Séculos
    XVIII e XIX*, edited by IPEA. Brasília: Instituto de Pesquisa Econômica
    Aplicada, 2000.
Gutiérrez, Horácio. "O Tráfico de Crianças Escravas para o Brasil durante
    o Século XVIII." *Revista de História, São Paulo* 120 (1989): 59–73.
Hair, P. E. H. "Ethnolinguistic Continuity on the Guinea Coast." *Journal of
    African History* 8, no. 2 (1967): 247–68.
    "From Language to Culture: Some Problems in the Systemic Analysis of the
    Ethnohistorical Records of the Sierra Leone Region." In *The Population
    Factor in African Studies*, edited by R. P. Moss and R. J. A. R. Rathbone,
    71–83. London: University of London Press, 1975.
    "Koelle at Freetown: An Historical Introduction." In *Polyglotta Africana*, by
    Sigismund Wilhelm Koelle, 7–17. edited by P. E. H. Hair and David
    Dalby. Graz: Akademische Druck, U. Verlagsanstalt, 1965.
    "The Enslavement of Koelle's Informants." *Journal of African History* 6, no. 2
    (1965): 193–203.
Hall, Gwendolyn Midlo. "African Ethnicities and the Meanings of 'Mina.'"
    In *Trans-Atlantic Dimensions of Ethnicity in the African Diaspora*, edited
    by Paul E. Lovejoy and David V. Trotman, 65–81. New York: Continuum,
    2003.
Harms, Robert W. *River of Wealth, River of Sorrow: The Central Zaire Basin in
    the Era of the Slave and Ivory Trade, 1500–1891.* New Haven: Yale
    University Press, 1981.
Hawthorne, Walter. *From Africa to Brazil: Culture, Identity, and an Atlantic
    Slave Trade, 1600–1830.* New York: Cambridge University Press, 2010.
    "Nourishing a Stateless Society during the Slave Trade: The Rise of Balanta
    Paddy-Rice Production in Guinea-Bissau." *Journal of African History* 42, no.
    1 (2001): 1–24.
    *Planting Rice and Harvesting Slaves: Transformations along the Guinea-Bissau
    Coast, 1400–1900.* Portsmouth: Heinemann, 2003.
    "The Production of Slaves Where There Was No State: The Guinea-Bissau
    Region, 1450–1815." *Slavery and Abolition* 20, no. 2 (1999): 97–124.
Heintze, Beatrix. "Angola nas Garras do Tráfico de Escravos: As Guerras do
    Ndongo (1611–1630)." *Revista Internacional de Estudos Africanos* 1
    (1984): 11–59.
    "Luso-African Feudalism in Angola? The Vassal Treaties of the Sixteenth to the
    Eighteenth Century." *Revista Portuguesa de História* 18 (1980): 111–31.
    *Pioneiros Africanos: Caravanas de Carregadores na África Centro-Ocidental
    entre 1850 e 1890.* Translated by Marina Santos. Lisbon: Caminho, 2002.

Henriques, Isabel Castro. "A Organização Afro-Portuguesa do Tráfico de Escravos (Séculos XVII-XIX)." In *A Rota dos Escravos: Angola e a Rede do Comércio Negreiro*, edited by João Medina and Isabel Castro Henriques, 124–73. Lisbon: Cegia, 1996.

Percursos da Modernidade em Angola: Dinâmicas Comerciais e Transformações Sociais no Século XIX. Translated by Alfredo Margarido. Lisbon: Instituto de Investigação Científica Tropical, 1997.

Herbert, Eugenia W. "Smallpox Inoculation in Africa." *Journal of African History* 16, no. 4 (1975): 539–59.

Heywood, Linda M. *Contested Power in Angola, 1840s to the Present*. Rochester: University of Rochester Press, 2000.

"Slavery and Its Transformation in the Kingdom of Kongo, 1491–1800." *Journal of African History* 50, no. 1 (2009): 1–22.

Heywood, Linda M., and John K. Thornton. *Central Africans, Atlantic Creoles, and the Foundation of the Americas, 1585–1660*. New York: Cambridge University Press, 2007.

Heywood, Linda, and John Thornton. "African Fiscal Systems as Sources for Demographic History: The Case of Central Angola, 1799–1920." *Journal of African History* 29, no. 2 (1988): 213–28.

Higman, B. W. *Slave Populations of the British Caribbean, 1807–1834*. 2 vols. Baltimore: Johns Hopkins University Press, 1984.

Hilton, Anne. "Family and Kinship among the Kongo South of the Zaire River from the Sixteenth to the Nineteenth Centuries." *Journal of African History* 24, no. 2 (1983): 189–206.

The Kingdom of Kongo. New York: Clarendon Press, 1985.

Hoover, Jeffrey J. "The Seduction of Ruweej: Reconstructing Ruund History (The Nuclear Lunda: Zaire, Angola, Zambia)." Ph.D., Yale University, 1978.

Hubbell, Andrew. "A View of the Slave Trade from the Margin: Souroudougou in the Late Nineteenth-Century Slave Trade of the Niger Bend." *Journal of African History* 42, no. 1 (2001): 25–47.

Huggins, Nathan Irvin. *Black Odyssey: The Afro-American Ordeal in Slavery*. New York: Pantheon Books, 1977.

Inikori, Joseph E. "Introduction." In *Forced Migration: The Impact of the Export Slave Trade on African Societies*, edited by Joseph E. Inikori, 13–59. New York: Africana Publishing Company, 1982.

"The Import of Firearms into West Africa, 1750–1807: A Quantitative Analysis." *Journal of African History* 18, no. 3 (1977): 339–68.

Jadin, Louis. "Rapport sur les Recherches aux Archives d'Angola du 4 Juillet au 7 Septembre 1952." *Bulletin des Séances de l'Institut Royal Colonial Belge*, no. 24 (1953).

James, C. L. R. *The Black Jacobins: Toussaint Louverture and the San Domingo Revolution*. 2nd edn. New York: Vintage Books, 1963.

Janzen, John. *Lemba, 1650–1930: A Drum of Affliction in Africa and the New World*. New York: Garland, 1982.

Johnson, Marion. "The Cowrie Currencies of West Africa. Part II." *Journal of African History* 11, no. 3 (1970): 331–53.

Bibliography

Karasch, Mary C. *Slave Life in Rio de Janeiro, 1808–1850.* Princeton: Princeton University Press, 1987.
   "The Brazilian Slavers and the Illegal Slave Trade, 1836–1851." M.A., University of Wisconsin, 1967.
Kea, Raymond A. "Firearms and Warfare on the Gold and Slave Coasts from the Sixteenth to the Nineteenth Centuries." *Journal of African History* 12, no. 2 (1971): 185–213.
Kennedy, John Norman. "Bahian Elites, 1750–1822." *Hispanic American Historical Review* 53, no. 3 (1973): 415–39.
Klein, Herbert S. "African Women in the Atlantic Slave Trade." In *Women and Slavery in Africa,* edited by Claire C. Robertson and Martin A. Klein, 29–38. Madison: University of Wisconsin Press, 1983.
   The Middle Passage: Comparative Studies in the Atlantic Slave Trade. Princeton: Princeton University Press, 1978.
   "The Portuguese Slave Trade From Angola in the Eighteenth Century." *Journal of Economic History* 32, no. 4 (1972): 894–918.
Klein, Herbert S., and Francisco Vidal Luna. *Slavery in Brazil.* New York: Cambridge University Press, 2010.
Klein, Martin A. "The Impact of the Atlantic Slave Trade on the Societies of the Western Sudan." *Social Science History* 14, no. 2 (1990): 231–53.
   "The Slave Trade and Decentralized Societies." *Journal of African History* 42, no. 1 (2001): 49–65.
Klein, Martin A., and Paul E. Lovejoy. "Slavery in West Africa." In *The Uncommon Market: Essays in the Economic History of the Atlantic Slave Trade,* edited by Henry A. Gemery and Jan S. Hogendorn, 181–212. New York: Academic Press, 1979.
Lapa, José Roberto do Amaral. *A Bahia e a Carreira da Índia.* Estudos Históricos, 42. São Paulo: Hucitec, Unicamp, 2000.
Law, Robin. "Ethnicities of Enslaved Africans in the Diaspora: On the Meanings of 'Mina' (Again)." *History in Africa* 32 (2005): 247–67.
   "Ethnicity and the Slave Trade: 'Lucumi' and 'Nago' as Ethnonyms in West Africa." *History in Africa* 24 (1997): 205–19.
   "Legal and Illegal Enslavement in West Africa, in the Context of the Trans-Atlantic Slave Trade." In *Ghana in Africa and the World: Essays in Honor of Adu Boahen,* edited by Toyin Falola, 513–33. Trenton: Africa World Press, 2003.
   The Slave Coast of West Africa, 1550–1750: The Impact of the Atlantic Slave Trade on an African Society. Oxford: Clarendon Press, 1991.
Le Veen, E. Philip. "The African Slave Supply Response." *African Studies Review* 18, no. 1 (1975): 9–28.
Lopo, Júlio de Castro. "Uma Rica Dona de Luanda." *Portucale,* 2, 3, no. 16–17 (1948): 129–38.
Lovejoy, Paul E. "Ethnic Designations of the Slave Trade and the Reconstruction of the History of Trans-Atlantic Slavery." In *Trans-Atlantic Dimensions of Ethnicity in the African Diaspora,* edited by Paul E. Lovejoy and David V. Trotman, 9–42. New York: Continuum, 2003.

"Internal Markets or an Atlantic-Sahara Divide? How Women Fit into the Slave Trade of West Africa." In *Women and Slavery: Africa, the Indian Ocean, and the Medieval North Atlantic*, edited by Gwyn Campbell, Suzanne Miers, and Joseph C. Miller, 1: 259–79. Athens: Ohio University Press, 2007.

"Transatlantic Transformations: The Origins and Identities of Africans in the Americas." In *Africa, Brazil, and the Construction of Trans-Atlantic Black Identities*, edited by Boubacar Barry, Elisée Soumonni, and Livio Sansone, 81–112. Trenton: Africa World Press, 2008.

Transformations in Slavery: A History of Slavery in Africa. 2nd edn. New York: Cambridge University Press, 2000.

Lovejoy, Paul E., and David Richardson. "The Business of Slaving: Pawnship in Western Africa, c.1600–1810." *Journal of African History* 42, no. 1 (2001): 67–89.

"Trust, Pawnship, and Atlantic History: The Institutional Foundations of the Old Calabar Slave Trade." *American Historical Review* 104, no. 2 (1999): 333–55.

MacGaffey, Wyatt. "Lineage Structure, Marriage and the Family amongst the Central Bantu." *Journal of African History* 24, no. 2 (1983): 173–87.

Machado, Pedro. "Cloths of a New Fashion: Indian Ocean Networks of Exchange and Cloth Zones of Contact in Africa and India in the Eighteenth and Nineteenth Centuries." In *How India Clothed the World: The World of South Asian Textiles, 1500–1850*, edited by Giorgio Riello and Tirthankar Roy, 53–84. Leiden: Brill, 2009.

Maestri Filho, Mário José. *A Agricultura Africana nos Séculos XVI e XVII no Litoral Angolano*. Porto Alegre: Universidade Federal do Rio Grande do Sul, 1978.

Mamigonian, Beatriz Gallotti. "To Be a Liberated African in Brazil: Labour and Citizenship in the Nineteenth Century." Ph.D., University of Waterloo, 2002.

Manchester, Alan K. "The Transfer of the Portuguese Court to Rio de Janeiro." In *Conflict and Continuity in Brazilian Society*, edited by Henry H. Keith and S. F. Edwards, 148–83. Columbia: University of South Carolina Press, 1969.

Mann, Kristin. *Slavery and the Birth of an African City: Lagos, 1760–1900*. Bloomington: Indiana University Press, 2007.

Manning, Patrick. *Slavery and African Life: Occidental, Oriental, and African Slave Trades*. New York: Cambridge University Press, 1990.

Marques, João Pedro. *Os Sons do Silêncio: O Portugal de Oitocentos e a Abolição do Tráfico de Escravos*. Lisbon: Imprensa de Ciências Sociais, 1999.

Martin, Phyllis M. "Family Strategies in Nineteenth Century Cabinda." *Journal of African History* 28, no. 1 (1987): 65–86.

The External Trade of the Loango Coast, 1576–1870: The Effects of Changing Commercial Relations on the Vili Kingdom of Loango. Oxford: Clarendon Press, 1972.

Martins Filho, Amilcar, and Roberto B. Martins. "Slavery in a Non-Export Economy: Nineteenth Century Minas Gerais Revisited." *Hispanic American Historical Review* 63, no. 3 (1983): 537–68.

McCulloch, Merran. *The Ovimbundu of Angola*. London: International African Institute, 1952.

Meillassoux, Claude. *The Anthropology of Slavery: The Womb of Iron and Gold*. Translated by Alide Dasnois. Chicago: University of Chicago Press, 1991.

"The Role of Slavery in the Economic and Social History of Sahelo-Sudanic Africa." In *Forced Migration: The Impact of the Export Slave Trade on African Societies*, edited by Joseph E. Inikori, translated by R. J. Gavin, 74–99. New York: Africana Publishing Company, 1982.

Mello, Evaldo Cabral de. *A Fronda dos Mazombos: Nobres Contra Mascates, Pernambuco, 1666–1715*. São Paulo: Companhia das Letras, 1995.

Olinda Restaurada: Guerra e Açúcar no Nordeste, 1630–1654. Rio de Janeiro: Editora Forense-Universitária, 1975.

Metcalf, George. "A Microcosm of Why Africans Sold Slaves: Akan Consumption Patterns in the 1770s." *Journal of African History* 28, no. 3 (1987): 377–94.

Miers, Suzanne, and Igor Kopytoff. "African 'Slavery' as an Institution of Marginality." In *Slavery in Africa: Historical and Anthropological Perspectives*, 3–81. Madison: University of Wisconsin Press, 1977.

Milheiros, Mário. *Índice Histórico-Corográfico de Angola*. Luanda: Instituto de Investigação Científica de Angola, 1972.

Miller, Joseph C. "Central Africa during the Era of the Slave Trade, c.1490s–1850s." In *Central Africans and Cultural Transformations in the American Diaspora*, edited by Linda M. Heywood, 21–69. New York: Cambridge University Press, 2002.

"Imbangala Lineage Slavery." In *Slavery in Africa: Historical and Anthropological Perspectives*, edited by Suzanne Miers and Igor Kopytoff, 205–33. Madison: University of Wisconsin Press, 1977.

"Imports at Luanda, Angola: 1785–1823." In *Figuring African Trade: Proceedings of the Symposium on the Quantification and Structure of the Import and Export and Long-Distance Trade of Africa in the Nineteenth Century, c.1800–1913 (St. Augustin, 3–6 January 1983)*, edited by Gerhard Liesegang, Helma Pasch, and Adam Jones, 162–244. Berlin: Dietrich Reimer Verlag, 1986.

"Legal Portuguese Slaving from Angola: Some Preliminary Indications of Volume and Direction, 1760–1830." *Revue Française d'Histoire d'Outre-Mer* 62, no. 226–27 (1975): 135–76.

"Slave Prices in the Portuguese Southern Atlantic, 1600–1830." In *Africans in Bondage: Studies in Slavery and the Slave Trade*, edited by Paul E. Lovejoy, 43–77. Madison: University of Wisconsin, 1986.

"The Imbangala and the Chronology of Early Central African History." *Journal of African History* 13, no. 4 (1972): 549–74.

"The Numbers, Origins, and Destinations of Slaves in the Eighteenth-Century Angolan Slave Trade." *Social Science History* 13, no. 4 (1989): 381–419.

"The Numbers, Origins, and Destinations of Slaves in the Eighteenth-Century Angolan Slave Trade." In *The Atlantic Slave Trade: Effects on Economics, Societies, and Peoples in Africa, the Americas and Europe*, edited by Joseph E. Inikori and Stanley L. Engerman, 2nd edn., 77–115. Durham: Duke University Press, 1998.

"The Political Economy of the Angolan Slave Trade in the Eighteenth Century." *Indian Historical Review* 15 (September 1988): 152–87.

"The Significance of Drought, Disease and Famine in the Agriculturally Marginal Zones of West-Central Africa." *Journal of African History* 23, no. 1 (1982): 17–61.

"The Slave Trade in Congo and Angola." In *The African Diaspora: Interpretative Essays,* edited by Martin L. Kilson and Robert I. Rotberg, 75–113. London: Harvard University Press, 1976.

Way of Death: Merchant Capitalism and the Angolan Slave Trade, 1730–1830. Madison: University of Wisconsin Press, 1988.

"Women as Slaves and Owners of Slaves: Experiences from Africa, the Indian Ocean World, and the Early Atlantic." In *Women and Slavery: Africa, the Indian Ocean, and the Medieval North Atlantic,* edited by Gwyn Campbell, Suzanne Miers, and Joseph C. Miller, 1: 1–39. Athens: Ohio University Press, 2007.

Moorman, Marissa J. *Intonations: A Social History of Music and Nation in Luanda, Angola, from 1945 to Recent Times.* Athens: Ohio University Press, 2008.

Moreno Fraginals, Manuel. *The Sugarmill: The Socioeconomic Complex of Sugar in Cuba, 1760–1860.* New York: Monthly Review Press, 1976.

Murray, David R. *Odious Commerce: Britain, Spain, and the Abolition of the Cuban Slave Trade.* New York: Cambridge University Press, 1980.

Nardi, Jean Baptiste. *O Fumo Brasileiro no Período Colonial: Lavoura, Comércio e Administração.* São Paulo: Brasiliense, 1996.

Northrup, David. *Trade without Rulers: Pre-Colonial Economic Development in South-Eastern Nigeria.* Oxford: Clarendon Press, 1978.

Nunn, Nathan. "Historical Legacies: A Model Linking Africa's Past to Its Current Underdevelopment." *Journal of Development Economics* 83 (2007): 157–75.

Nwokeji, G. Ugo. "African Conceptions of Gender and the Slave Traffic." *William and Mary Quarterly* 58, no. 1 (2001): 47–68.

The Slave Trade and Culture in the Bight of Biafra: An African Society in the Atlantic World. New York: Cambridge University Press, 2010.

Oppen, Achim von. *Terms of Trade and Terms of Trust: The History and Contexts of Pre-Colonial Market Production around the Upper Zambezi and Kasai.* Münster: LIT Verlag, 1994.

Ortiz, Fernando. *Los Negros Esclavos.* Havana: Editorial de Ciencias Sociales, 1975.

Paquette, Gabriel. *Imperial Portugal in the Age of Atlantic Revolutions: The Luso-Brazilian World, c.1770–1850.* New York: Cambridge University Press, 2013.

Parreira, Adriano. *Economia e Sociedade em Angola na Época da Rainha Jinga, Século XVII.* Lisbon: Estampa, 1990.

Patterson, Orlando. *Slavery and Social Death: A Comparative Study.* Cambridge: Harvard University Press, 1982.

Pearce, Justin. *Political Identity and Conflict in Central Angola, 1975–2002.* New York: Cambridge University Press, 2015.

Pélissier, René. *História das Campanhas de Angola: Resistência e Revoltas, 1845–1941*. 2 vols. Lisbon: Editorial Estampa, 1997.

Pinto, Virgílio Noya. *O Ouro Brasileiro e o Comércio Anglo-Português: Uma Contribuição aos Estudos da Economia Atlântica no Século XVIII*. 2nd edn. São Paulo: Companhia Editora Nacional, 1979.

Redinha, José. *Distribuição Étnica de Angola*. Luanda: Centro de Informação e Turismo de Angola, 1962.

Ribeiro, Alexandre Vieira. "A Cidade de Salvador: Estrutura Econômica, Comércio de Escravos e Grupo Mercantil (c.1750-c.1800)." Doctorate, Universidade Federal do Rio de Janeiro, 2009.

"O Comércio de Escravos e a Elite Baiana no Período Colonial." In *Conquistadores e Negociantes: Histórias de Elites no Antigo Regime nos Trópicos. América Lusa, Séculos XVI a XVIII*, edited by João Luís Ribeiro Fragoso, Carla Maria de Carvalho de Almeida, and Antônio Carlos Jucá de Sampaio, 311–35. Rio de Janeiro: Civilização Brasileira, 2007.

"O Tráfico Atlântico de Escravos e a Praça Mercantil de Salvador, c. 1680–1830." M.A., Universidade Federal do Rio de Janeiro, 2005.

Ribeiro Júnior, José. *Colonização e Monopólio no Nordeste Brasileiro: A Companhia Geral de Pernambuco e Paraíba (1759–1780)*. São Paulo: HUCITEC, 1976.

Richards, A. "Some Types of Family Structure amongst the Central Bantu." In *African Systems of Kinship and Marriage*, edited by A. R. Radcliffe-Brown and Cyril Daryll Forde. London: Oxford University Press, 1964.

Richardson, David. "Prices of Slaves in West and West Central Africa: Toward an Annual Series, 1698–1807." *Bulletin of Economic Research* 43, no. 1 (1991): 21–56.

"West African Consumption Patterns and Their Influence on the Eighteenth Century English Slave Trade." In *The Uncommon Market: Essays in the Economic History of the Atlantic Slave Trade*, edited by Henry A. Gemery and Jan S. Hogendorn, 303–30. New York: Academic Press, 1979.

Roberts, Richard L. *Warriors, Merchants, and Slaves: The State and the Economy in the Niger Valley, 1700–1914*. Stanford: Stanford University Press, 1987.

Robertson, Claire C., and Martin A. Klein. "Women's Importance in African Slave Systems." In *Women and Slavery in Africa*, edited by Claire C. Robertson and Martin A. Klein, 3–25. Madison: University of Wisconsin Press, 1983.

Rodney, Walter. *How Europe Underdeveloped Africa*. Washington D.C.: Howard University Press, 1982.

Rodrigues, Jaime. *De Costa a Costa: Escravos, Marinheiros e Intermediários do Tráfico Negreiro de Angola ao Rio de Janeiro, 1780–1860*. São Paulo: Companhia das Letras, 2005.

Russell-Wood, A. J. R. "Colonial Brazil: The Gold Cycle, c.1690–1750." In *The Cambridge History of Latin America*, edited by Leslie Bethell, 2: 547–600. New York: Cambridge University Press, 1984.

Sampaio, Antônio Carlos Jucá. "Famílias e Negócios: A Formação da Comunidade Mercantil Carioca na Primeira Metade do Setecentos." In *Conquistadores e Negociantes: Histórias de Elites no Antigo Regime nos*

Trópicos. América Lusa, Séculos XVI a XVIII, edited by João Luís Ribeiro Fragoso, Antônio Carlos Jucá de Sampaio, and Carla Maria de Carvalho de Almeida, 225–64. Rio de Janeiro: Civilização Brasileira, 2007.

Sanborn, Melinde Lutz. "Angola and Elizabeth: An African Family in the Massachusetts Bay Colony." *New England Quarterly* 72, no. 1 (1999): 119–29.

Santos, Catarina Madeira. "Um Governo 'Polido' para Angola: Reconfigurar Dispositivos de Domínio (1750-c.1800)." Doctorate, Universidade Nova de Lisboa, 2005.

Santos, Corcino Medeiro dos. "Relações de Angola com o Rio de Janeiro (1736–1808)." *Estudos Históricos*, no. 12 (1973): 7–68.

Santos, José de Almeida. *Vinte Anos Decisivos de uma Cidade*. Luanda: Câmara Municipal de Luanda, 1970.

Santos, Maria Emília Madeira. *Nos Caminhos de África: Serventia e Posse (Angola, Século XIX)*. Lisbon: Instituto de Investigação Científica Tropical, 1998.

Viagens de Exploração Terrestre dos Portugueses em África. Lisbon: Centro de Estudos de Cartografia Antiga, 1978.

Schenck, Marcia C., and Mariana P. Cândido. "Uncomfortable Pasts: Talking about Slavery in Angola." In *African Heritage and Memories of Slavery in Brazil and the South Atlantic World*, edited by Ana Lúcia Araújo, 213–52. Amherst: Cambria Press, 2015.

Schrag, Norm. "Mboma and the Lower Zaire: A Socioeconomic Study of a Kongo Trading Community, c.1785–1885." Ph.D., Indiana University, 1985.

Schultz, Kirsten. "The Transfer of the Portuguese Court and Ideas of Empire." *Portuguese Studies Review* 15, no. 1–2 (2007): 367–91.

Schwartz, Stuart B. *Sugar Plantations in the Formation of Brazilian Society, Bahia, 1550–1835*. New York: Cambridge University Press, 1985.

Shumway, Rebecca. *The Fante and the Transatlantic Slave Trade*. Rochester: University of Rochester Press, 2011.

Silbering, Norman J. "British Prices and Business Cycles, 1779–1850." *Review of Economics and Statistics* 5 (1923): 223–47.

Slenes, Robert W. "'Malungu, Ngoma Vem!:' África Coberta e Descoberta no Brasil." *Revista USP* 12 (1991): 48–67.

Sluiter, Engel. "New Light on the '20. and Odd Negroes' Arriving in Virginia, August 1619." *William and Mary Quarterly*, 3, 54, no. 2 (1997): 395–98.

Smith, David Grant. "The Mercantile Class of Portugal and Brazil in the Seventeenth Century: A Socioeconomic Study of the Merchants of Lisbon and Bahia, 1620–1690." Ph.D., University of Texas, 1975.

Soares, Mariza de Carvalho. *Devotos da Cor: Identidade Étnica, Religiosidade e Escravidão no Rio de Janeiro, Século XVIII*. Rio de Janeiro: Civilização Brasileira, 2000.

Solar, Peter M., and Klas Rönnbäck. "Copper Sheathing and the British Slave Trade." *Economic History Review* Early view (2014): 1–24.

Sousa, Ana Madalena Trigo de. "Uma Tentativa de Fomento Industrial na Angola Setecentista: A 'Fábrica do Ferro' de Nova Oeiras (1766–1772)." *Africana Studia* 10 (2007): 291–308.

Souza, Marina de Mello e. *Reis Negros no Brasil Escravista: História da Festa de Coroação de Rei Congo*. Belo Horizonte: Editora UFMG, 2002.

Sparks, Randy J. *Where the Negroes Are Masters: An African Port in the Era of the Slave Trade*. Cambridge: Harvard University Press, 2014.

Stilwell, Sean. *Slavery and Slaving in African History*. New York: Cambridge University Press, 2014.

Strickrodt, Silke. *Afro-European Trade in the Atlantic World: The Western Slave Coast, c.1550-c.1885*. James Currey, 2015.

Thompson, Edward Palmer. *Customs in Common*. New York: The New Press, 1991.

Thornton, John K. *A Cultural History of the Atlantic World, 1250–1820*. New York: Cambridge University Press, 2012.

  Africa and Africans in the Making of the Atlantic World, 1400–1800. 2nd edn. New York: Cambridge University Press, 1998.

  "African Political Ethics and the Slave Trade." In *Abolitionism and Imperialism in Britain, Africa, and the Atlantic*, edited by Derek R. Peterson, 38–62. Athens: Ohio University Press, 2010.

  "As Guerras Civis no Congo e o Tráfico de Escravos: A História e a Demografia de 1718 a 1844 Revisitadas." *Estudos Afro-Asiáticos* 32 (1997): 55–74.

  "Precolonial African Industry and the Atlantic Trade, 1500–1800." *African Economic History*, no. 19 (1990): 1–19.

  "The African Experience of the '20. and Odd Negroes' Arriving in Virginia in 1619." *William and Mary Quarterly* 55, no. 3 (1998): 421–34.

  "The Art of War in Angola, 1575–1680." *Comparative Studies in Society and History* 30, no. 2 (1988): 360–78.

  "The Chronology and Causes of Lunda Expansion to the West, c.1700–1852." *Zambia Journal of History* 1 (1981): 1–14.

  The Kingdom of Kongo: Civil War and Transition, 1641–1718. Madison: University of Wisconsin Press, 1983.

  "The Slave Trade in Eighteenth Century Angola: Effects on Demographic Structures." *Canadian Journal of African Studies* 14, no. 3 (1980): 417–27.

  Warfare in Atlantic Africa, 1500–1800. New York: University College London Press, 1999.

Tilly, Louise, and Joan W. Scott. *Women, Work, and Family*. New York: Holt, Rinehart and Winston, 1978.

Vansina, Jan. "Ambaca Society and the Slave Trade c.1760–1845." *Journal of African History* 46, no. 1 (2005): 1–27.

  How Societies Are Born: Governance in West Central Africa before 1600. Charlottesville: University of Virginia Press, 2004.

  "It Never Happened: Kinguri's Exodus and Its Consequences." *History in Africa* 25 (1998): 387–403.

  Kingdoms of the Savanna: A History of Central African States until European Occupation. Madison: University of Wisconsin Press, 1966.

  "More on the Invasions of Kongo and Angola by the Jaga and the Lunda." *Journal of African History* 7, no. 3 (1966): 421–29.

  "Portuguese vs Kimbundu: Language Use in the Colony of Angola (1575-c.1845)." *Bulletin Des Séances de l'Academie Royale Des Sciences d'Outre Mer* 47 (March 2001): 267–81.

"The Foundation of the Kingdom of Kasanje." *Journal of African History* 4, no. 3 (1963): 355–74.

Vellut, Jean-Luc. "Notes sur le Lunda et la Frontière Luso-Africaine (1700–1900)." *Études d'Histoire Africaine* 3 (1972): 61–166.

Venâncio, José Carlos. *A Economia de Luanda e Hinterland no Século XVIII: Um Estudo de Sociologia Histórica.* Lisbon: Editorial Estampa, 1996.

Verger, Pierre. *Fluxo e Refluxo: O Tráfico de Escravos entre o Golfo de Benin e a Bahia de Todos os Santos dos Séculos XVII a XIX.* São Paulo: Corrupio, 1987.

Vila Vilar, Enriqueta. *Hispanoamerica y el Comercio de Esclavos.* Seville: Escuela de Estudios Hispano-Americanos, 1977.

Vos, Jelmer. "The Kingdom of Kongo and Its Borderlands, 1880–1915." Ph.D., School of Oriental and African Studies, 2005.

Walvin, James. *Crossings: Africa, the Americas, and the Atlantic Slave Trade.* London: Reaktion Books, 2013.

Wells, Tom Henderson. *The Slave Ship Wanderer.* Athens: University of Georgia Press, 1967.

Whatley, Warren, and Rob Gillezeau. "The Fundamental Impact of the Slave Trade on African Economies." In *Economic Evolution and Revolution in Historical Time,* edited by Paul Rhode, Joshua Rosenbloom, and David Weiman, 111–34. Stanford: Stanford University Press, 2011.

Wheeler, Douglas L. "Angolan Woman of Means: D. Ana Joaquina Dos Santos E Silva, Mid-Nineteenth Century Luso-African Merchant-Capitalist of Luanda." *Santa Barbara Portuguese Studies Review* 3 (1996): 284–97.

"The Portuguese in Angola, 1836–1891: A Study in Expansion and Administration." Ph.D., Boston University, 1963.

Wiesner, Merry E. *Women and Gender in Early Modern Europe.* 2nd edn. New York: Cambridge University Press, 2000.

Williams, David M. "Abolition and the Re-Deployment of the Slave Fleet, 1807–11." *Journal of Transport History* 11, no. 2 (1973): 103–15.

Williams, Eric. *Capitalism and Slavery.* Chapel Hill: University of North Carolina Press, 1994.

Ximenes, Cristina Ferreira Lyrio. "Joaquim Pereira Marinho: Perfil de um Contrabandista de Escravos na Bahia, 1828–1887." M.A., Universidade Federal da Bahia, 1999.

E) ELECTRONIC SOURCES

Eltis, David, David Richardson, Manolo Florentino, and Stephen D. Behrendt. "Voyages: The Trans-Atlantic Slave Trade Database." Online database, 2008. www.slavevoyages.org/.

Eltis, David, and Philip Misevich. "African Origins: Portal to Africans Liberated from Transatlantic Slave Vessels." Online database, 2009. www.african-origins.org/.

Handler, Jerome S., and Michael L. Tuite Jr. "The Atlantic Slave Trade and Slave Life in the Americas: A Visual Record." Online database, 2008. http://hitch cock.itc.virginia.edu/Slavery/.

Hoare, Robert. "WorldClimate: Weather and Climate Data Worldwide." Online database, 1996. www.worldclimate.com/.

"Internet Archive," 1996-. https://archive.org/.

"Merriam-Webster Dictionary Online," 2011. www.merriam-webster.com/.

Paul M. Lewis, ed. "Ethnologue: Languages of the World," 16th edn. Online database, 2009. www.ethnologue.com/.

Index